Transportation Analysis and Feasibility Study:
Sabino Canyon Recreation Area
Coronado National Forest

Prepared for the U.S. Forest Service

February 2010

John A. Volpe National Transportation Systems Center
Research and Innovative Technology Administration
U.S. Department of Transportation

REPORT DOCUMENTATION PAGE

1. REPORT DATE (DD MM YYYY)	2. REPORT TYPE	3. DATES COVERED (From To)
2-16-10	Final	12/2008 - 2/2010

4. TITLE AND SUBTITLE	5a. CONTRACT NUMBER
Transportation Analysis and Feasibility Study: Sabino Canyon Recreation Area, Coronado National Forest	09-IA-11030510-009

5b. GRANT NUMBER

5c. PROGRAM ELEMENT NUMBER

6. AUTHOR(S)	5d. PROJECT NUMBER
Frances Fisher	VXF9

Alex Linthicum
Eric Plosky
David Spiller

5e. TASK NUMBER

5f. WORK UNIT NUMBER

7. PERFORMING ORGANIZATION NAME(S) AND ADDRESS(ES)	8. PERFORMING ORGANIZATION REPORT NUMBER
U.S. Department of Transportation Research and Innovative Technology Administration John A. Volpe Transportation Systems Center 55 Broadway, Cambridge, MA 02142	DOT-VNTSC-USDA-10-01

9. SPONSORING/MONITORING AGENCY NAME(S) AND ADDRESS(ES)	10. SPONSOR/MONITOR'S ACRONYM(S)
Coronado National Forest 300 West Congress Tucson, AZ 85701	USDA USFS

11. SPONSOR/MONITOR'S REPORT NUMBER(S)

12. DISTRIBUTION/AVAILABILITY STATEMENT

Public distribution/availability

13. SUPPLEMENTARY NOTES

14. ABSTRACT

This report provides an overview of the historic and current visitation, environmental and infrastructure conditions as Sabino Canyon Recreation area in the Coronado NF in Tucson, AZ. Transportation goals were defined and specific potential solutions were identified in the following categories: Access Management; Bicycle, Pedestrian and Equestrian; Communications; Infrastructure; Management; Motorized Solutions; School Groups. These specific potential solutions were then grouped and analyzed as alternative scenarios. The analysis was done to support the Sabino Canyon Recreation Concept Plan which is being done subsequent to this study; all NEPA compliance will be conducted as part of the Recreation Concept Plan.

15. SUBJECT TERMS

USFS, recreation area, transportation, alternative transportation, bicycle, management, flooding

16. SECURITY CLASSIFICATION OF:			17. LIMITATION OF ABSTRACT	18. NUMBER OF PAGES	19a. NAME OF RESPONSIBLE PERSON
a. REPORT	b. ABSTRACT	c. THIS PAGE	NA	156	Frances Fisher, Volpe Center
None	None	None			19b. TELEPHONE NUMBER (Include area code) 617-494-3442

Report Notes

This report was prepared by the U.S. Department of Transportation John A. Volpe National Transportation Systems Center in Cambridge, Massachusetts in agreement with the USDA Forest Service, Region 3, Coronado National Forest in Tucson, Arizona. The project team was let by Eric Plosky and Frances Fisher of the Systems Operations and Assessment Division at the Volpe Center. Larry Pratt, Developed Recreation Project Manager at Coronado National Forest was the primary contact at the Forest.

This effort was undertaken in fulfillment of Interagency Agreement 09-IA-11030510-009, Sabino Canyon Transportation Analysis and Feasibility Study, signed in November 2008.

Acknowledgements

U.S. Forest Service

Diane Carroll-Cobb
Recreation Planner

Tom Cassell
Civil Engineer

Johnnie Coburn
Law Enforcement Officer

Tim Connor
Range/Watershed

Mike Culbert
Recreation Fee Program Supervisor

Veronica Forrest
Visitor Center Manager

Celeste Gordon
Recreation/Special Uses Program Manager

Stan Helin
District Ranger

Rachel Hohl
Dispersed Recreation Manager

Walter Keyes
Roads Engineer

Kathy Makansi
Archaeologist

Larry Pratt
Developed Recreation Project Manager

Devin Quintana
Cartographer

Misty Shafiqullah
Engineering Staff

Ken Simons
Business Management Officer

Jim Sutton
Special Uses Resource Clerk

Joshua Taiz
District Wildlife Staff

Sherry Tune
District Ranger

Stakeholder representatives

Jessica Bassi
Facilities Project Manager, Catalina Foothills School District 16

Keith Bauman
Vice President, Friends of Sabino Canyon

Peter Bengtson
Southern Arizona Hiking Club

Fred Blatt
Secretary, Friends of Sabino Canyon

Claudia Bray
Treasurer, Sabino Canyon Volunteer Naturalists

Dave Bushell
President, Friends of Sabino Canyon

Cherie Campbell
Director of Transportation Planning, Pima Association of Governments

Jonathan Crowe
Principal Planner, Pima County Department of Transportation

Brian Duffy
President, Southern Arizona Rescue Association

Howard Dutt
Parks and Recreation Department, City of Tucson

Bill Florence
Treasurer, Southern Arizona Rescue Association

Jan Galvin
Kindergarten Program Leader, Sabino Canyon Volunteer Naturalists

Bernard Goldstein
Coordinator, Coronado Mounted Assistance Unit

Marta Gunderson
Principal, Canyon View Elementary School

Bill Kaufman
Board Member, Friends of Sabino Canyon

David Lazaroff
Independent Naturalist

Deb Langeloh
Board Member, Sabino Volunteer Patrol

Martha Lemen
President, Sonoran Desert Mountain Bicyclists

Sgt. Scott Lowing
Deputy Sherriff, Pima County Sheriff Department

Jude McCarthy
Recreation, Canyon Ranch

David McCray
Sabino Canyon Manager, Public Lands Interpretive Association

Bob McGee
SunTran Scheduling, City of Tucson

Louise Misztal
Conservation Associate, Sky Island Alliance

Don Morehart
Treasurer, Sabino Volunteer Patrol

Jan Nusbaum
Board Member, Sabino Volunteer Patrol

Marylee Peterson
President, Sabino Volunteer Patrol

Sgt Bill Phillips
Pima County Sheriff Department

Mykle Raymond
Operations Leader, Southern Arizona Rescue Association

Donn Ricketts
President, Sabino Canyon Tours, Inc.

Tom Thivener
Bicycle and Pedestrian Programs, City of Tucson

John Zukas
Transit, City of Tucson

Jay Zuckerman
President, Sabino Canyon Ranch

Executive summary

Sabino Canyon Recreation Area, part of the Coronado National Forest, is located just outside Tucson, Arizona. The recreation area is a popular retreat for local residents, schoolchildren on field trips, naturalists, and visitors from all over the world. Sabino Canyon contains one of only two perennial streams flowing into the Tucson Basin and a unique riparian environment, providing habitat for a massive number of plant and animal species. The environment, the plants and animals, and presence of virtually car-less transportation infrastructure contribute to the popularity of the canyon among visitors.

An estimated 520,000 people visit Sabino Canyon each year by private vehicle alone. An unknown number of additional people visit on foot or bicycle from nearby residential neighborhoods. Many factors contribute to the canyon's popularity, shape visitor usage, and ultimately affect both the internal and external transportation systems. These key factors include environmental conditions, the presence and condition of transportation infrastructure, and conflicts between different user groups and stakeholders.

Growing pressure on the Sabino Canyon transportation system, especially after a damaging flood in 2006, led the Coronado National Forest to apply to the federal Transit in the Parks (TRIP) program for funds to conduct a comprehensive study that would analyze existing conditions and formulate several alternatives that could be considered for the future. This report, produced by the U.S. Department of Transportation Volpe Center, is the final result of that study. However, this report is not considered a "decision document" and was not intended to fulfill the requirements of the National Environmental Policy Act or other U.S. Forest Service (USFS) compliance requirements; it is a feasibility study that does not recommend a "preferred alternative."

Environmental conditions

Sabino Canyon is home to riparian habitats that are sustained by Sabino Creek. Relatively rare in desert areas, these habitats provide food and shelter to plant and animal species. Sabino Canyon is officially recognized as a critical habitat for the Gila chub, a species of fish that is federally protected by the Endangered Species Act.

Dry, warm desert conditions contribute to the popularity of Sabino Canyon and the entire Tucson area. Average daily temperatures allow for outdoor activity year-round, predominantly during the day in the winter and during early morning or evening hours in the summer.

The watershed supplying Sabino Creek covers 35.5 square miles in the Santa Catalina Mountains and draws visitors year-round. As USFS staff stated, "People come to where the water is." But over the last 75 years, there has been a trend of weaker continuous flow in Sabino Creek and stronger isolated rain storms. Record-breaking floods in 2006 caused 240 debris flows in the surrounding mountains and $2 million in damage to the road and bridges. The bridges and dam, originally intended to create pools of water for people to enjoy, have instead collected soil and silt.

Presence and condition of transportation infrastructure

Since 1978, when private vehicles were permanently banned from the canyon road, visitors have been attracted to Sabino Canyon's 3.8 miles of relatively vehicle-free, paved road on which to walk, jog, and bicycle. A tram provides motorized transportation within the recreation area and has become an attraction itself, shuttling between 100,000 and 160,000 people in and out of Sabino and Bear Canyons each year.

Popular usage, natural events, and old age have contributed to degradation of the road, bridges, and tram system. The flooding that occurred in 2006 and subsequent damage to the Sabino Canyon road required 1 ½ years to repair and restore. Despite the attraction of the road for many users, some have questioned the time and expenditures required for restoration, given that future flooding could cause comparable – or worse – damage.

Non-motorized transportation system users (such as hikers and cyclists) point out conflicts between the tram and the natural environment. Some visitors have complained that the diesel trams, built in the 1970s, are loud and smelly and that the audio emanating from the loudspeakers, used by the tram drivers to interpret natural and cultural themes to passengers, carries up and down the canyon.

User group and stakeholder conflicts

The continued popularity of Sabino Canyon has led to conflicts between diverse user groups. These issues were documented 15 years ago in Sabino Canyon's 1993 Recreation Concept Plan and continue today. Cyclists, pedestrians, and the tram vie for time and space on the road. In 1992, after aggressive behavior by some cyclists was reported, biking hours were limited to mornings and evenings and prohibited completely on Wednesdays and Saturdays. Still, as mentioned above, conflicts between humans and nature (weather/climate, flora, and fauna) are also frequent.

Nearby residents are inconvenienced by illegal parking on North Sabino Canyon Road during weekends in the peak season.

Traffic created by parents dropping children off at nearby elementary and middle schools hinders egress from the recreation area.

Themes and goals

Based on the data collected to document existing conditions as a baseline for analysis, five themes stood out as key areas of focus for Sabino Canyon.

- Theme 1 – Public safety.
- Theme 2 – Infrastructure preservation, maintenance, and management.
- Theme 3 – Mobility, accessibility, and connectivity.
- Theme 4 – Visitor experience.
- Theme 5 – Environmental stewardship.

These themes were used in conjunction with the 1993 Sabino Canyon Recreation Concept Plan to identify goals for Sabino Canyon and its transportation system. The following five goals were identified to focus transportation planning efforts based on shared values and beliefs.

- Financial sustainability (FS) – Maintain assets and operate systems in a cost-effective and financially sustainable way.
- Public safety (PS) – Improve public safety and reduce visitor risk with respect to natural disasters and user conflicts.
- Historical and cultural sites (HCS) – Preserve, protect, and restore unique historical and cultural sites within Sabino Canyon.
- Natural and ecological resources (NER) – Preserve, protect, and restore the natural and ecological resources within Sabino Canyon.
- Access and circulation (AC) – Provide access to and circulation within Sabino Canyon for all visitors as the basis for an enjoyable experience.

The themes and goals were then used to develop criteria to analyze each of the specific transportation solutions, or elements, developed during the study.

Elements

Following completion of the goals and criteria, a list of 80 transportation interventions, or "elements," was compiled. Each element specifically addressed one or more issues identified in the review of existing conditions. These elements were categorized into issue areas, and each element was assigned a number within the appropriate category. Issue areas include:

- AM – Access Management Elements.
- BPE – Bicycle, Pedestrian, and Equestrian Elements.
- COM – Communications Elements.
- INF – Infrastructure Elements.
- MGMT – Management Elements.
- MOT – Motorized Elements.
- SCH – School Elements.

After identifying the elements, they were discussed with USFS staff and the public stakeholder group. Some elements were then consolidated with other elements; found to meet no identified need; characterized as significantly unpopular; or considered infeasible and dropped from the list. The remaining elements were evaluated based on the criteria associated with the goals of Sabino Canyon and then summarized individually.

Filtered list of transportation elements

Element ID	Element description
AM 01	Create a new internal road connecting the current and future parking areas or redevelop the existing interior access road for public access to the new overflow lot.
AM 02	Institute 24-hour access control.
AM 03	Develop south-side access-egress from lot to avoid conflicts with school.
AM 04	Install a traffic signal at the recreation area entrance.
AM 05	Expand public transit service to Sabino Canyon Recreation Area.
AM 06	Stripe and widen shoulders of roads to improve bicycle access.
AM 07	Create off-road path connecting to greenway for bikes and pedestrians.
AM 08	Encourage walking or cycling to the recreation area from nearby neighborhoods.
AM 09	Improve Bear Canyon access point.
AM 10	Dedicated right-turn lane into Sabino Canyon parking lot.
AM 11	Create new broad walking path from new parking lot directly to Cactus Picnic Area.
AM 12	Install a southbound right-turn lane from Sabino Canyon Road to Skyline.
BPE 01	Initiate bicycle guided tours of Sabino Canyon.
BPE 02	Create a grade-separated bike and/or pedestrian trail.
BPE 03	Stripe an at-grade bike and/or pedestrian trail using the existing road width, widening where possible.
BPE 04	Provide bicycle parking at trail-heads.
BPE 05	Develop equestrian tours.
BPE 06	Create additional or improve infrastructure for equestrian users.
COM 01	Install mile markers and directory kiosks with distances to infrastructure and amenities.
COM 02	Advertise that the tram runs on bio-diesel fuel.
COM 03	Improve the frequency and accuracy of visitor communications via the website.
COM 04	Expand information delivery methods to include new distribution channels.
COM 05	Use variable message signs for disseminating parking and safety messages.
COM 06	Collect parking lot utilization and disseminate in real-time via the web and/or variable message signs on approach roads.
INF 01	Create alternate trail network that avoids stream crossings and facilitates evacuation.
INF 02	Relocate the visitor center farther up the canyon and shuttle between it and the parking lots.
INF 03	Widen road to reduce user conflicts.
INF 04	Widen the bridges and bridge approaches.
INF 05	Redesign bridges to improve flow and reduce sedimentation issues; keep historic look but change engineering.
INF 06	Regularly maintain culverts to maintain desired (conceptualized at the creation of the bridges) water flow.
INF 07	Develop new bridges for pedestrians (or tram) off of the existing roadway network.
INF 08	Eliminate planned overflow parking.
MGMT 01	Create and disseminate a disaster evacuation, rescue, and communication plan.
MGMT 02	Develop aggregation points to shelter-in-place or facilitate evacuation for visitors within Sabino Canyon up to the end of Sabino Canyon Road.
MGMT 03	Develop flood detection and early warning system.
MGMT 04	Update and enforce time-separation strategies for different user types.
MGMT 05	Require the tram vehicles to conform to specified noise and air quality requirements.
MGMT 06	Include/enforce shuttle service requirements in special-use permit.
MGMT 07	Transfer ownership of the tram vehicles to USFS and continue operation by a contractor.
MGMT 08	Provide the tram as a fare-free service for visitors.
MGMT 09	Charge an expanded amenity recreation fee to pay for fare-free shuttle service.
MGMT 10	Institute a frequent rider pass.

Element ID	Element description
MGMT 11	Develop a parking reservation system.
MGMT 12	Charge entry fee for all users, per person.
MGMT 13	Maintain existing tram operation and service concept.
MOT 01	Use trams for evacuation.
MOT 02	Remove the tram.
MOT 03	Develop aerial tram service.
MOT 04	Electric carts could be provided for mobility-impaired visitors by reservation.
MOT 05	Rent electric bicycles to assist people to get up canyon.
MOT 06	Create an on-demand and/or reservation system for the mobility-impaired.
MOT 07	Replace with in-kind vehicle of same size/function.
MOT 08	Replace vehicles with larger or smaller vehicles but run at equivalent capacity.
MOT 09	Replace trams with an enclosed vehicle design.
MOT 10	Upgrade interpretation method/technology.
MOT 11	Add passenger safety equipment.
MOT 12	Limit hours/days/seasons of tram.
MOT 13	Limit tram route to lower canyon only.
MOT 14	Connect new parking lot to visitor center via tram.
MOT 15	Replace Sabino Canyon shuttle with more developed shuttle service in Bear Canyon.
MOT 16	Develop separate shuttle options and/or routes within CNF (to Mt. Lemmon and/or additional parking areas).
SCH 01	Provide free tram shuttle to transport student groups within the canyon.
SCH 02	Relocate educational facilities or build trails so that students can walk from the parking lot.
SCH 03	Purchase vehicle specifically for student group travel.

These individual elements were then packaged into five alternatives that focus on different types of transportation changes. In addition, a number of elements were grouped as recommended long-range operations and management strategies that could be combined with any of the alternatives. These alternatives include:

- Long-range operations and management elements (could be combined with any of the alternatives listed below).
- Alternative 0 – No Action.
- Alternative 1 – Parking management and capacity control.
- Alternative 2 – Expanded non-motorized use.
- Alternative 3 – Fare-free shuttle.
- Alternative 4 – Infrastructure improvements.

The proposed alternatives are designed to provide examples of how the elements can be combined to produce specific scenarios, none of which should be seen as binding. As USFS moves forward with the development of the updated Sabino Canyon Recreation Concept Plan, the existing alternatives should be used as a starting point, with new combinations of elements used to produce the forest's desired outcome.

Next steps

By summarizing the natural environment of Sabino Canyon, its history, the surroundings, and the people who use the canyon, key themes and goals for Sabino Canyon became apparent. This document provides a foundation for current and future planning for Sabino Canyon, particularly focusing on the transportation systems surrounding and within the canyon.

As noted above, this document is not designed to provide a specific plan of action for transportation at Sabino Canyon, but instead to identify several potential solutions to specific transportation issues that were identified. It is expected that as the Sabino Canyon Recreation Concept Plan goes ahead, and a preferred alternative is developed as part of that effort, transportation elements from this study can be combined to develop the appropriate transportation system to meet the future desired goals for Sabino Canyon and its visitors.

Chapter VI provides an example of how a number of elements can be combined to create very different experiences within the canyon and how these alternatives can be analyzed and compared to each other. There are a number of long-range operations and management elements that could benefit Sabino Canyon regardless of direction defined by the Recreation Concept Plan.

Table of contents

I.   Introduction

Sabino Canyon Recreation Area, part of the Coronado National Forest, is located just outside Tucson, Arizona. The recreation area is a popular retreat for local residents, schoolchildren on field trips, naturalists, and visitors from all over the world. Sabino Canyon contains one of only two perennial streams flowing into the Tucson Basin and a unique riparian environment, providing habitat for a massive number of plant and animal species. The environment, the plants and animals, and presence of virtually car-less transportation infrastructure contribute to the popularity of the canyon among visitors.

An estimated 520,000 people arrive at Sabino Canyon each year by private vehicle. An unknown number of additional people visit on foot or bicycle from nearby residential neighborhoods. Many factors contribute to the canyon's popularity, shape visitor usage, and ultimately affect both the internal and external transportation systems. These key factors include environmental conditions, presence and condition of transportation infrastructure, and user group and stakeholder conflicts.

Growing pressure on the Sabino Canyon transportation system, especially after a damaging flood in 2006, led the Coronado National Forest to apply to the federal Transit in the Parks (TRIP) program for funds to conduct a comprehensive planning study to analyze existing conditions and formulate several alternatives that could be considered for the future. The TRIP program, administered by the Federal Transit Administration, the U.S. Department of the Interior, and the U.S. Forest Service (USFS), aims to promote alternative transportation methods (including bus shuttles and nonmotorized systems) as a way of improving the visitor experience and reducing resource damage on federal lands.

The Sabino Canyon funding request was approved, and the Coronado National Forest established an interagency agreement with the U.S. Department of Transportation Volpe Center to conduct the work. This report is the final result of that study. However, this report is not considered a "decision document" and was not intended to fulfill the requirements of the National Environmental Policy Act (NEPA) or other USFS compliance requirements; it is a feasibility study that does not recommend a "preferred alternative." It was envisioned that the results of this study could be considered as part of the separate effort to update the Sabino Canyon Recreation Concept Plan, as part of which it is expected that the Coronado National Forest *will* identify a preferred alternative, complying with the NEPA process and other applicable requirements.

Purpose

The goal of this report is to identify potential transportation solutions to issues that have been identified at Sabino Canyon. Examples of future transportation systems are provided to show a variety of future transportation conditions within the Canyon. As the preferred alternative is developed for the Sabino Canyon Recreation Concept Plan, transportation elements from this study can be combined to develop the appropriate transportation system to meet the future desired goals for Sabino Canyon and its visitors.

Overview

As the popularity of Sabino Canyon continues to grow, it becomes necessary to review the current transportation system of the canyon and make plans for the future. This report describes the existing conditions and transportation issues at Sabino Canyon (Chapter II), highlights key themes (Chapter III), defines goals and criteria (Chapter IV), presents transportation solutions or elements (Chapter V), and combines elements to suggest five comprehensive transportation alternatives (Chapter VI). Chapter VII discusses financial opportunities that USFS may pursue to implement the elements and alternatives. Chapter VIII provides concluding remarks, and appendices follow. This report provides a basis upon which USFS and Sabino Canyon stakeholders may continue to discuss transportation in the context of broader recreation goals and ultimately move forward with updates to the existing transportation system.

II. Existing conditions

Existing conditions at Sabino Canyon Recreation Area are presented in the following six sections:

1. Location and history;
2. Visitation;
3. Natural environment;
4. Transportation infrastructure;
5. Sabino Canyon tram; and
6. User and stakeholder groups.

Location and history

Sabino Canyon Recreation Area is situated northeast of the city of Tucson, as shown in Figure 1. The recreation area is located in the eastern foothills of the Santa Catalina Mountains and is within the Santa Catalina Ranger District, one of five administrative units of the Coronado National Forest. Located within a 45-minute drive of most residential areas in Tucson, the canyon is accessible via Interstate 19 from the south and Interstate 10 from the northwest and southeast. South Kolb Road and East Speedway Boulevard provide access from Interstate 10 to the south and west, respectively.

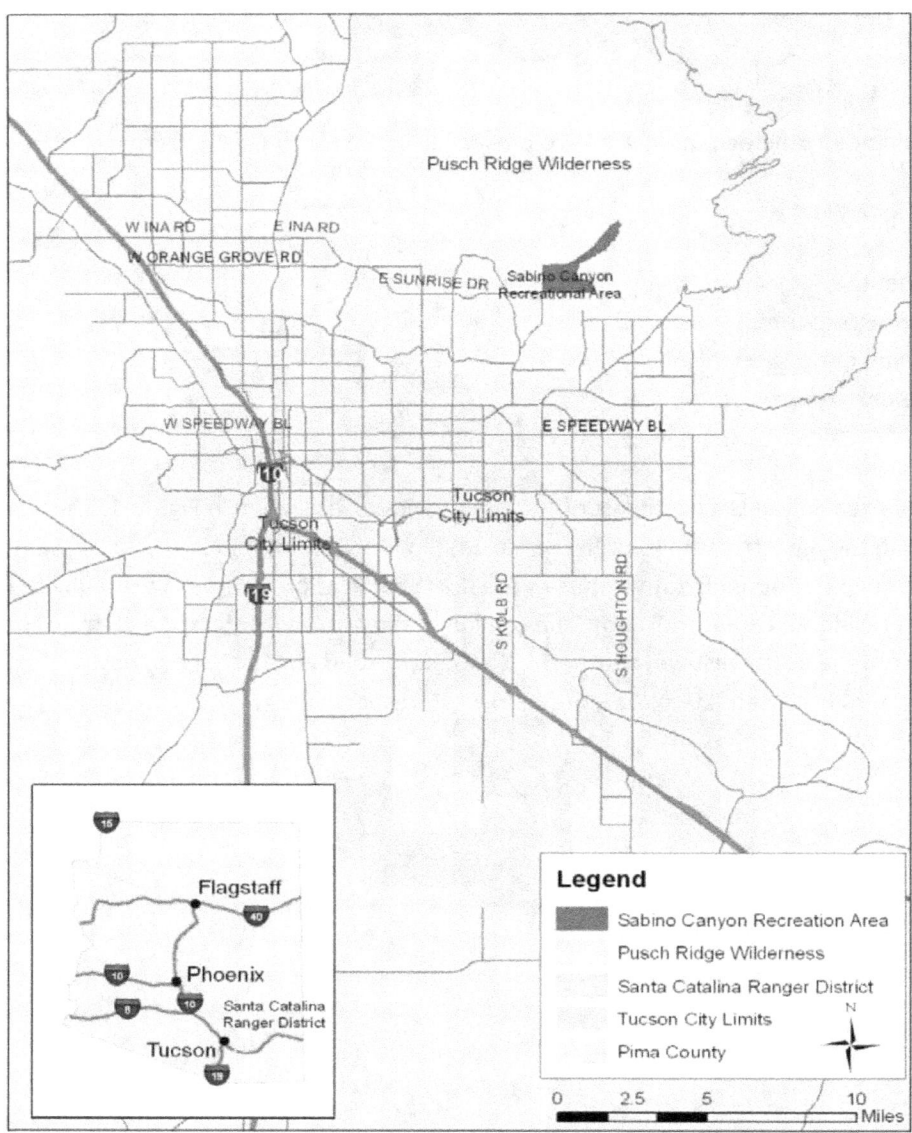

Figure 1 – Sabino Canyon Recreation Area in relation to Tucson, Arizona[1]

The recreation area is roughly 2 square miles in area and is bordered to the north and east by the Pusch Ridge Wilderness, another part of the Santa Catalina Ranger District, and residential developments to the south and west.

Sabino Canyon was not always located near residential and commercial development. Population and land area of Tucson is shown in Figure 2. In 1902, when Sabino Canyon was initially protected as part of the Santa Catalina Forest Reserve, the population of Tucson was about 7,500 and was largely contained within a four square-mile area located in what is today downtown Tucson. By the mid-to-late 1930s, the

---

[1] GIS files provided by Pima County Department of Transportation.

Emergency Relief Administration, the Works Progress Administration, and the Civilian Conservation Corps had built roads, nine bridges (technically considered 'vented low-water crossings'), ranger facilities, and a dam in the canyon.[2] The population of Tucson had quadrupled to over 32,000. By the mid-1970s, the population had increased tenfold. Today, over 750,000 people currently live in the Tucson metropolitan area, which includes parts of Pima County.

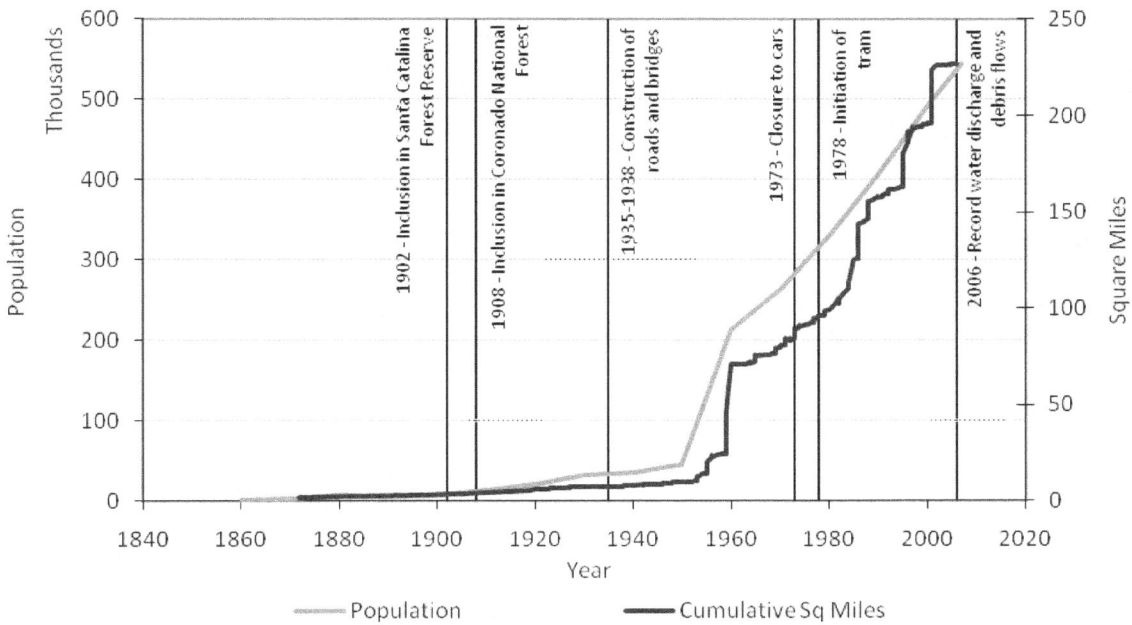

Figure 2 – Tucson population and annexation history with selected Sabino Canyon milestones[3,4,5]

Following construction of Upper Sabino Canyon Road, many visitors made specific day trips to Sabino Canyon to explore, picnic, and hike. Driving up the 3.8 mile road to picnic, scenic, and hiking areas was a popular activity. It was reported that on Easter weekend in 1967, over 4,000 visitors and almost half as many private vehicles were in Sabino Canyon at once. On busy weekends, the roads would become so congested that people and vehicles became trapped until others left.[6]

In 1973, a flood destroyed several of the bridge approaches and precipitated temporary closure of the road. In 1978, after a period of review of safety issues and public concerns, the road was permanently closed to unauthorized private vehicles and a tram service was initiated to transport visitors up and into the canyon. Weekend visitation remained high while changes in land use introduced a new set of users.

---

[2] Friends of Sabino Canyon (2008). *Newsletter Archives: Winter 2004 Newsletter*. Accessed at http://sabinocanyon.org/archives.htm on March 18, 2009.

[3] Bureau of the Census (October 24, 2001). *Decennial Censuses, Arizona Counties, Cities, Places, 1860-1990*. Accessed at http://www.tucsonaz.gov/planning/data/census/decennial/decennials.pdf on February 18, 2009.

[4] Bureau of the Census (2009). *Tucson City, Arizona – Population Finder – American Factfinder*. Accessed at http://factfinder.census.gov/servlet/SAFFPopulation?_submenuId=population_0&_sse=on on April 1, 2009.

[5] City of Tucson (January 2007). *City of Tucson Calendar Year Annual Summary of Growth*. Accessed at http://www.tucsonaz.gov/planning/data/general/annual.pdf on February 18, 2009.

[6] Coronado National Forest, Santa Catalina Ranger District (December 1993). *Sabino Canyon Recreation Concept Plan: Recommendations for Restoration and Enhancement*. USDA Forest Service.

Recently, nearby urban development has increased. Aerial photographs from 1993 and 2009, shown in Figure 3, demonstrate changes in the recreation area's immediate vicinity.

Figure 3 – Aerial photographs depict the parking lot and main entrance to Sabino Canyon. The photo on the left was taken in 1993. The photo on the right was taken in 2009[7].

While weekend and day trips to the canyon are still popular, this nearby development has inspired a whole new group of users: local residents who visit the recreation area one or more times a week and on weekends for shorter periods of time. Local residents come to walk, jog, or bicycle. As shown in Figure 4, there are now roughly 75 residential parcels within ¼ mile and 500 within ½ mile of entrances to the canyon along the local road network. There are 275 residential parcels within ¼ mile, and 725 within ½ mile, of entrances to the recreation area as the crow flies. Roughly 2,000 parcels are within one mile, which is less than a five-minute drive.

---

[7] Google Earth.

⠂ Recreation area entrances	⠂ Residential parcels within 1/4 mile
Sabino Canyon Recreation Area	Residential parcels within 1/2 mile
⌐ ⌐ ⌐ Distances from entrances, 1/4 and 1/2 mile	Residential parcels farther than 1/2 mile

Figure 4 – Residential parcels near Sabino Canyon Recreation Area. On the left are parcels located within 1/4 and 1/2 mile from recreation area entrances as the crow flies. On the right are parcels located within 1/4 and 1/2 mile of recreation area entrances along the street network. The Bear Canyon Entrance was included in these calculations (although few residential parcels are near it)[8].

Visitation

The public may visit Sabino Canyon Recreation Area at any time of day. They may arrive by private vehicle, on foot, on horseback, or by bicycle. Several attempts have been made to quantify visitation to Sabino Canyon Recreation Area, though none to date has been comprehensive.

Main entrance fee booth vehicle counts

Vehicle counts are made by the Forest Service cashier at the main entrance fee booth. These data are limited because i) the Forest Service is not able to staff the booth 24 hours a day, ii) beginning in April 2008, counts were no longer taken for vehicles entering with long-term passes, iii) the counts only capture visitors arriving by private automobile.

During the hottest months of the year (June through August), people may visit as early as 4:00 a.m. and as late as 11:00 p.m. Monitoring of the booths may begin as early as 6:00 a.m. and end as late as 6:30 p.m. Forest Service employees may only work up to 10-hour shifts, thus booth operations vary based on staff schedules and availability. There is a 'fee tube' located at the entrance gate that facilitates

---

[8] Pima County Department of Transportation (2009). FTP Server GIS Data Download.

collection of entrance fees during hours when the fee booth is unmanned. In late 2008, the Forest Service monitored compliance of those who arrive early to the recreation area by checking private vehicles in the lot for long-term passes or signs of voluntary payment. No data, however, has been collected regarding the number of people using the recreation area during these times.

The main entrance is split into two lanes. The right gate is manned during daytime hours to collect entrance fees for automobiles. Entrance fees are charged for each automobile and are $5 (Day Pass), $10 (Week Pass), and $20 (Annual Pass).[9] National and interagency passes are sold or waived through as well, including Golden Age, Golden Eagle Passport, Golden Eagle Hologram, and the America the Beautiful – National Parks and Federal Recreational Lands Pass.

Figure 5 shows the number of passes sold in FY2005 through FY2008. This figure does not represent annual visitations as some visitors buy passes elsewhere.

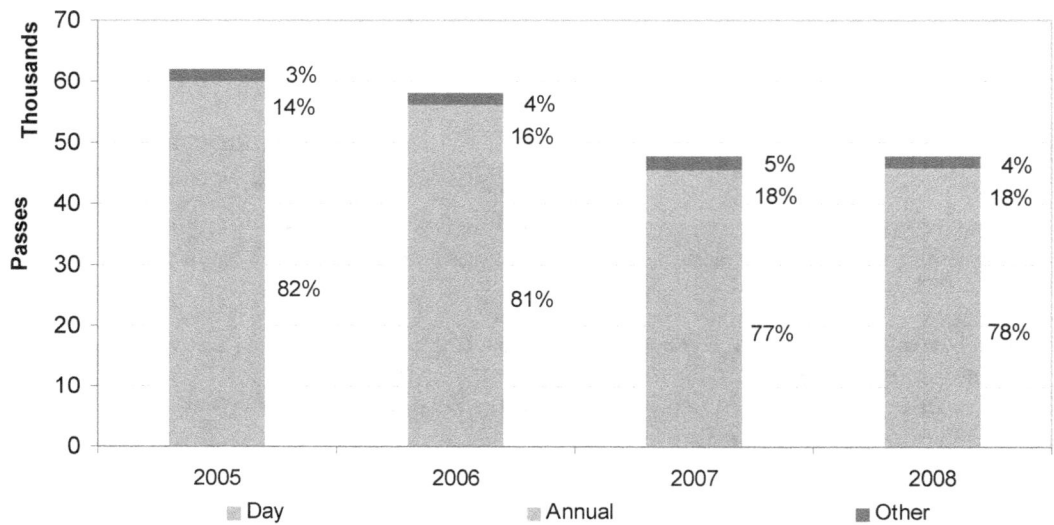

Figure 5 – Number and type of visitation passes sold at Sabino Canyon Recreation Area

The cashier at the main entrance gate counts private vehicles as they enter and categorizes them as either being charged a fee or being waived through with a pass. The left gate became unmanned in April 2008 and is now used as an entrance for pass holders.[10] Counts are not made for private vehicles entering through this gate. Anecdotally, some Forest Service staff members have heard people in Tucson describing how to cheat the fee booth: "If you stay left, it's free."

Despite issues with the fee booth counts, they provide an indication of visitation during daytime hours when the recreation area is busiest. Annual visitation from FY2002 through FY2008 is shown in Figure 6. Several atypical circumstances during this time are summarized in

---

[9] USDA Forest Service (2008). *Coronado National Forest: Passes, Permits, and Fees.* Accessed at http://www.fs.fed.us/r3/coronado/forest/passes/fees/fees.shtml on February 2, 2009.
[10] Telephone conversation with Veronica Forrest, Visitor Center Manager (February 11, 2009).

Table 1. Monthly private vehicle counts reported by the main entrance booth are shown in Figure 7.

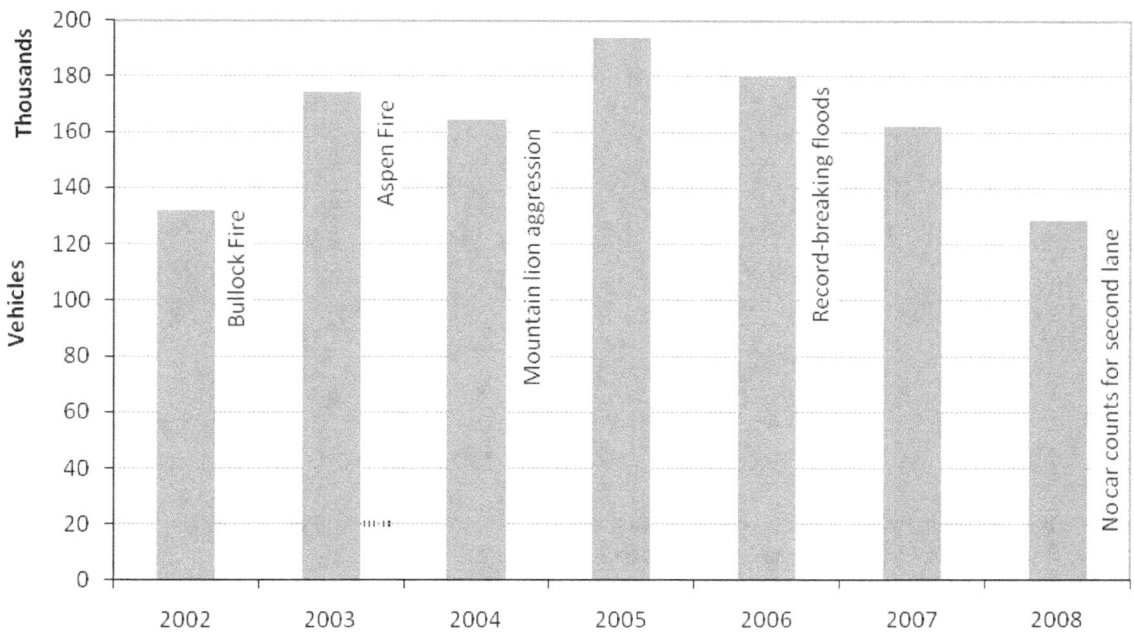

Figure 6 – Annual vehicle counts reported by entrance fee booth, FY2002-2008

Table 1 – Atypical circumstances at Sabino Canyon, FY2002-2008

Begin Date	End Date	Comments
May 26, 2002	Jul 18, 2002	Closed due to Bullock Fire
Jul 04, 2003	Jul 24, 2003	Closed due to Aspen Fire
Mar 04, 2004	Mar 30, 2004	Closed due to mountain lion aggression
Aug 2006	Oct 2006	Tram suspended on Upper Sabino Canyon Road due to debris flow damage
Oct 2006	Apr 2007	Tram resumed to Shuttle Stop 4 on Sabino Canyon Road
Apr 14, 2008	Present	Cars no longer counted in second fee booth entrance lane

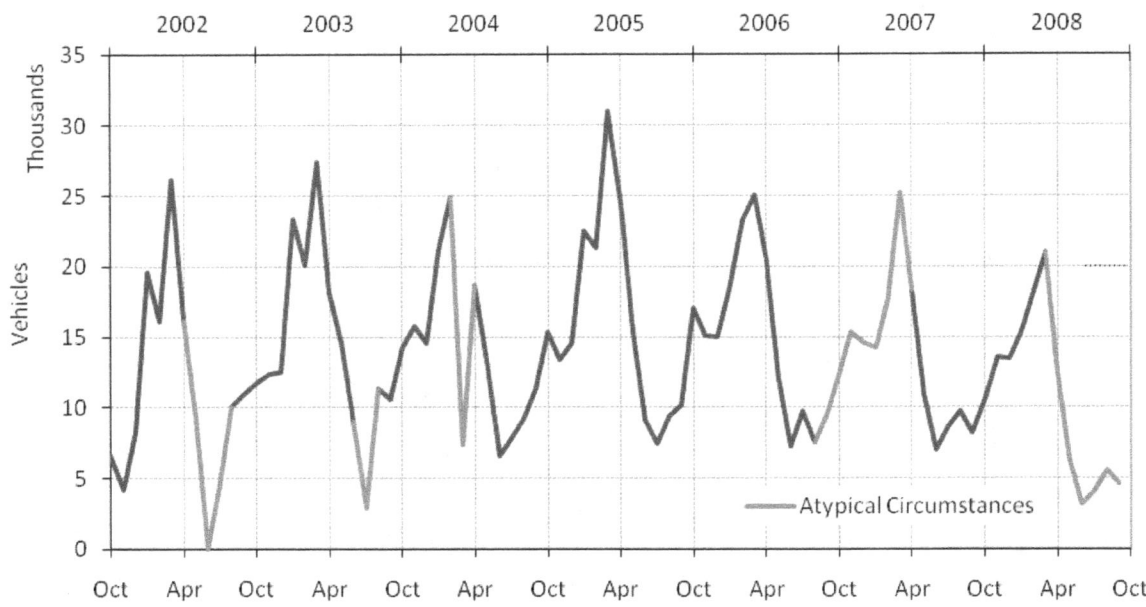

Figure 7 – Monthly vehicle counts reported by entrance fee booth, FY2002-2008. Peak visitation occurs between December and April. Non-peak visitation occurs between May and November.

Inductive loop traffic counter data

The Forest Service operated an inductive loop traffic counter non-continuously from 1995 to 2001 at the main entrance gate. While operating, it counted all vehicles entering the parking lot, 24 hours a day. The loop counter dataset contains significant time gaps which prevents aggregation by month or year. Furthermore, the counts do not capture visitors arriving on foot or by bicycle.

Despite the drawbacks of the inductive loop traffic counter data, they may be used to suggest average hourly and daily visitation patterns for those visitors arriving by private vehicle. Because a majority of visitors arrive by private vehicle, these data may be used as a proxy for all visitations. Figure 8 shows daily visitation patterns. Weekends and peak season visitation is generally higher than weekday and off-peak season visitation.

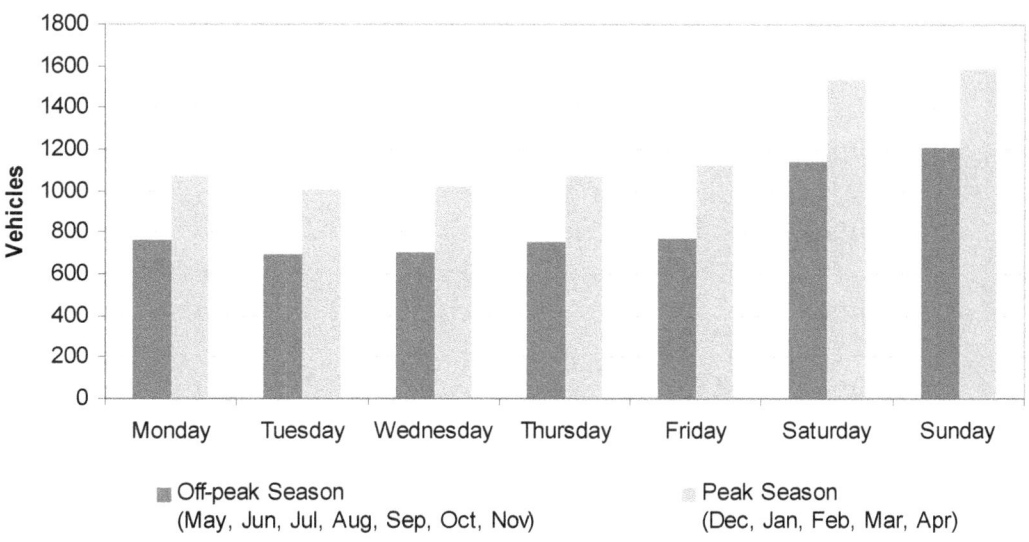

Figure 8 – Average vehicle counts reported by day of week and season. Inductive loop counter data reported only for 1,353 days during which the counter ran 24 hours, 1995-2001.

Figure 9 shows hourly arrival patterns. In the peak season, hourly arrival trends for weekday and weekend visitation are similar. More people tend to come earlier on the weekends, beginning at 5:00 a.m. Arrivals peak for both weekdays and weekends at around 10:00 a.m. and taper off quickly until about 2:00 p.m. when they level out. After 2:00 p.m., weekend arrivals decrease faster than weekday arrivals until 6:00 p.m. when arrivals decrease at the same rate.

In the off-peak season, arrivals begin earlier and end later than in the peak season to take advantage of cooler temperatures in the early morning and evening hours. Arrivals for both weekdays and weekends peak around 6:00 a.m. Weekday arrivals peak again at 6:00 p.m., possibly reflecting after-work visits. After 6:00 p.m., weekend and weekday arrivals have the same volume and decrease at the same rate during the off-peak season.

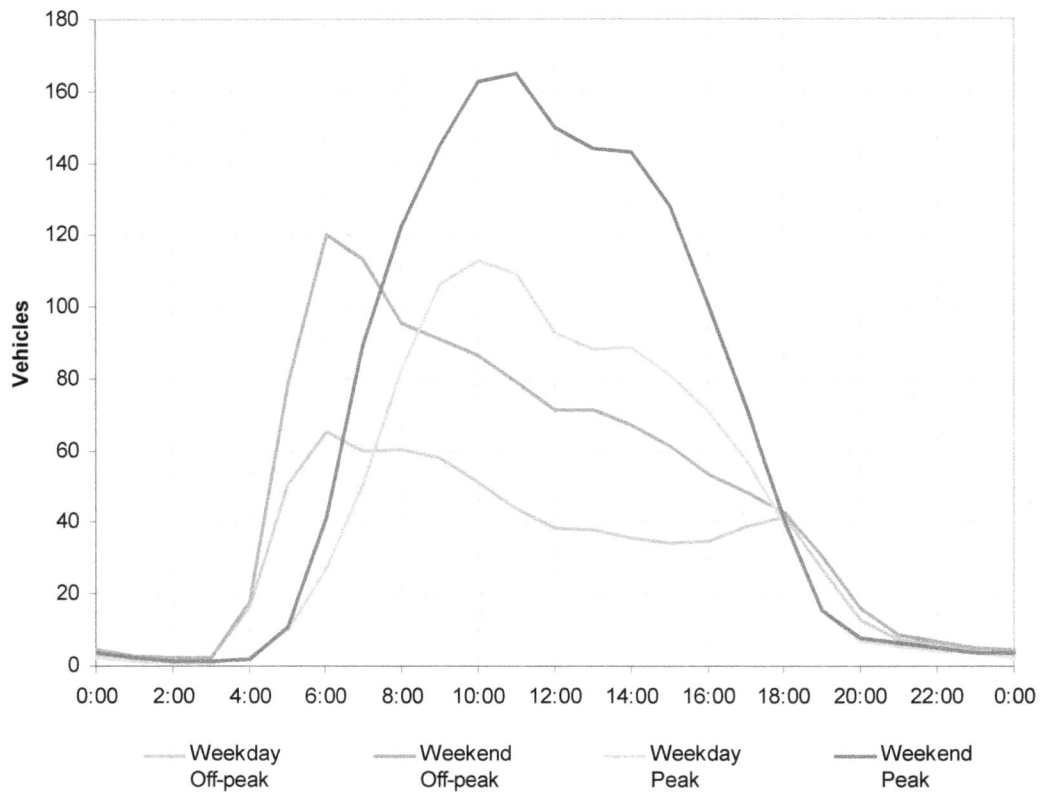

Figure 9 – Average vehicle counts reported by hour, type of day, and season. Inductive loop counter data reported only for 1,353 days during which the counter ran 24 hours, 1995-2001.

National Visitor Use Monitoring studies

National Visitor Use Monitoring (NVUM) studies conducted by the Forest Service in 2001 and 2007 for Coronado National Forest do not specifically report visitation and use statistics for Sabino Canyon.[11] Several factors limited the usefulness and applicability of these studies for the current effort at Sabino Canyon Recreation Area.[12,13] First, the data for the recreation area was aggregated with data for the remainder of Coronado National Forest. Second, although data were aggregated by land use type, Sabino Canyon Recreation Area was included as undeveloped "General Forest Area" (GFA). Sabino Canyon contains a great deal more infrastructure and attracts more visitors than other GFAs, thus GFA statistics are not representative of Sabino Canyon. Third, the methods used to conduct the two surveys differed, thus limiting the ability to make comparisons between them.

[11] USDA Forest Service Region 3 (2008). Coronado National Visitor Use Monitoring Results. p 17.
[12] Telephone conversation with Doak McDuffie, Monday, March 16, 2009, 3:00 PM EST.
[13] Email from Doak McDuffie (Forest Service) to Larry Pratt (Forest Service), March 10, 2009, 4:21 PM EST. *Re: NVUM Data Sabino Specific.*

Natural environment

The geography, climate, hydrology, ecology, and plant and animal biology contribute to the popularity of Sabino Canyon. This section documents these characteristics as well as the concept of natural carrying capacity and the impacts of the transportation system on the natural environment.

Geography

As shown in Figure 10, Sabino Canyon is one of several parallel canyons emanating northeast to southwest from Mount Lemmon and the Santa Catalina Mountains. Upper Sabino Canyon Road, the 3.8 mile road that traverses part of the length of Sabino Canyon, begins at 2,700 feet above sea level and climbs to an altitude of roughly 3,300 feet. Saddleback Ridge to the southeast is roughly 4,300 to 5,000 feet. The top of Thimble Peak rests at 5,300 feet. Mount Lemmon, located 14 miles north, peaks at over 9,100 feet.

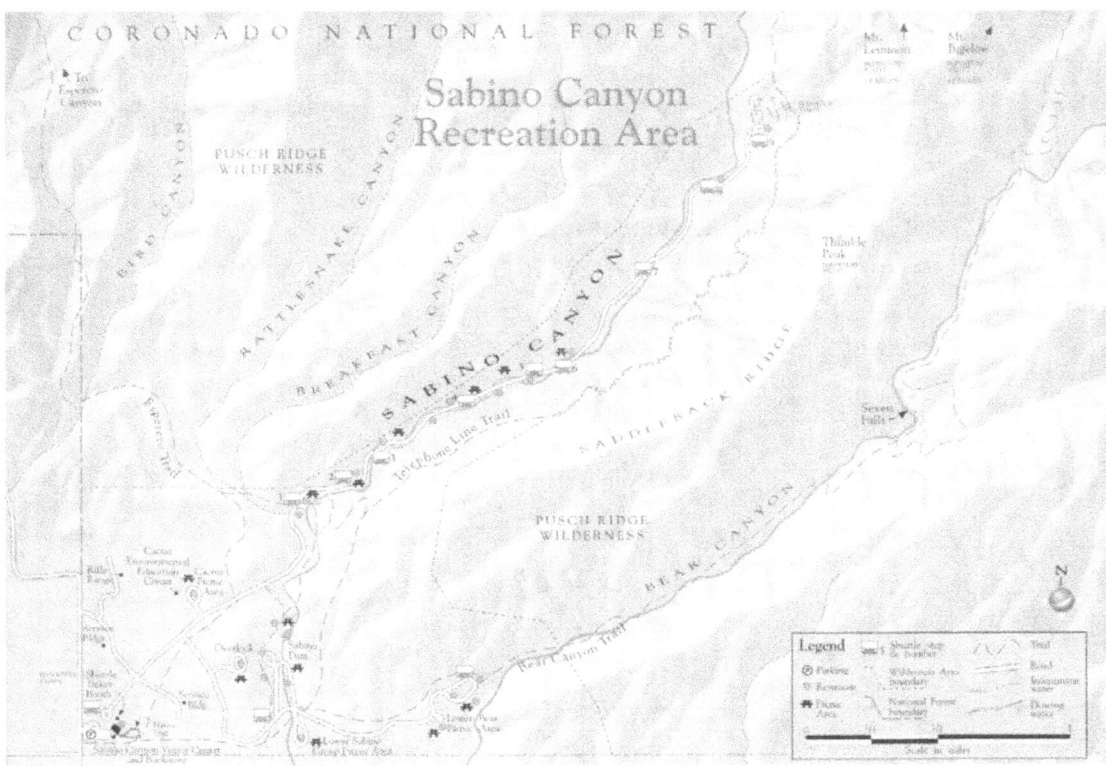

Figure 10 – Sabino Canyon Recreation Area, Coronado National Forest[14]

Climate

Tucson's desert climate is one of extremes. Differences between daily high and low temperatures are commonly more than 30 degrees Fahrenheit. Figure 11 shows seasonal variations in temperature while Figure 12 shows hourly variations in temperature in the months of January and July. The most comfortable times to visit the canyon are during the day in December through April and in the morning and evenings in May through November.

---

[14] Sabino Canyon Tours, http://www.sabinocanyon.com/imgCore/maps/SabinoCanyon_Map.pdf

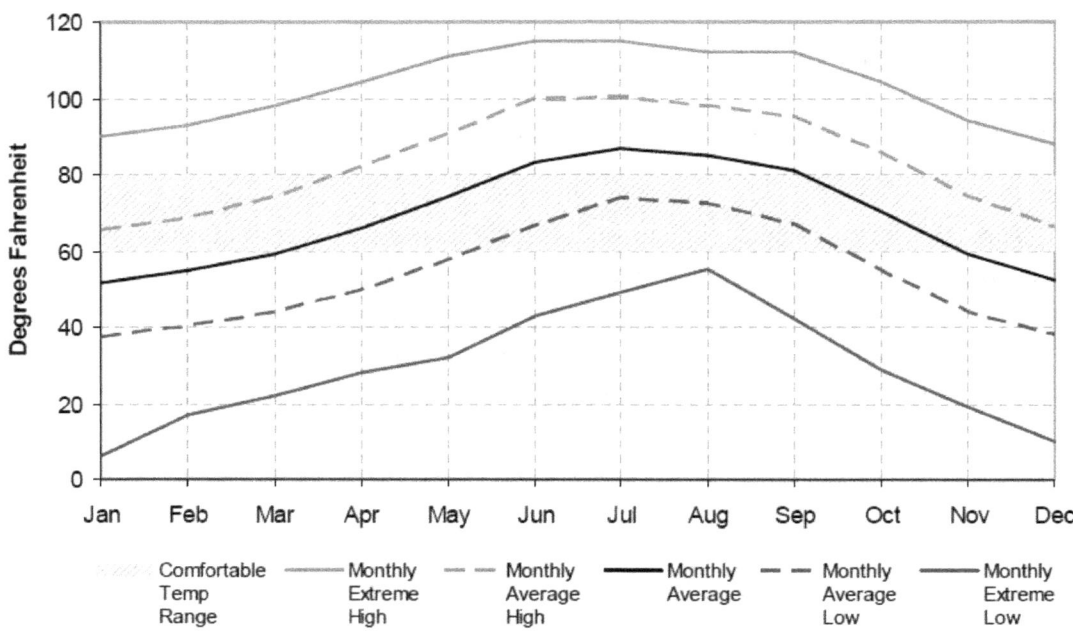

Figure 11 – Tucson seasonal variations in temperature, 1894 to 2008[15]

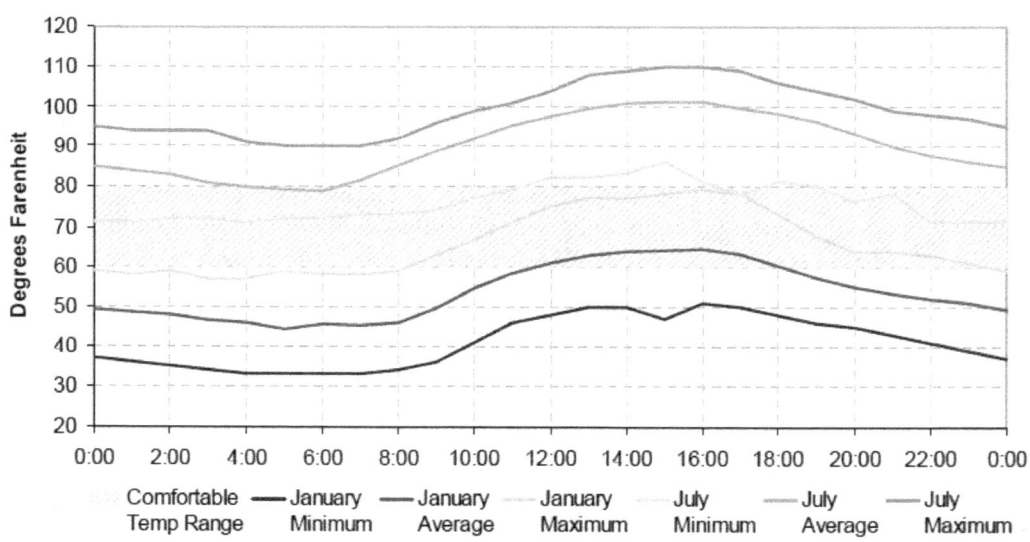

Figure 12 – Hourly temperature variations, January and July 2005[16]

The 1991 Interpretive Plan suggests caution using data from nearby weather stations to characterize conditions in Sabino Canyon. The canyon is subject to cold air drainage, shortened periods of sunshine,

[15] Western Regional Climate Center (2009). Station 028815: University of Arizona Tucson.
[16] Western Regional Climate Center (2009). Station 23160: Tucson International Airport.

and variations in elevation. The temperature and rainfall in Sabino Canyon is variable and unpredictable and may be best characterized by extreme temperature and rainfall statistics rather than averages.[17]

Sunrise in the winter months varies from 6:30 a.m. to 7:15 a.m. Sunrise in the summer months varies from 5:00 a.m. to 5:30 a.m.

Hydrology

Monthly average precipitation amounts at Sabino Canyon are shown in Figure 13. Mount Lemmon, part of the Sabino Creek watershed, and Tucson are shown for comparison. Summer rainfall consists of localized thundershowers from July through September. Winter rainfall consists of widespread, gentle showers from December through March. Figure 14 shows maximum and minimum monthly extremes as measured at the Sabino Canyon weather station.

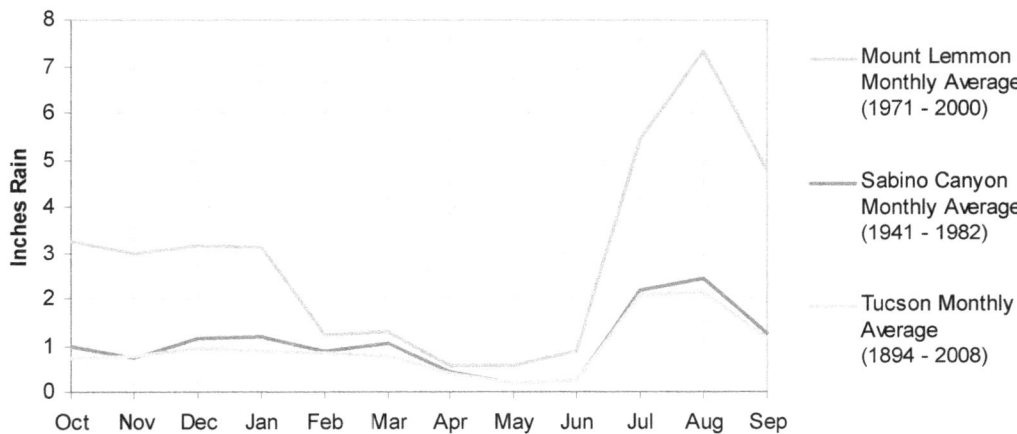

Figure 13 – Monthly average precipitation by water year at Mount Lemmon, Sabino Canyon, and University of Arizona, Tucson. Each of the weather stations was operational at different points in time as noted in the chart legend.[18]

---

[17] Walker, W., Lazaroff, D., and Whittlesey, S. (1991). *Sabino Canyon Interpretive Plan*. Coronado National Forest. 115 pp.
[18] Western Regional Climate Center (2009). Station 028815: University of Arizona Tucson; Station 027355: Sabino Canyon; Station 025732: Mount Lemmon, Arizona.

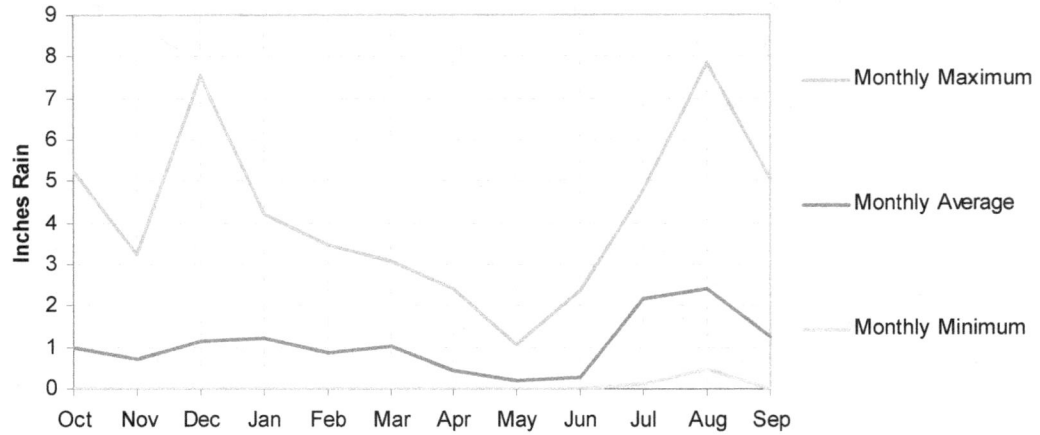

Figure 14 – Monthly maximum, average, and minimum rainfall measured at the Sabino Canyon weather station, 1941-1982[19]

Sabino Creek is one of only two perennial streams flowing into the Tucson Basin (the other being Cienega Creek).[20] As shown in Figure 15, the creek's watershed consists of an area of roughly 35.5 square miles in the Santa Catalina Mountains. It collects snow or rain from canyons (including Marshall Gulch, Lemmon Canyon, West Fork Sabino Canyon, Spencer Canyon, Rose Canyon, Pine Canyon, Palisade Canyon, and Box Camp Canyon) and water from natural springs (including Huntsman, Box, Apache, and Mud). Water drops nearly 6,000 feet along its 15 mile course from Summerhaven, Arizona, near the peak of Mount Lemmon, to Sabino Canyon Recreation Area.[21] Beyond Sabino Canyon, Sabino Creek flows into Tanque Verde Creek and several other rivers until it reaches the Colorado River and flows into the Gulf of California, roughly 400 miles away.

[19] Western Regional Climate Center. Station 027355: Sabino Canyon.
[20] Walker, W., Lazaroff, D., and Whittlesey, S. (1991). *Sabino Canyon Interpretive Plan*. Coronado National Forest. 115 pp.
[21] Ibid.

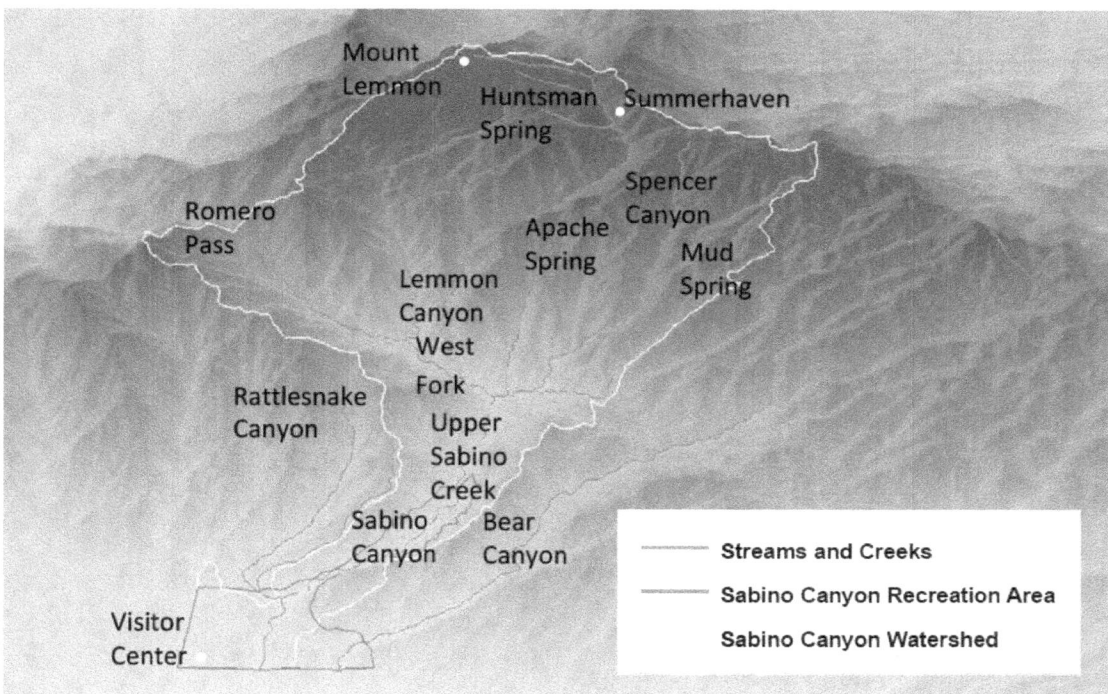

Figure 15 – Sabino Creek watershed[22]

Upper Sabino Creek has perennial water flow while Lower Sabino Creek has intermittent flow. During drought periods in the spring and fall, the sun may evaporate water in the lower creek down to a few perennial pools and the discharge slows dramatically, as shown in Figure 16.[23] Attempts to create man-made pools behind Sabino Canyon's nine bridges (technically considered 'vented low-water crossings') and a lake behind Sabino Dam have largely failed, collecting soil and sediment over time instead of water. Due to evaporation and permeable soils, flowing water rarely reaches Tanque Verde Creek. Instead, it sinks into the sandy creek bed and eventually into an underground aquifer that supplies Tucson with drinking water and sustains riparian vegetation along Sabino Creek.[24]

---

[22] GIS files provided by the Forest Service.
[23] Ibid.
[24] Kroesen, K. and Wilbor, S. (August 2006). *Sabino Creek Important Bird Area: A Habitat Guide for Landowners*. Tucson Audubon Society, Tucson, AZ. 34pp

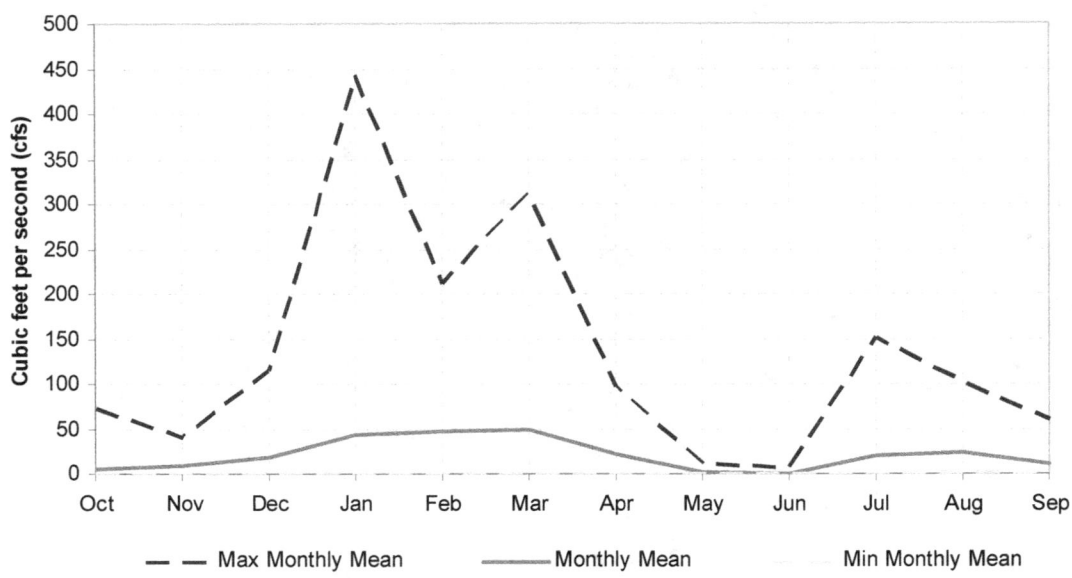

Figure 16 – Monthly mean water discharge in Lower Sabino Canyon, 1988-2006 by water year[25]

Large peak flows are commonly associated with flooding of Sabino Creek during the rainy seasons. Canyon visitors are warned about the possible dangers of walking near the creek. Although it may not be raining in the lower canyon, rain on top of the Santa Catalina Mountains can cause sudden flashfloods in the canyon. Sabino Creek can experience sudden and sometimes dangerous floods, particularly during the summer monsoon storms.

Figure 17 shows the annual number and percentage of days that i) have no water discharge and ii) have discharge that meets or exceeds the minimum flood conditions of 15 cubic feet per second (cfs) at Bridge 8. During the same time period, peak average daily discharges are shown in Figure 18. Absolute maximum discharges are shown in Figure 19.

---

[25] U.S. Geological Survey (2008). Water-Data Report 2007, Sabino Creek (09484000).

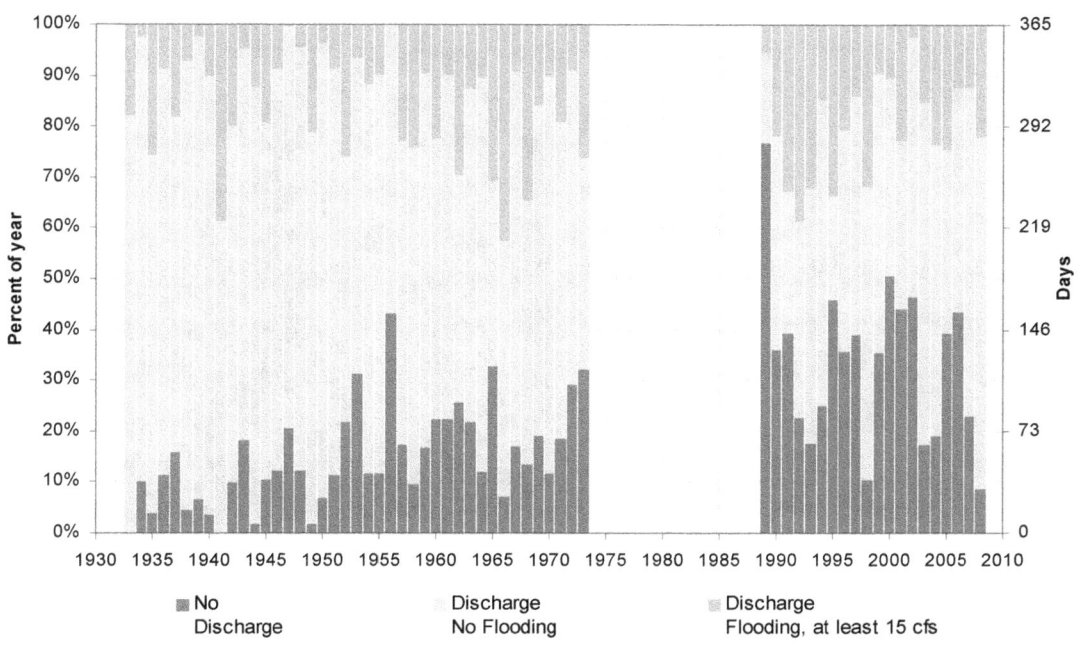

Figure 17 – Water discharge measured at lower Sabino Creek, June 1932 through March 2009 except for October 1974 to January 1988[26]

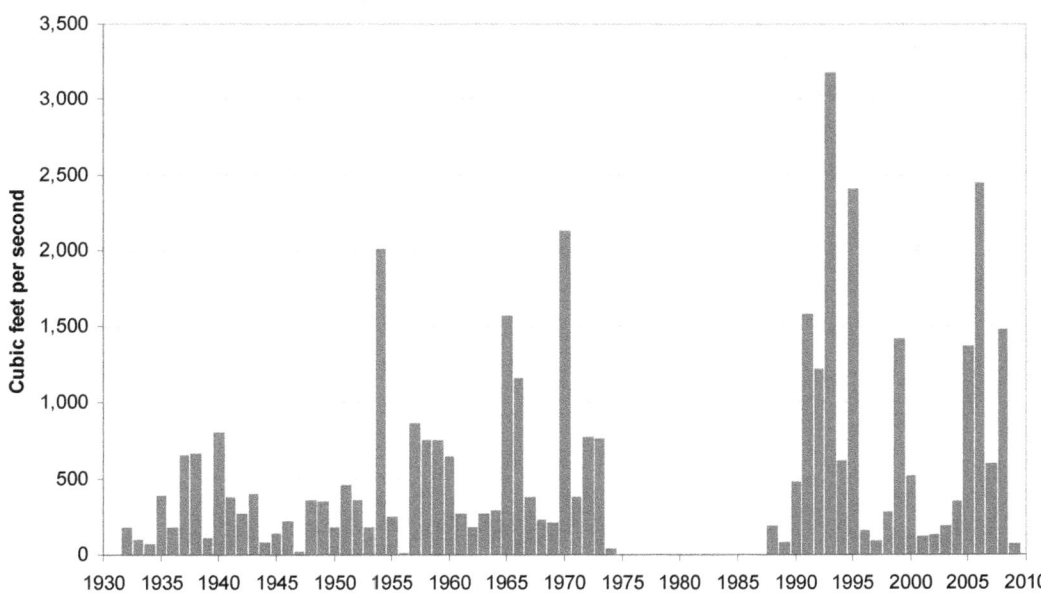

Figure 18 – Peak average daily water discharge measured at lower Sabino Creek. June 1932 through March 2009 except for October 1974 to January 1988[27]

---

[26] U.S. Geological Survey (2008). *National Water Information System: Web Interface*. Site 09484000, Sabino Creek near Tucson Arizona. Accessed at http://waterdata.usgs.gov/nwis on March 16, 2009.

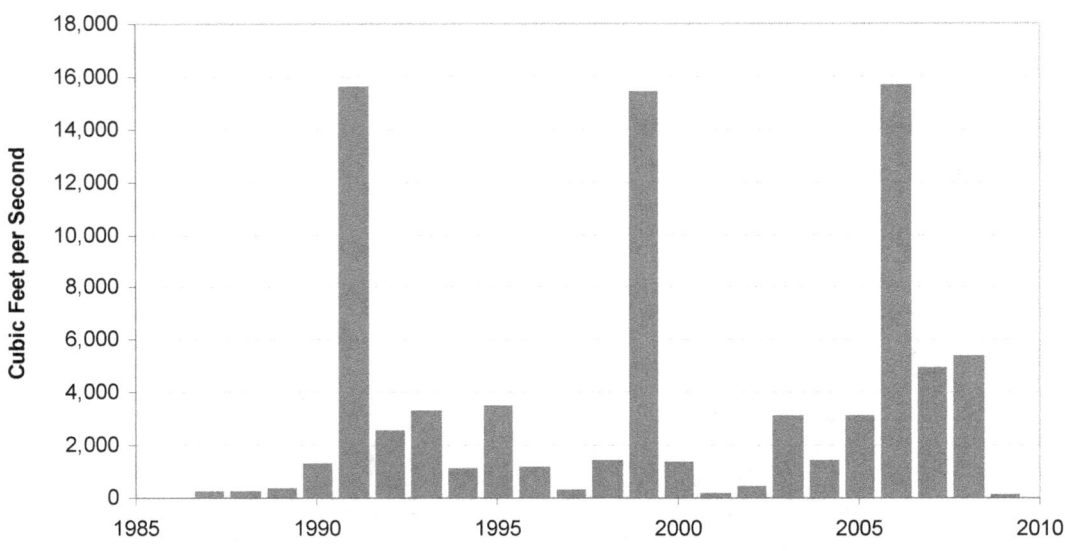

Figure 19 – Peak water discharge measured at lower Sabino Creek. Only available January 1988 through March 2009[28]

As shown in Figure 19, flooding in late July and early August 2006 resulted in the highest water discharge rate and debris flow slurries in the historic record of Sabino Canyon. Rainfall from July 27-30 saturated the creek bed so that heavy storms on July 31 and August 1 caused record peak stream flows of 15,700 cfs. The maximum three-day precipitation measured was 12.04 inches, an event that has a recurrence interval (RI) of 1,000 years. Ninety-two percent of the precipitation resulted in run off.[29] Soil saturation caused over 240 debris flows, three of which traveled in proximity to the mountain front. Prior to the 2006 floods, only five debris flows, all small, were known to have occurred in the Santa Catalina Mountains[30]. Debris flows can carry sediment ranging from sand to large boulders. Though they are part of the natural cycle, these flows can create massive destruction to the built environment. Locations of debris flows in Sabino Canyon resulting from the 2006 flood are shown in Figure 20. Examples of resulting damage to the road are shown in Figure 21.

---

[27] Ibid.

[28] Ibid.

[29] Webb, R.H., Magirl, C.S., Griffiths, P.G., Youberg, A., and Pearthree, P.A. (2008). Slopes Fail, Debris Flows in Extremis. *Southwest Hydrology*, November/December 2008, p8.

[30] Webb, R.H., Griffiths, P.G., Magirl, C.S., Boyer, D., Pytlak, E., Shoemaker, C., Schaffner, M., Pearthree, P.A., and Youberg, A. (2007). *Santa Catalina Debris Flows*. USGS, AZGS, NOAA. 70pp.

Figure 20 – Debris flows in Sabino Canyon, July 31 and August 1, 2006[31]

Figure 21 – Aerial (left) and ground (right) photos of debris flow deposits burying the end of the tram road in Sabino Canyon. The tram road turnaround is beneath the boulder pile in the ground view; note Lee Allison and Todd Shipman of the AZGS for scale. Large white arrow points to the location of buried rest room facilities. Aerial photo provided by R.H. Webb.[32]

To educate and protect visitors to the canyon about dangerous flood events, in 2008 the Forest Service participated in a joint event sponsored by the National Weather Service (NWS) titled "Thunderstorm Safety Awareness Week." This annual and week-long event is held in June and highlights safety and

[31] Webb, R.H., Griffiths, P.G., Magirl, C.S., Boyer, D., Pytlak, E., Shoemaker, C., Schaffner, M., Pearthree, P.A., and Youberg, A. (2007). *Santa Catalina Debris Flows*. USGS, AZGS, NOAA. 70pp.
[32] Pearthree, P., and Youberg, A. (2006). Recent Debris Flows and Floods in Southern Arizona. *Arizona Geology*, Vol. 36, No. 3.

hazards associated with thunderstorms, lightning, and flash flooding. The partnership had previously focused on mainly urban issues, including crossing flooded washes in a car, keeping out of flood waters in the storm run-off system, and avoiding outdoor activities during lightning. The Forest Service became involved to highlight the hazards associated with outdoor recreation in canyons and mountains during thunderstorms and periods of greater rainfall. A week following the media-covered event a significant storm system came to Tucson. The Forest Service and partners were able to leverage the previous media coverage and disseminate specific predictions of rainfall amounts and stream crossing closures to the public. Warning messages and outreach included links to NWS websites and other web-based information as well as numbers to call for the latest conditions. The storm dumped a lot of rain, and the Forest Service responded by closing roads and stream crossings at Sabino Canyon. The Forest Service also now deploys field staff earlier in the morning than usual (often at 5:00 a.m.) to assess the hazards and safety considerations during and after storms. These active management techniques precipitated a decrease in rescues caused by high water in Sabino Canyon from 126 in 2007 to 1 in 2008. Thunderstorm Safety Awareness Week, now called Monsoon Safety Awareness Week, has been adopted by all NWS offices in Arizona and New Mexico along with offices located in El Paso, Texas and Las Vegas, Nevada.

Ecology

Sabino Canon Recreation Area consists of five major natural communities: aquatic, riparian woodland, mesquite bosque, desert scrub, and grassland.[33] The riparian areas are particularly unique and valued natural resources. Riparian habitat and its associated greenery, water features, and wildlife are significant attractions for visitors. Statewide, it is estimated only 5 percent of this habitat remains, yet riparian habitat provides food and shelter to 80 percent of the state's wildlife for some portion of their life cycle[34]. Sabino Creek is one of the few remaining locations within urban Tucson where riparian habitat may still be protected.

Sabino Creek's aquatic habitats are home to the Gila chub, a fish species listed as endangered in the United States under the Endangered Species Act and monitored by the U.S. Fish and Wildlife Service (USFWS). Sabino Creek contains 6.9 miles of critical habitat for the Gila chub, from the southwest forest boundary to the West Fork of Sabino Canyon[35]. The exact boundary of the Gila chub's critical habitat is a corridor defined by a 300-foot buffer extending to either side of Sabino Creek's normal high water mark. This critical habitat is characterized by primary constituent elements (PCEs), or the physical and biological features that are essential to the conservation and restoration of Gila chubs. Some of the key features of the PCE's include:

Perennial pools, areas of higher velocity, and areas of shallow water among plants or eddies;

- Seasonally appropriate water temperatures for all life stages;

[33] Coronado National Forest, Santa Catalina Ranger District (December 1993). *Sabino Canyon Recreation Concept Plan: Recommendations for Restoration and Enhancement.* USDA Forest Service.

[34] Kroesen, K., and Wilbor, S. (2006). *Sabino Creek Important Bird Area: A Habitat Guide for Landowners.* Tucson Audubon Society. 34 pp.

[35] Department of the Interior, Fish and Wildlife Service (2005). 50 Code of Federal Regulations (CFR) Part 17: Endangered and Threatened Wildlife and Plants; Listing Gila chub as Endangered With Critical Habitat; Final Rule. *Federal Register*, Vol. 70, No. 211, Wednesday, November 2, 2005. Accessed at http://www.fws.gov/southwest/es/arizona/Documents/SpeciesDocs/GilaChub/Final/Gila%20chub%20final%20rule.pdf on March 25, 2009.

- Reasonable water quality;
- Access to invertebrates and aquatic plants for food;
- Sufficient cover consisting of downed logs in the water channel, submerged aquatic vegetation, submerged large tree root wads, undercut banks with sufficient overhanging vegetation, large rocks and boulders with overhangs, a high degree of stream-bank stability, and a healthy, intact riparian vegetation community;
- Minimal competition from non-native species; and
- Streams that maintain a natural flow pattern including periodic flooding.[36]

Flooding, mentioned earlier, is an important component of the riparian ecosystem because it:

- Scrapes the ground, making bare patches for seeds to grow;
- Transports seeds away from parent plants so that new plants do not compete for water and sun with older plants;
- Washes away salts that crust on the earth's surface and brings nutrients to improve the soil;
- Breaks off tree limbs and removes dead wood, clearing more space for sunlight; and
- Raises the water table.[37]

Naturally occurring wildfires are beneficial and are part of the natural cycle of ecosystems such as those found in the Santa Catalina Mountains. By removing overhead vegetation, fire opens soil up to increased solar radiation and warming during the day. Loss of vegetation also allows soils to become cooler more quickly at night, allows more rain to reach the soil's surface, and results in decreased transpiration which allows soil to retain more moisture. Some plants are fire intolerant, while others are tolerant and some even require fire to germinate. These plants rely on fire to decrease competition among competitors and create local environments that foster successful propagation. Two notable wildfires have occurred in the Santa Catalina Mountains since 2000.

In 2002, the Bullock Fire burned from May 21st to June 5th.[38] Ignited by humans, the fire burned roughly 30,000 acres of land and no structures were lost. The cost of fighting the fire was $14 million. Sabino Canyon Recreation Area was closed from May 26th to July 18th.

In 2003, the Aspen Fire burned from June 17th to July 18th.[39] Ignited by humans, the fire burned roughly 85,000 acres of land and destroyed 340 homes and businesses in the town of Summerhaven.[40] Damages to utilities including electric and phone lines, water and sewer facilities, and roads totaled $4.1 million. The cost of fighting the fire was roughly $17 million, and the Forest Service is spending $2.7 million to prevent soil loss. Sabino Canyon Recreation Area was closed from June 4th to June 24th.

---

[36] Ibid.

[37] Webb, R.H., Griffiths, P.G., Magirl, C.S., Boyer, D., Pytlak, E., Shoemaker, C., Schaffner, M., Pearthree, P.A., and Youberg, A. (2007). *Santa Catalina Debris Flows*. USGS, AZGS, NOAA. 70pp.

[38] Wildfire Alternatives (WALTER) (2004). *Catalina Mountains: Fire History*. University of Arizona. Accessed at http://walter.arizona.edu/overview/study_areas/catalina_fire_hist.asp on March 26, 2009.

[39] National Interagency Fire Center. *Fire Information - Wildland Fire Statistics: Wildland Fire Season 2003*. Accessed at http://www.nifc.gov/fire_info/fire_summaries/summary_2003.htm on March 26, 2009.

[40] Aspen Fire. (2008, October 25). In *Wikipedia, The Free Encyclopedia*. Accessed at http://en.wikipedia.org/w/index.php?title=Aspen_Fire&oldid=247562300 on March 26, 2009.

Biology

In addition to the previously mentioned Gila chub, Sabino Canyon is home to an array of reptiles and amphibians, birds, insects, mammals, fish, and plants.[41]

Sabino Canyon is a world-renowned spot to see unique reptiles, including the giant spotted whiptail, the tiger rattlesnake, and the collared lizard among others.

Sabino Canyon is a popular spot for ornithologists to bird watch. Over 100 species of birds have been identified there, including Roadrunner, Gila woodpecker, Red-tailed Hawk, Black Phoebe, Belted Kingfisher, and Great Blue Heron.[42] The migration of Cedar Waxwings is a popular attraction in the spring and fall.[43] Hummingbird research is conducted in Sabino Canyon due to its location along the intercontinental migration routes of many species. Mexican spotted owls, listed as threatened by the federal government, sometimes come down from the Santa Catalina Mountains in the colder winter months. Audubon's Important Bird Area (IBA) Program in Arizona reviewed and approved Sabino and Bear Creeks as an IBA in 2004 because they provide shelter to significant populations of species listed as "Species of Conservation Concern."[44]

Sabino Canyon is home to a unique species of damselfly, the Sabino Canyon Damselfly.[45] This species is neither endangered nor threatened, but it is unique and cherished by naturalists and canyon visitors. Other invertebrates including water tigers, diving beetles, and invasive crayfish live in the canyon as well.[46]

Small mammals including bobcats, raccoons, foxes, coatis, ring-tailed cats, ground-squirrels, and many others live in the creek floodplain. Large mammals include whitetail deer, javelinas, and mountain lions. The increasing presence of people spurred by tourism and nearby development have accustomed both deer and mountain lions to humans. In 2004, mountain lions began to act aggressively toward humans. Though there were no fatalities in Sabino Canyon, there were unsuccessful lion attacks on humans in nearby Ventana Canyon. The Arizona Fish & Game Department has removed aggressive lions from the vicinity of Sabino Canyon.

The Forest Service is seeking to restore populations of several species in Sabino Canyon and the Santa Catalina Mountains. One species is the bighorn sheep, the population of which declined sharply in the 1980s due to degrading habitat quality resulting from encroaching development, increase of brush, and lack of wildfires. Lowland leopard frogs, Gila top minnows, and Mexican garter snakes, the last two of which are endangered, are also being planned for repopulation in Sabino Canyon.

Forest Service and the Arizona Fish & Game Department eradicated non-native fish from Sabino Creek including green sunfish, largemouth bass, and catfish. Kingfisher, heron, and crayfish are known to prey on Gila chub. Fish are most vulnerable in summer when water flow is diminished and hot temperatures

---

[41] Telephone conversation with Joshua Taiz, Santa Catalina District Biologist, Forest Service. March 24, 2009.
[42] Kroesen, K., and Wilbor, S. (2006). *Sabino Creek Important Bird Area: A Habitat Guide for Landowners*. Tucson Audubon Society. 34 pp.
[43] Phone conversation with Joshua Taiz, Santa Catalina District Biologist, Forest Service. March 24, 2009.
[44] Kroesen, K., and Wilbor, S. (2006). *Sabino Creek Important Bird Area: A Habitat Guide for Landowners*. Tucson Audubon Society. 34 pp.
[45] Phone conversation with Joshua Taiz, Santa Catalina District Biologist, Forest Service. March 24, 2009.
[46] Kroesen, K., and Wilbor, S. (2006). *Sabino Creek Important Bird Area: A Habitat Guide for Landowners*. Tucson Audubon Society. 34 pp.

evaporate pools of water. These are the same pools that attract people. One popular pool that people swim in is known as 'The Crack,' located beyond Bridge 9.

Vegetation along Sabino Creek includes cottonwoods, willows, ashes, elderberries, other native trees, and non-native grasses. Shrubs consist of water-loving plants such as buttonbushes, native cotton, white-ball acacia, desert honeysuckle, and many others. On the floor of the floodplain, there are native wildflowers and grasses, although some non-native weeds have invaded.[47] In the drier canyon environments live numerous desert scrub species including saguaro, cholla cacti, velvet mesquite (also found in mesquite bosque environments, thick forests near water), and palo verde trees. Invasive plant species, such as buffelgrass, giant reeds, and green fountain grass monopolize the canyon's water source, using up to four times as much hydration as their surrounding native plants[48]. Giant reeds also endanger waterfowl that depend on the bugs and insects in riparian zones for food. Volunteers in late 2008 and early 2009 worked to remove non-native species.

Carrying capacity

The 1993 Sabino Canyon Recreation Concept Plan refers to studies from the 1970s that determined that maintaining a maximum capacity of 2,200 persons at one time would prevent irreversible damage to the natural and built environments at the recreation area[49]. Given the passage of time, the Forest Service is uncertain of the validity of methods and results of the carrying capacity study.

Visitor demand is managed de facto during peak times by limited parking capacity. Although visitors may access the recreation area via several alternative transportation modes including walking, biking, and buses, access by private automobile is the most popular mode. The parking lot accommodates 372 vehicles.[50] If each vehicle holds an average of 3.0 people (the average size of groups that visit Coronado National)[51], the size of the lot constrains automobile visitation to an average of roughly 1,100 visitors at any given time. Since the recreation area does not track arrivals of visitors by alternative modes, it does not know whether the 2,200 person carrying capacity cited in the 1993 Recreation Plan is exceeded. There are plans to add parking for an additional 130 vehicles, bringing the potential average of total automobile visitors at one time to 1,500.

Impacts of transportation system on the natural environment

The bridges prevent the natural flow of water in Sabino Creek and cause unnatural buildup of sediment in the creek bed. This unintended result of the bridges is in direct competition with the primary constituent elements of the Gila chub's critical habitat, to prevent unnecessary sedimentation and allow natural water flow. Because the bridges were built prior to the listing of the Gila chub, they are included in the baseline of the critical habitat.

[47] Kroesen, K., and Wilbor, S. (2006). *Sabino Creek Important Bird Area: A Habitat Guide for Landowners.* Tucson Audubon Society. 34 pp.
[48] Hartman, K. Arizonans Even the Score for Underdog Trees, Plants (March 22, 2009). Associated Content. Accessed at http://www.associatedcontent.com/article/1584433/arizonans_even_the_score_for_underdog.html on March 24, 2009.
[49] Coronado National Forest, Santa Catalina Ranger District (December 1993). *Sabino Canyon Recreation Concept Plan: Recommendations for Restoration and Enhancement.* USDA Forest Service.
[50] Email from Larry Pratt, "RE: Carrying Capacity Study", Thursday, January 08, 2009 5:30 PM
[51] Email from Larry Pratt, "Visitors Per Vehicle Estimates for Sabino Canyon", Wednesday, May 13, 2009 7:29 PM.

During flooding events, sediment is deposited on the bridges. Removing it is an environmental and operational issue.

The bridges affect upstream and downstream movement of species in Sabino Canyon. They prevent invasive fish species from moving upstream and competing with or preying on the Gila chub. They also bolster populations of invasive crayfish by creating tranquil habitats.

The 12-foot tall dam also prevents upstream movement of invasive fish species.

With respect to the tram, no causal relationship has been defined between the degradation of natural species and the tram, the tram's diesel exhaust, or the noise generated by the tram's loud speaker use.

Transportation infrastructure

Development history[52]

In the 1930s, the Works Projects Administration (WPA) and the Civilian Conservation Corps (CCC) undertook a series of development projects within the area. A four-mile paved road with nine stone bridges (technically 'vented low-water crossings') was constructed in the canyon bottom. Dams were built, creating pools for recreational visitors. Extensive camping and picnic facilities were constructed. Plans called for extending the road and constructing a large dam farther up the canyon (in an area now congressionally-designated a Wilderness Area), but funding shortfalls prevented completion of the project.

For more than 30 years, residents and tourists were free to drive their personal vehicles within the canyon. The narrow, winding roads were designed for 1930s traffic, however, and by the 1960s, traffic jams and vehicle exhaust fumes were commonplace on weekends and holidays. The very experience that many people were coming to enjoy was being destroyed.

In the 1960s and 1970s, the Forest Service invested heavily in the infrastructure of the recreation area. New roads were built, electricity and water-sewer lines were installed, and many new restrooms and recreation facilities were constructed. The first visitor center in the Forest Service's Southwest Region was erected here in 1963. Visitation skyrocketed.

In 1973, a flood destroyed several approaches to river crossings in the upper canyon, and the road was closed temporarily to private vehicles to accommodate installation of sewer lines. The closure provided an opportunity to address the problems in the canyon, including noise and air pollution, litter, vandalism, rowdiness, and congestion. Debate included whether or not private vehicles should be permanently banned in the canyon. At issue, in part, was to continue providing access to Sabino Canyon to disabled communities.[53]

A draft environmental statement was issued in 1975 outlining the concept of a public transportation system in the canyon. The four primary objectives for the system were to:

---

[52] This history is taken from a case study of the bus shuttle system by T. Quinn; T. Quinn, *A Public Utility Model for Managing Public Land Recreation Enterprises*, USDA/Forest Service, Pacific Northwest Research Station, General Technical Report PNW-GTR-543, May 2002.
[53] U.S. Department of Agriculture, Forest Service Memorandum (October 24, 1988). "History of Shuttle System in Sabino Canyon."

- Enhance the experience of forest visitors;
- Emphasize the natural and environmental factors of this experience;
- Provide interpretive and educational services and opportunities; and
- Maintain and improve the quality of the ecosystem (soil, water, air, vegetation, and wildlife).

A tram system was recommended as the best solution to pollution and vehicle congestion issues in the canyon. In 1978, a parking lot, ticket booth, new restrooms, and roofed shelters for waiting visitors were constructed near the Visitor Center. Tram service began that year to Upper Sabino Canyon and was extended to Lower Sabino Canyon and Bear Canyon in 1981.[54,55] The tram operation changed management in 1985, and the present operator, Sabino Canyon Tours, Inc., has provided service since.

The remainder of this section will describe the transportation infrastructure in and around Sabino Canyon Recreation Area, including roads, vented low-water crossings, parking, trails, tram infrastructure and operations, and access. An overview of the recreation area and its infrastructure is provided in Figure 22.

---

[54] Walker, W., Lazaroff, D., and Whittlesey, S. (1991). *Sabino Canyon Interpretive Plan*. Coronado National Forest. 115 pp.

[55] Coronado National Forest, Santa Catalina Ranger District (December 1993). *Sabino Canyon Recreation Concept Plan: Recommendations for Restoration and Enhancement*. USDA Forest Service.

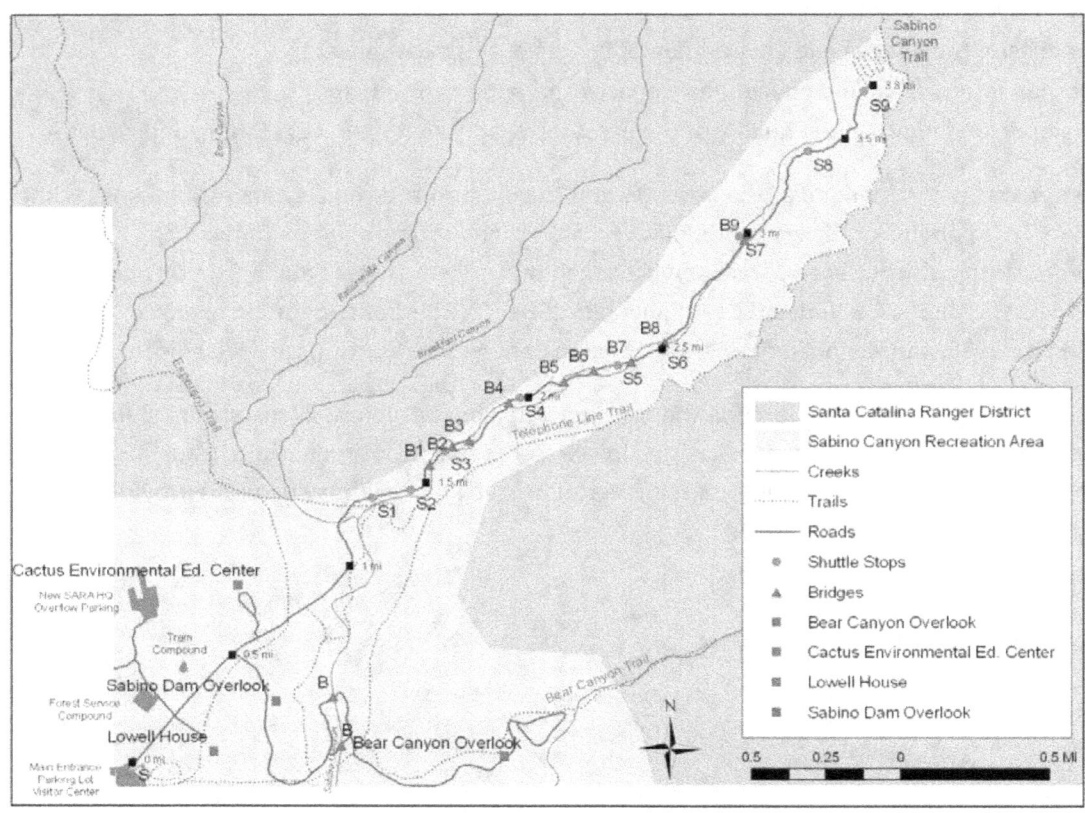

Figure 22 – Sabino Canyon Recreation Area[56]

Roads

Upper Sabino Canyon Road and Bear Canyon Road are within the recreation area. The ideal maintenance schedule for these federally-owned roads is shown in Table 2. The annualized maintenance cost under this idealized schedule would be $120,000. In addition to regular maintenance needs, Emergency Relief for Federally Owned Roads (ERFO) projects are initiated as needed (roughly every seven years) and may be on the order of $1 million.[57]

---

[56] GIS files provided by the Forest Service.
[57] Email from Walt Keyes, April 6, 2009.

Table 2 – Maintenance schedule for roads[58]

Frequency	Cost	Description
1 year	$30,000	Work on the shoulders, asphalt, stones, and ditch clean out for road and parking lot.
7 years	$350,000	Maintaining asphault with crack, fog, slurry, and chip sealing and restriping
50 years	$2,000,000	Grind pavement, lay new asphault mat and installing shouldering by placing aggregate, shaping, and compacting

Upper Sabino Canyon Road

Upper Sabino Canyon Road is narrow with rolling grades and contains nine tram stops. The road is closed to private motorized vehicles. The key road geometric characteristics are presented in Table 3 and the road elevation is presented in Figure 23.

Table 3 – Road geometries, Upper Sabino Canyon Road[59]

Location	Grades (%)	Length (ft)	Comments
Deadman Hill	8-11	350	Majority of Roadway is under 10%, steepest near crest
Bridge 1	8-10	50	
Bridge 3			Tight radius
Bridge 4			Tight radius
Bridge 5	10-14	40	
Bridge 6	8-10	50	
Ocho Grande (below crossing)	8-10	300	
Ocho Grande (dip section)	-10 to +10	40	40' vertical curve length
Stop 8 to Stop 9	7-12	2,900	Majority of roadway is 7-9%

Figure 23 – Upper Sabino Canyon Road elevation

As shown in Figure 24, the cross-section width and the turning radii at crossing entrances and exits are the most restrictive elements of the road and may constrain vehicle types.

---

[58] Ibid.
[59] Telephone conversation with Tom Cassell, March 2009.

Figure 24 – The bridge and tram widths require that pedestrians wait for the tram to cross. Sharp corners of bridge approaches may constrain choice of tram vehicles. Courtesy: USDOT Volpe Center.

Bear Canyon Road

Vehicle access to Bear Canyon Road is off of Upper Sabino Canyon Road, approximately ¾ miles north of the Visitor Center. Foot traffic can access Bear Canyon Road off of North Bear Canyon Road. Only a fraction (roughly 1-5 percent) of visitors use the lower canyon area for recreation compared with the number of visitors who use the upper canyon area.[60] Bear Canyon Road consists of two 9' lanes with 1' shoulders at intermittent spots. There are three tram stops in Bear Canyon. The topography is less restricted than that of Upper Sabino Canyon Road and has only two low water crossings. Storm events have less effect on the operation of Bear Canyon Road and it is usually restored earlier than Upper Sabino Canyon Road. Grades are also less, reaching an 8 percent maximum. There is a severe, 120-degree turn at the far end of the road. The existing tram has articulated joints and front and rear steering axles, thus off-tracking of the body of the tram is limited. In other words, there is little room needed to accommodate the swing of the vehicle body relative to the track width of the wheels, and the vehicle can negotiate relatively tight turns. Though there used to be a loop turnaround in Bear Canyon, this has been replaced with a new turnaround ½ mile outside the mouth of the canyon. The last ½ mile of unimproved road in the vicinity of the federally-designated Wilderness Area is now closed to all traffic except emergency and service vehicles.

Bridges

There are 11 bridges in the recreation area, nine along Upper Sabino Canyon Road, and two along Bear Canyon Road, and one decommissioned bridge near the Lower Sabino Picnic Area. Technically, the structures are not bridges but vented low-water crossings that are most properly considered part of the

---

[60] Personal communications, Walter Keyes, Road Engineer, Forest Service.

pavement structure, as they have subsurface and arched concrete culverts for drainage of the creek.[61] The cross-section width is 8' 6" +/- 1". There are no transition or tangent segments prior to the crossings. Single-lane operation is required to traverse the crossings, and pedestrians and cyclists are often forced to wait for passage of the tram.

The crossings are Portland cement mortared rock masonry walls with cast-in-place reinforced concrete decks. The two main "vents" are arched, cast-in-place concrete culverts with flat concrete bottoms, many of which have become plugged with channel fill over time. It is believed additional corrugated drainage pipes are set at a lower elevation and probably also plugged with fill. The crossing decks are constrained on the sides by rock masonry extensions of the walls on both ends of the crossing. In the center the deck functionally extends over the top of the rock masonry except for what appears to be decorative 'dragon teeth', which are individual stones set on top of the rock masonry in the center section of the crossing. Three bridges are shown in Figure 25.

Figure 25 – Bridges of Upper Sabino Canyon Road. Note the decorative 'dragon teeth' in set in the rock masonry (bottom). Courtesy: USDOT Volpe Center.

---

[61] Ibid.

Although the bridges are designed to allow passage of low-water flows, the bridges and road surfaces do flood when discharge rates exceed relatively low discharge limits. **Table 4** shows the discharge rates that induce flooding over the various bridges in Sabino Canyon. Furthermore, the culverts under the decks are not regularly cleaned, and when blocked, the bridges act like dams. When water flow is high, the water rises from drainage of the watershed and drains downstream over the surface of the pavement. Each flooding event also increases bed sedimentation, thereby increasing stream elevation and the relative frequency of flooding.

Table 4 – Discharge rates for flooding at bridges on Upper Sabino Canyon Road[62]

Bridge	Minimum flood conditions (cfs)
1	18
2	24
3	30
4	34
5	30
6	18
7	65
8	15
9	65

The 2006 debris flows in Sabino Canyon caused damage at 16 sites within the recreation area, four of which were assessed in an Emergency Relief for Federally Owned Roads (ERFO) Design Study Report (DSR). The four sites included:

- Bridge 5 site repairs;
- Rockfall containment site repairs;
- Bridge 9 site repairs; and
- Tram stop 9 site repairs.

Repairs to two of the four sites were expected by the Damage Survey Report (DSR) to cost $1.15 million, and the total cost for all repairs paid for all the repairs was $2 million.

Trails

There are four main hiking trails and numerous connector routes in Sabino Canyon Recreation Area. The main trails, shown in Figure 22, are Esperero Trail, Telephone Line Trail, Sabino Canyon Trail, and Bear Canyon Trail. The trails are generally primitive and are not Americans with Disabilities Act (ADA)-accessible. The trailhead to the Telephone Line Trail is at Tram Stop 1 on Upper Sabino Canyon Road. This trail is essentially a loop with a second trailhead at Stop 9. This trail proceeds from the turnaround

---

[62] Sustainability of semi-Arid Hydrology and Riparian Areas (2008). *Sabino Canyon Hydrology*. University of Arizona. Accessed at http://www.sahra.arizona.edu/sabinocanyon/flash/index.html on March 19, 2009.

site at Stop 9 to the east across the old switch-back trail. This trail has been recommended for upgrade to ADA accessibility standards, if feasible.[63]

Sabino Canyon tram

Tram ridership

The tram service itself has become an attraction at Sabino Canyon. Many visitors come solely to experience the canyon via the tram. Though they may disembark and walk between several stops, they usually ride the beginning and end portions of the road, especially given the steep incline between Tram Stops 7 and 9. Some visitors choose to walk back down the road from Stop 9. Of those, many board the tram again at some point. The tram provides assistance to those who are not comfortable fording crossings during minor flood conditions, free of charge.

Figure 26 shows annual tram ridership compared with estimated annual recreation area visitation. Recreation area visitation is estimated by multiplying average vehicle occupancy of 3.0[64] by the number of private vehicles that enter Sabino Canyon Recreation Area. This estimation does not include visitors who arrive by other means. Figure 26 suggests that during an average year, roughly 25-30 percent of visitors who arrive by private vehicle ride the tram.

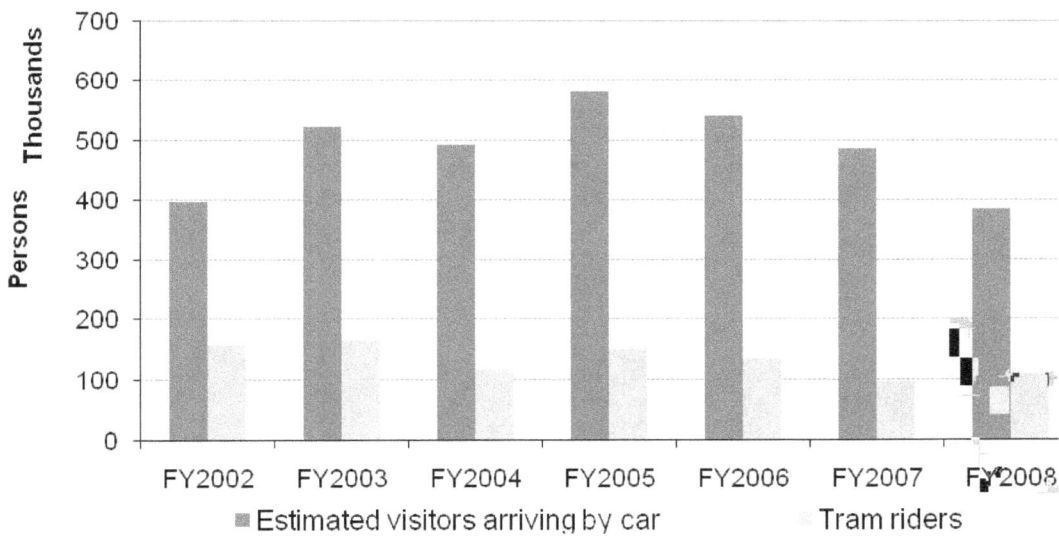

Figure 26 – Annual tram ridership (obtained from ticket sales) compared with estimated average monthly visitation of recreation area visitors arriving by private vehicle, FY2002-2008

Figure 25 shows the monthly tram ridership compared with estimated visitation from October 2002 through September 2008. While all years show similar winter peaking, atypical conditions previously described in Table 1 greatly impact the service. For example, ridership in the March 2004 was far below normal due to the canyon closings caused by mountain lion aggression. Following the 2006 floods, the

---

[63] Federal Highway Administration Central Federal Lands Highway Division (September 2007). *Design Study Report, Sabino Canyon ERFO Improvements*. p. 31.
[64] Email from Larry Pratt, "Visitors Per Vehicle Estimates for Sabino Canyon", Wednesday, May 13, 2009 7:29 PM.

Sabino Canyon tram service was suspended from August through October of the same year, when it opened to Stop 4. In April 2007, the remainder of the road reopened through Tram Stop 9.

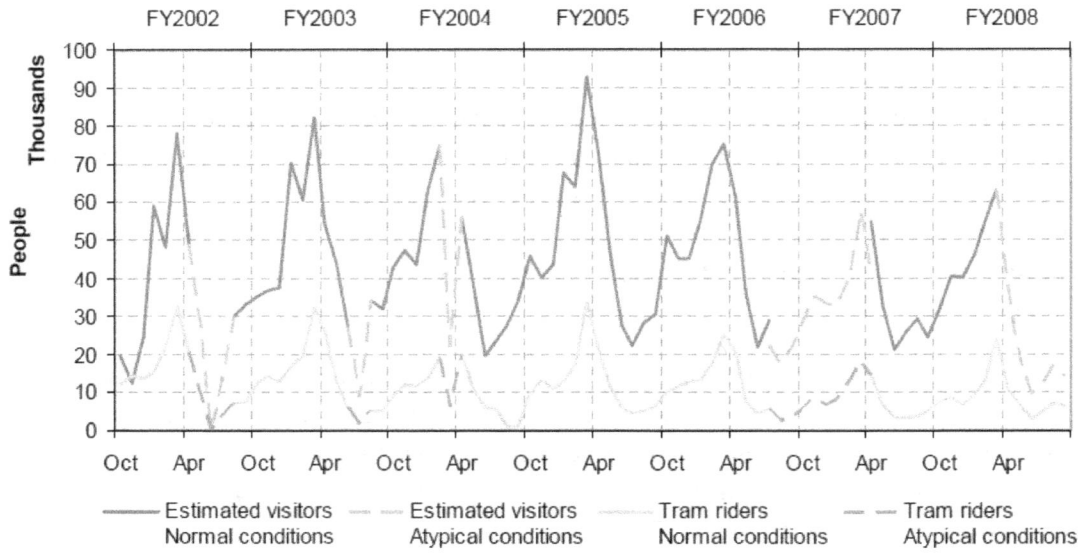

Figure 27 – Estimated visitation of visitors arriving by automobile and tram riders (obtained from ticket sales). Descriptions of atypical conditions are summarized in Table 1. Data courtesy of Forest Service and Sabino Canyon Tours, Inc.

Figure 28 depicts average monthly tram ridership and estimated visitors. Again, riders and visitation are high in winter months and comparatively lower in summer months.

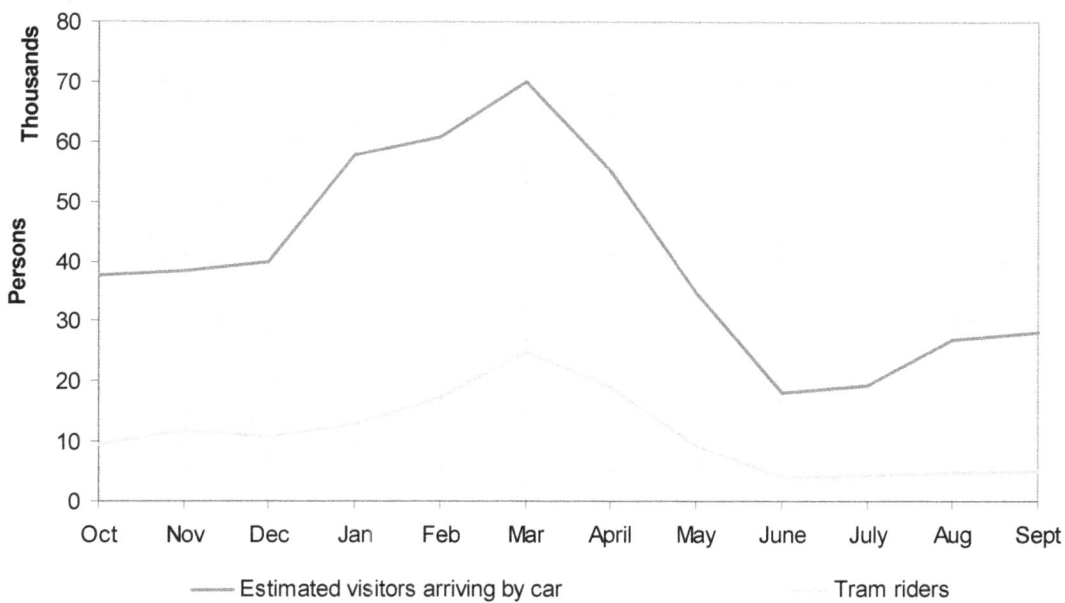

Figure 28 – Average monthly tram ridership (obtained from ticket sales) compared with estimated average monthly visitation of recreation area visitors arriving by private vehicle, FY2002-2008. Sabino Canyon Tours and USDA Forest Service.

Hourly tram ridership was not available, thus Figure 29 shows estimated hourly tram ridership based on arrival rates of private automobiles, adjusted for monthly tram ticket sales. The estimation methodology is presented in Appendix A. Ridership is estimated to be highest in the morning hours, particularly on weekdays and weekends in the peak season, December through April, and declines throughout the day. Actual ridership may not drop off as drastically throughout the day as estimated because some riders buy their tickets early but may not ride until later. The tram is estimated to be more popular on weekends than weekdays.

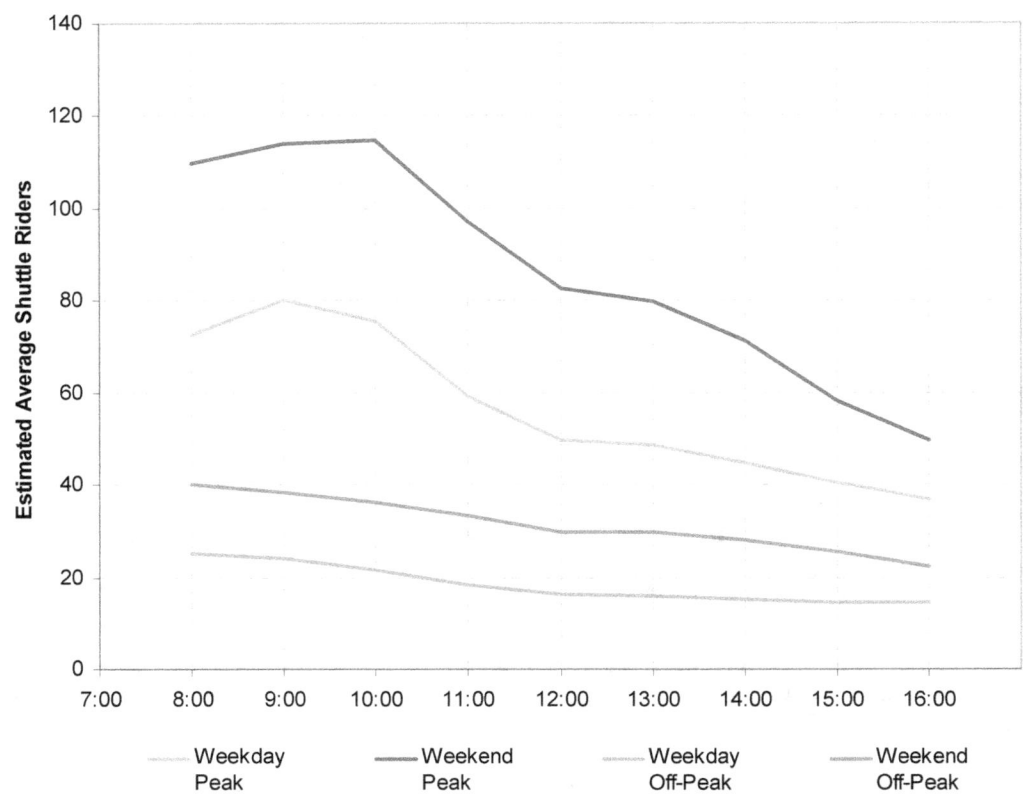

Figure 29 – Hourly tram ridership estimated using monthly tram rider counts and hourly private automobile arrivals.

Tram operator

Sabino Canyon Tours, Inc., has been operating the tram service at Sabino Canyon since 1985 under a special use permit granted by the Forest Service. At the time of writing, Sabino Canyon Tours is negotiating a new permit.[65] It has been operating under an addendum to its most recent one-year special use permit which terminated on January 31, 2009.[66,67] Section II.A of the permit requires an annual operating plan to be prepared by the tram operator. The current operations plan was originally written for the period 2004 through 2006 and specifies tram run types, routes, fee structure, schedule, and interpretation requirements.[68]

---

[65] USDA Forest Service (2009). Special Use Term Permit, Sabino Canyon Tours, Inc., SAN4015-03. Draft.

[66] Telephone conversation with James Sutton, Forest Service. Tuesday, January 27, 2009.

[67] Telephone conversation with James Sutton, Forest Service. Friday, March 27, 2009.

[68] USDA Forest Service (2004). Sabino Canyon Tours, Inc. Three-Year Operation and Maintenance Plan, 2004-2006.

Runs

Upper Sabino Canyon Run

The Upper Sabino Canyon Run is an out-and-back route covering all 3.8 miles of Sabino Canyon Road.[69] The ride takes 1.5 hours (45 minutes one-way), and is accompanied by interpretive narration by the driver. The tram crosses the nine bridges originally constructed by the WPA and CCC and makes nine stops along the route. The bridges are not much wider than the trams, and pedestrians, cyclists, and other trams are forced to wait on one side until a tram has completely crossed. Tram frequency is 30 minutes with three trams operating simultaneously. Ticket holders may embark or disembark at any stop as often as they wish.

Bear Canyon Run

The Bear Canyon Run is an out-and-back route on a paved road 2 miles in length (one-way). The tram leaves once an hour, on the hour. There are three stops along the route which is not narrated. As with The Upper Sabino Canyon Run, ticket holders may embark or disembark at any stop as often as they wish.

Evening runs

Three nights a month from April through December, with the exception of the monsoon rain months of July and August, the tram runs to Upper Sabino Canyon.

Chartered runs

Groups may choose to charter the trams. Charter fees in addition to individual ticket fares are charged based on time of day and amount of time. Daytime weddings are charged only individual ticket fares. The bride and groom ride free.

Whitewater runs

When bridge crossings are unsafe due to flood conditions, trams travel to Tram Stop 2 and stop for 10 minutes. The tram then proceeds to the Lower Sabino area, using the Bear Canyon Road and stopping for 10 minutes before returning to the ticket booth area. These runs offer safe observation of the rushing creek water and are offered at reduced fares.

Fee structure

Fees for the tram's various runs are shown in Table 5. Currently, Sabino Canyon Tours accepts only cash for tram ticket sales. A small fee booth for the tram service is located roughly six feet from the Visitor Center. The fee booth is wired with electricity and a phone line.

---

[69] Sabino Canyon Tours, Inc. (2006). *Sabino Canyon Tours at Sabino Canyon, Tucson, Arizona*. Accessed at http://www.sabinocanyon.com/ on March 27, 2009.

Table 5 – Fee structure for tram runs. Children under 3 ride free

Run Type	Fee Type	Fee
Upper Sabino Canyon Run (Day and Night)	Adult (13 yrs and older)	$7.50
	Child (3-12 years)	$3.00
Bear Canyon Run	Adult	$3.00
	Child	$1.00
Whitewater Runs	Adult	$3.00
	Child	$1.00
Charter Fares (Do not include individual fares)	Day (9am-5pm)	$500/hr
	Night (5pm-9am)	$700 1st hr; $500 each additional hr

Schedule

The tram operates on a winter and summer schedule. During the summer, weekday service ends at 4:00 p.m. and weekend and holiday service ends at 4:30 p.m. The operating schedule is shown in Table 6.

Table 6 – Tram operating schedule

Season	Months	Days	Start Time	End Time
Winter	mid-December - June	All days	9:00 AM	4:30 PM
Summer	July - mid-December	Weekdays	9:00 AM	4:00 PM
Summer	July - mid-December	Weekends and Holidays	9:00 AM	4:30 PM

Interpretation

The special use permit specifies that the interpretive narration is to be kept as factual as possible. It may be reviewed by a Forest Service liaison officer as deemed necessary. Interpretation is provided during the Sabino Canyon Run and is performed by the driver, whose narration is spoken into a microphone and broadcast to riders via speakers mounted throughout the trams. The Operations and Maintenance Plan specifies the Forest Service and Sabino Canyon Tours are to cooperate to determine the best speaker technology for use by tram vehicles. The goals are to clearly communicate with passengers and to minimize aural disturbances throughout the remainder of the recreation area.

Vehicles

Sabino Canyon Tours owns and operates six trams for the Upper Sabino Canyon Run and one tram for the Bear Canyon Run.[70] Four of the vehicles run on B-35 biodiesel and three run on gasoline with both types having a fuel economy between 8.5 – 10 miles per gallon. Vehicle capacity range from 48 – 64 passengers each with a total capacity of 372 seats. Each vehicle is equipped with a two-way radio communication system for contact with the ticket booth, the vehicle compound office, and other mobile units. The vehicle compound office, located less than ¼ mile from Upper Sabino Canyon Road, is used for storage, fueling, and maintenance of the tram vehicles.

---

[70] Telephone conversation with Donn Ricketts, Sabino Canyon Tours, Inc. Wednesday, February 4, 2009.

The tram vehicles are considered by many to be old. Specific dates of manufacture of the vehicles were not available, but it is believed that the current fleet has been in use since Sabino Canyon Tours began operation in 1985. For its capital programs, the Federal Transit Administration (FTA) defines the minimum useful life of the most heavy-duty vehicles to be 12 years or over 500,000 miles. Trams are considered lighter duty vehicles which have correspondingly shorter service life.

Granular ridership data

Although monthly ridership data was provided, hourly ticket sales or ridership for a multi-year period could be used to uncover daily trip demand patterns seasonally, on weekdays, weekends, and holidays. Ticket sales by route could help quantitatively differentiate demand between the Sabino and Bear Canyon routes. Boarding and alighting statistics could quantitatively characterize popularity of destinations and travel patterns within Sabino Canyon as many riders also walk between stops. Ticket sales by ticket type (adult or child) could help determine average weight loads of tram trips and be used to calculate tram revenues.

Vehicle dimensions

Vehicle axle type, turning radius, width, length, and weight of the trams and trailers could be used to help better understand vehicle features that successfully navigate Upper Sabino Canyon Road.

Revenues and costs

Financial information including revenues and capital, operations, and maintenance costs could be used as a basis to examine the financial feasibility of alternative routes, schedules, and alternative vehicles.

Access

Visitors access Sabino Canyon Recreation Area in private automobiles, on bicycles, foot, and horseback, and in vans, tour buses, and school buses. Though access has not been characterized quantitatively, the Forest Service observes that the majority of visitors arrive by private automobile.

As shown in Figure 30, North Sabino Canyon Road defines the west boundary of Sabino Canyon Recreational Area and provides access to the main entrance, visitor center, and parking lot. North of the main entrance and across the street are Canyon View Elementary School and Esperero Canyon Middle School. Beyond that is an administrative entrance, followed by numerous subdivisions.

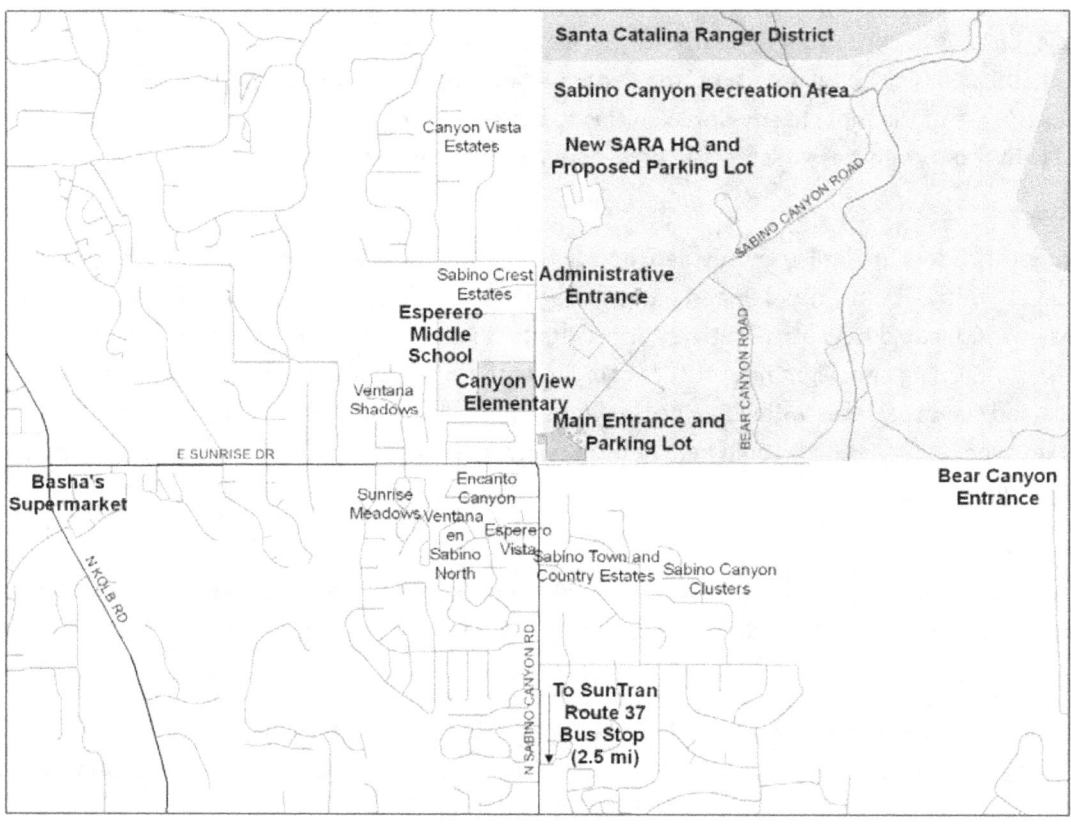

Figure 30 – Sabino Canyon Recreation Area local surrounding area and entrances[71]

Private vehicle

Private vehicles are the primary means of accessing the recreation area. Visitors with private vehicles may experience congestion when leaving the canyon between 7:00 and 8:00 a.m. on weekdays when neighboring schools are in session. During this time, parents queue up northbound on North Sabino Canyon Road waiting to drop their children off at Canyon View Elementary and Esperero Canyon Middle Schools. After parents leave the schools, they queue up southbound on North Sabino Canyon at the signalized intersection with East Sunshine Drive. Most visitors exiting the canyon must make a left to go southbound on North Sabino Canyon Road and must therefore cross two lanes of traffic. Visitors have reported long waits to exit the canyon. Traffic counts just north of the intersection of North Sabino Canyon Road with East Sunshine Drive during the morning and afternoon peak hours indicate a two-way traffic count of 978 vehicles and 522 vehicles respectively.[72] Traffic counts for this intersection are shown in Figure 31.

---

[71] GIS files provided by Pima County DOT and the Forest Service.

[72] Data provided by Aichong Sun, Travel Demand Modeling Manager, Pima Association of Governments; data collected by Pima County Department of Transportation on November 19, 2008.

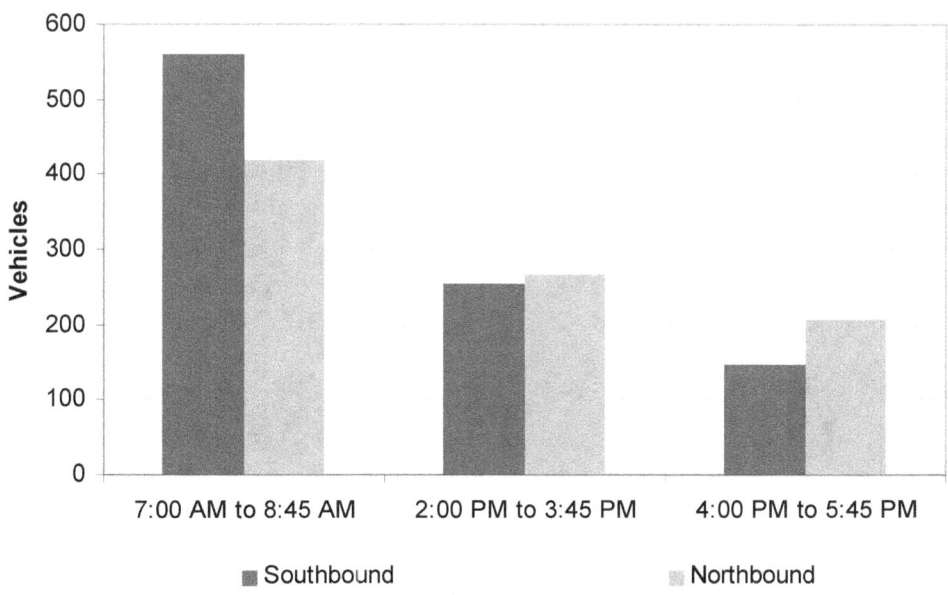

Figure 31 – Vehicle counts for North Sabino Canyon Road taken at the intersection with East Sunshine Drive[73]

Walking/cycling

The Forest Service has observed many repeat visitors coming on foot or bicycle from nearby neighborhoods. These patrons effectively utilize Sabino Canyon Recreation Area as a neighborhood park. They include exercisers, mothers with strollers, retired persons, and others who visit the recreation area one or more times a week. Patrons who arrive on foot or bicycle are not required to pay an entrance fee.

Vans and buses

Groups visit the recreation area in vans and buses. Vans usually hold 15 people and are from local resource centers, churches, and schools. Buses may hold between 20 and 50 visitors depending on the vehicle, and generally transport tourists rather than locals. Buses avoid paying an entrance fee by parking at the nearby Basha's Supermarket after dropping off passengers outside the recreation area.

Public bus

SunTran is the public transit operator in Tucson. The nearest SunTran bus stop is located 3.2 miles from the entrance to Sabino Canyon Recreation Area. This stop, located at the intersection of North Sabino Canyon Road and East Cloud Road, is serviced by SunTran Route 37 at half-hour increments. Service begins at about 5:40 a.m. and runs until 7:15 p.m. Northbound buses generally arrive at 7 and 37 minutes past each hour. Southbound buses generally arrive at 14 and 44 minutes past each hour.[74] Bicycle racks are mounted on the front of every SunTran bus.

---

[73] Ibid.

[74] SunTran (2008). "Route 37 – Pantano." Accessed at http://suntran.com/pdf/routes/Fall_08_Route_37.pdf on February 2, 2009.

Entrances

There are three entrances to the recreation area. As shown in Figure 30, the entrances are described in the following sections.

Main entrance

The main entrance is located off of North Sabino Canyon Road, just north of the intersection with Sunrise Drive. This entrance, operated by the Forest Service, accommodates automobiles, bicycles, tour buses, or pedestrians. There are two gates at the main entrance which are shown in Figure 32. At peak visiting times the queuing space for vehicles at the fee booth is sometimes exceeded, which results in congestion on North Sabino Canyon Road.

Figure 32 – Main entrance fee booths, shown from behind. The vehicle pictured is entering through the right lane[75].

The main entrance is next to a 372-space parking lot that is adjacent to the visitor center, shown in Figure 33 and Figure 34. During weekends in the peak season (December-April) the lot can fill to capacity. The Forest Service estimates that during the busiest times, each space may turn over four to six times a day, bringing the total number of daily parked private vehicles to between 1,500 and 2,200.[76] If the lot is full, some visitors park illegally in emergency lanes and spaces for disabled persons. Illegally parked vehicles in the lot are issued warnings and fines by the Forest Service. On-street parking along North Sabino Canyon Road is expressly prohibited. Illegally parked vehicles on nearby streets are issued warnings and fines by Pima County.[77]

---

[75] Google StreetView.

[76] Email from Larry Pratt, "RE: Carrying Capacity Study", Thursday, January 08, 2009 5:30 PM.

[77] Serda, M. (February 1, 2009). "Serenity of Sabino Canyon interrupted with parking nightmare." KOLD News 13. Accessed at http://www.kold.com/Global/story.asp?S=9769043 on February 2, 2009.

Figure 33 – Sabino Canyon Recreation Area parking lot[78]

Figure 34 – Aerial photograph of Sabino Canyon Recreation Area main entrance and parking lot[79]

To mitigate parking demand, the Forest Service recommends pass holders avoid peak hours (December through April, Saturday and Sunday, 10:00 a.m. to 2:00 p.m.). People who do arrive during peak hours, but cannot find a parking spot, are advised to leave the lot for a few minutes and then come back. Parked vehicles often leave the lot in waves that are correlated with the return of the tram to the visitor center.

---

[78] Google StreetView.
[79] Google Maps.

The Forest Service does not temporarily close the lot since there is a high volume of circulation and turn over. The Forest Service provides parking refunds to drivers who cannot find parking. There may be as many as five refunds on a peak-season day.

The earthwork is complete for an additional parking lot at the former Tucson Rod and Gun Club site.[80] The lot is expected to include 130 spaces.[81] A pedestrian access path exists from the intersection of North Sabino Canyon Road and East Sunrise Drive directly to the main parking lot.

Beyond the main entrance parking lot is the visitor center. Operated by the Forest Service, the visitor center contains a bookstore, meeting room, and staff to answer visitor questions related to the canyon. The bookstore is operated by the Public Lands Interpretive Association, a 501(c)(3) not-for-profit educational organization. Restrooms and drinking fountains are located in an out-building, and there are outdoor exhibits describing the natural resources of Sabino Canyon. Roughly 80 percent of the patrons who visit Sabino Canyon during the winter months and utilize the visitor center are from out of town.

Administrative entrance

As shown in Figure 35, an administrative entrance provides access from North Sabino Canyon Road to Upper Sabino Canyon Road in the recreation area. Accessible via this entrance is the Sabino Canyon Tours, Inc., vehicle compound, and the former site of the Tucson Rod and Gun Club, which is currently being converted to an overflow parking lot and the new headquarters for the Southern Arizona Rescue Association. This entrance is currently blocked by a gate and is not accessible by the general public. It is used as an entrance for private vehicles and buses transporting children on school field trips.

Figure 35 – Administrative entrance gate[82]

Bear Canyon entrance

A small, undeveloped entrance to Bear Canyon is operated by the Pima County Natural Resources, Parks, and Recreation Department. The Bear Canyon entrance has an unpaved parking area located at

[80] Email from Walter Keyes. "RE: Transportation Study Data Request," Monday, January 12, 2009 6:01 PM.
[81] Poole, B. (January 29, 2009). "Sabino Canyon lots overflowing, but parking laws must be obeyed," *TucsonCitizen.com*. Accessed at http://www.tucsoncitizen.com/ss/local/108965.php on February 19, 2009.
[82] Google StreetView.

the north end of Bear Canyon Road with room for about 10 vehicles. The Bear Canyon Entrance is large enough to accommodate horse trailers and is the primary entrance for horseback riders. Users can follow an undeveloped road north a short distance to access the Bear Canyon area of the Coronado National Forest and the Bear Canyon Trail. Bicyclists are not permitted beyond the end of the road where the trail enters a wilderness area. The parking area is open from dawn until dusk.[83]

User and stakeholder groups

The unique topography and climate, presence of water and riparian habitats, as well as a virtually car-less transportation infrastructure has fostered the popularity of Sabino Canyon for a diverse set of user and stakeholder groups. These groups differ with respect to preferred activities and spatial and temporal usage patterns. This has resulted in differing requirements and visions for Sabino Canyon and its future transportation system.

This section attempts to describe the various user and stakeholder groups at Sabino Canyon, their issues with current operations and policies at the recreation area, and their suggestions for future changes. Determination of user and stakeholder groups was done by the alternative transportation study team in consultation with the Forest Service. The groups discussed below are not mutually exclusive and may not be exhaustive. Members of one group may belong to one or more other groups.

User groups include:

- Cyclists;
- Hikers;
- Naturalists;
- Pedestrians (On-Road); and
- Sightseers.

Stakeholder groups include:

- Friends of Sabino Canyon;
- Neighborhoods and schools;
- Preservationists;
- Sabino Canyon Tours, Inc.;
- Sabino Canyon Volunteer Naturalists (SCVN); and
- Safety, security, and rescue personnel.

Descriptions and views of these groups were collected from comments from public meetings, recreation area users, and interviews with selected representatives of user and stakeholder groups. These sources are described briefly below. The number and breakdown of users has not been quantitatively determined.

---

[83] Pima County Natural Resource, Parks, and Recreation (NRPR) (2008). Accessed at http://www.pima.gov/nrpr/trails/bear_canyon/index.htm on February 2, 2009.

Handwritten public comments collected from the Sabino Canyon Recreation Area suggestion box were analyzed.[84] Specific comments are not definitively attributable to particular user groups, but the views contained in them have been represented as best as possible.

Following the devastating 2006 floods, 545 public comments were collected from August through November regarding the future of the recreation area.[85] Comments were collected via emails, public comment forms that were mailed to the District Ranger or left at the visitor center, and phone calls. Over 50 percent of the public felt the recreation area should "be returned to the way it was" prior to the floods and debris flows.

In December 2008 a group of stakeholders were invited to speak about the future of the transportation system in and around Sabino Canyon.

In late 2008 and early 2009 a series of focus groups were led by the Pima Association of Governments to obtain public input for the upcoming 2040 Regional Transportation Plan.[86]

Finally, individual interviews were conducted by the alternative transportation systems study team with representatives of user and stakeholder groups. Interviews focused on usage patterns, current issues, and future visions.

The remainder of this section combines analysis from each of these resources to document user and stakeholder groups and their associated usage patterns or activities, issues with the current transportation system, and suggestions for the future transportation system. User and stakeholder groups are listed in alphabetical order.

User groups

Cyclists

Cyclists enjoy Sabino Canyon because the 3.8-mile paved road provides a great uphill workout in a "beautiful riparian area" with no cars. Cyclists in Sabino Canyon generally consist of casual and recreational riders. Cycling is allowed in the recreation area prior to 9:00 a.m. and after 5:00 p.m. on all days except Wednesdays and Saturdays. Cyclists have been observed in the canyon as early as 4:30 a.m. in the summer months when cool temperatures and low pedestrian volumes favor cycling. Biking speed limits are 15 mph on roadways and 10 mph on bridges in the canyon.[87] Adherence to cycling rules is monitored by the Sabino Canyon Volunteer Bicycle Patrol. Cycling activity is summarized in Figure 36. Cycling is more popular in the non-winter months, the off-peak season, because temperatures are warmer in the mornings and evenings when cyclists have use of the canyon. The Volunteer Bicycle Patrol reports that bicycle demand varies on weekends and holidays depending on organized cycling events elsewhere. For example, during the weeks preceding cycling events in Tucson, such as El Tour de Tucson, cycling activity increases in Sabino Canyon. Activity returns to normal following the event. The Volunteer Bicycle Patrol reports that only one or two cyclists will use Bear Canyon Road to access Upper Sabino

---

[84] Provided by Larry Pratt (2008). Sabino_trans_comments0001.pdf
[85] Forest Service (2006). Sabino Canyon Public Comments Update: Comments from 8/12 – 11/9/06. 2 pp.
[86] Done, R. (2008). 2040 RTP Session 17. Pima Association of Governments. 22 pp.
[87] Arizona Daily Star (March 4, 1992). Sabino deal bans bikes Wednesdays, Saturdays. 631 words.

Canyon Road from their homes. Many people ride their bikes to the recreation area and may come from distances as far as 10 to 15 miles.

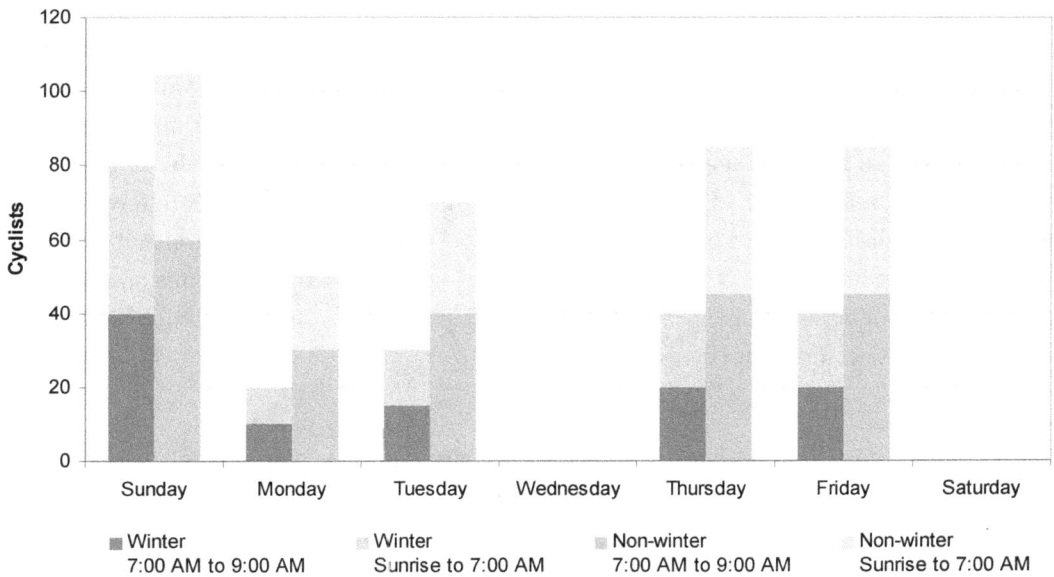

Figure 36 – Morning cycling activity by season observed by Sabino Canyon Volunteer Bicycle Patrol on Upper Sabino Canyon Road. Cycling is prohibited on Wednesdays and Saturdays.

Irresponsible cyclist behavior, including speeding and aggressiveness near pedestrians in the 1990s prompted the Forest Service to review the appropriateness of cycling in the canyon. To avoid a complete ban on cycling, bicycle advocacy groups negotiated restrictions[88] and settled on the current allowable times for cycling described above that became effective in March 1992. Since that time, the Sabino Canyon Volunteer Bicycle Patrol has monitored bicycle usage and speed. There have been no serious cyclist/pedestrian accidents since the restrictions were enacted though bicyclists sometimes have accidents on their own. Bicyclists acknowledge that it is up to them to avoid pedestrians, but they have expressed minor frustration with pedestrians who walk abreast in groups and are not focused on their surroundings.

The 1992 restrictions prompted the faster and more aggressive bicycle racing and training community to leave Sabino Canyon for Mount Lemmon, Saguaro National Park, and Gates Pass in Tucson Mountain County Park. Cyclists who have remained say that in the winter, early morning rides can be uncomfortably cold and there is not enough light for successful evening rides. Tucson's summer heat and longer days make morning and evening rides more feasible. Cyclists have also noted issues accessing Sabino Canyon on their bikes. Though shoulder improvements have been made for cyclists, not all cyclists are comfortable biking on the shoulders of nearby busy roads.

---

[88] Arizona Daily Star (January 1, 1992). *Sabino ban on bicycling is postponed.* 454 words.

Hikers

Hikers visit the canyon specifically to hike on the off-road trail network of the adjacent Pusch Ridge Wilderness. Hikers may use the road network or even the tram to access trailheads within the recreation area. Hikers may also consider themselves naturalists, though their primary activity in Sabino Canyon may not be interpretation. Hikers primarily arrive at Sabino Canyon via private automobile. Hikers may be individuals, part of small informal groups, or part of larger, more formal groups organized by the Southern Arizona Hiking Club or the Sabino Canyon Volunteer Naturalists. Hikers are similar to other user groups with respect to daily and seasonal visitation patterns. Hikers generally prefer to hike in the winter when the comfortable climate allows longer outings. Organized summer hikes are fewer in number and shorter in duration due to extreme temperatures. The most common complaint of hikers is the noise and smell of the diesel tram. The intensity of feelings against the tram depends on the individual and ranges from minor annoyance to major grievance. Other hikers have complained about poor directional markings on the trails themselves.

Naturalists

Naturalists include bird, lizard, and wildlife observers; amateur and professional ecologists, biologists, and geologists; and other visitors whose primary reason for visiting the canyon is to observe nature. These visitors may overlap with other visitor groups, particularly hikers. Naturalists are attracted to the riparian areas which are generally (and conveniently) near the road. Birders tend to concentrate in the lower canyon near the dam. Naturalists tend to visit Sabino Canyon when animal activity is high, such as early in the morning, late afternoon, and at dusk. Summer temperatures are comfortable during these times as well. Spring and fall are popular times for birders to witness numerous avian species as they migrate north or south, respectively.

Some naturalists are disturbed by the noise and exhaust from the trams' diesel engines and concerned about the noise and quality of the interpretation given on the tram. The 1991 Sabino Canyon Interpretive Plan outlined six issues with interpretation in the recreation area, including lack of financial, staff, and interpretive resources and incomplete or inaccurate messages delivered by tram drivers.[89] One naturalist commented the tram luckily does not conflict with the most likely and popular times to observe nature (early mornings, late afternoons, and after dark). Some naturalists are concerned about excessive development of visitor infrastructure in the canyon. Naturalists have an interest in balancing the impact of man-made structures (including the bridges and roads) with preserving and reintroducing native species and access to areas where wildlife can be observed.

Pedestrians (on-road)

Growth in residential development near Sabino Canyon has resulted in it becoming a popular daily destination for pedestrians. These users primarily use the paved road in Sabino and Bear Canyons and they arrive by private automobile. Pedestrians come throughout the day, particularly in winter, but prefer mornings and early evenings when the tram is not operating. On Wednesdays and Saturdays, bicyclists are prohibited from the Upper Sabino Canyon Road, thus increasing ease of use for pedestrians. Pedestrians generally avoid daytime hours in the summer when the temperature is

---

[89] Coronado National Forest, Santa Catalina Ranger District (December 1993). *Sabino Canyon Recreation Concept Plan: Recommendations for Restoration and Enhancement.* USDA Forest Service.

regularly over 100 degrees Fahrenheit. Walkers may come alone or walk in groups while socializing. There is some concern that regular walkers and joggers along Upper Sabino Canyon Road, particularly those who listen to personal audio devices, may forget that they are in a National Forest that is home to populations of animals which, while not normally aggressive to humans, can attack if startled.

Pedestrians who visit on weekday mornings are primarily concerned with ingress and egress to and from the recreation area. Between 7:15 and 8:00 a.m. North Sabino Canyon Road becomes significantly congested with parents dropping their children off at Canyon View Elementary School and Esperero Canyon Middle School. Users of the canyon needing to make a left turn south onto North Sabino Canyon Road must cross two lanes of bumper-to-bumper traffic. Complaints are that this is dangerous and impractical. Some drivers have reported long waits for a break in traffic. In addition to access, walkers and joggers have cited noise and fumes from the tram and potential interactions with "fast" and "rude" cyclists as ongoing issues.[90]

Sightseers

Sightseers include individuals or groups who are neither firmly included in any of the above categories nor belong to one of the stakeholder groups described below. Sightseers include tourists, tram passengers, picnickers, swimmers, and walkers who are not regular visitors to the canyon. Picnicking used to be a highly popular activity in the canyon, though restrictions on automobile use and the banning of alcohol in the canyon have significantly reduced its popularity.[91,92] Sightseers tend to visit during winter daytime hours, 9:00 a.m. to 5:00 p.m., especially on weekends. Organized tour groups visit the canyon on buses. Sabino Canyon is a popular destination for ElderHostel tours. Because sightseers are not frequent visitors and may be from out of town, there are no organizations that represent this user group. Issues and suggestions for sightseers are largely communicated verbally to Forest Service staff and written on comment sheets.

Most sightseer comments relate to operation of the tram and visitor infrastructure in the canyon. Sightseers have expressed a strong desire for quieter and environmentally-friendly alternative fuel vehicles and for the tram operator to accept credit and debit cards. Sightseers have requested more bathroom breaks and photo stops during the tram ride, as well as improved signage in addition to verbal instructions regarding tram safety. Sightseers have also noted a lack of conveniently-placed trash and recycling receptacles in the canyon and that at times the present receptacles overflow with refuse. Sightseers have also commented on the lack of shaded picnic tables.

Stakeholder groups

Friends of Sabino Canyon

Friends of Sabino Canyon (FOSC) is a 501(c)(3) charitable organization initiated in 1993 to preserve, protect and enhance Sabino Canyon Recreation Area. FOSC has a mailing list of 1,200 individuals. The organization raised $500,000 during its first 12 years of existence. Comparatively, it raised $750,000 in the last two years alone as part of its "Save Our Sabino" (SOS) initiative following the destructive 2006

---

[90] USDA Forest Service (2006). Sabino Canyon Public Comments Update: Comments from 8/12 – 11/9/06. 2 pp.
[91] Email from Donn Ricketts. Subject: "Don – Requst by L. Pratt on 93 Concept plan" (sic). Wednesday, October 22, 2008, 3:22 PM.
[92] Telephone conversation with Doak McDuffie, Acting Water Systems Manager, Forest Service, Monday, March 16, 2009.

floods. In the years following its inception, the Forest Service expressed the recreation area's funding needs to FOSC. The relationship and communication between the Forest Service and FOSC has evolved over time. Today, FOSC has taken a more active role by envisioning ideas for projects itself. The Forest Service then generates formal proposals for these projects which FOSC often provides matching grants to complete.

Recent and current issues perceived by FOSC include the increasing frequency of schools that are not able to fund transportation for field trips to the canyon; the need for regular annual trail maintenance, additional visitor parking, and the replacement of and improvement to visitor infrastructure at the tram stops.

Neighbors and schools

As shown in Figure 30, numerous developments are located near Sabino Canyon. There are no official access points from the recreation area to these neighborhoods. Canyon View Elementary School and Esperero Canyon Middle School are located across North Sabino Canyon Road from the recreation area entrance. Residents of nearby developments and students, faculty, and staff of the schools create and are affected by congestion near the main entrance of the recreation area. They are also more likely to be regular visitors to the canyon than those who live further away.

Similar to walkers, joggers, and other regular morning users of the canyon, nearby residents and the schools have noted significant congestion on North Sabino Canyon Road between the school entrances and East Sunrise Drive. This congestion is generated by parents dropping their children off at school. The schools have also noted illegal parking on weekends in school lots. Despite signs prohibiting Sabino Canyon visitors from parking in the lots, roughly 10 to 15 vehicles at a time may do so on busy winter weekends. The prohibition of Sabino Canyon visitor parking in the school lot is intended to leave the lots open to people who want to use the ball fields.

Preservationists

Preservationists represent a cross section of individuals from other user and stakeholder groups. These individuals express a preference to preserve and protect the nine bridges leading up into the canyon. While not currently listed on the National Register of Historic Places, the bridges are believed to be eligible for inclusion on the Register. This means that any proposed projects must be reviewed by the Advisory Council on Historic Preservation.

Sabino Canyon Tours, Inc.

Sabino Canyon Tours, Inc., has operated the tram service in Sabino Canyon Recreation Area since 1985 under a special use permit with the USDA Forest Service.[93] The company operates two routes, one on Upper Sabino Canyon Road and the other on Bear Canyon Road. The tram operator provides interpretation of the natural and built environments along Upper Sabino Canyon Road. The interpretation is delivered to tram passengers by the driver via a microphone and public address system. Both routes depart from the Sabino Canyon Recreation Area Visitor Center. The weekends during

---

[93] USDA Forest Service (2006). Sabino Canyon Tours, Inc. Three-Year Operation and Maintenance Plan, January 1, 2004 to December 31, 2006. 10 pp.

December and April (winter months) are the busiest. Long weekends such as Good Friday and Easter Sunday have historically been the busiest weekends for the tram during the entire year.

Sabino Canyon Tours, Inc., has suggested that the proposed overflow parking lot located near its vehicle compound will increase liability due to proximity of visitors and potential conflicts with private vehicles. The company also notes the potential for conflicts with pedestrians at peak visitation hours near bridges, especially when they are flooded.

Sabino Canyon Volunteer Naturalists

Sabino Canyon Volunteer Naturalists (SCVN) is a non-profit community group which contracts with the Forest Service to provide environmental education activities in the Sabino Canyon Recreation Area. The group consists of members of the community who enjoy nature and are trained to interpret the natural history of the Sonoran Desert and the riparian area surrounding Sabino Creek. SCVN runs a kindergarten program that operates Tuesday through Thursday during the school year at the Cactus Picnic Area. Numbers of kindergarten field trips by month and by year are shown in Figure 37 and Figure 38, respectively.

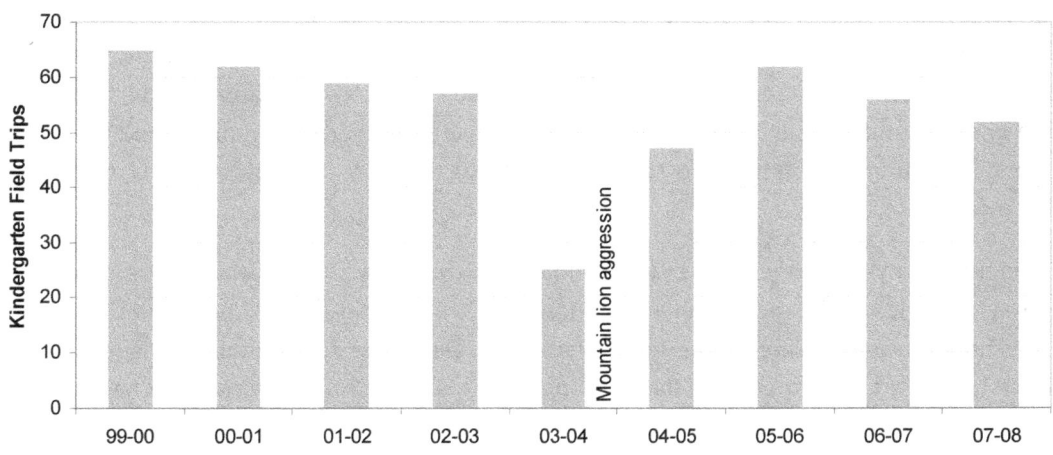

Figure 37 – SCVN kindergarten field trips by school year

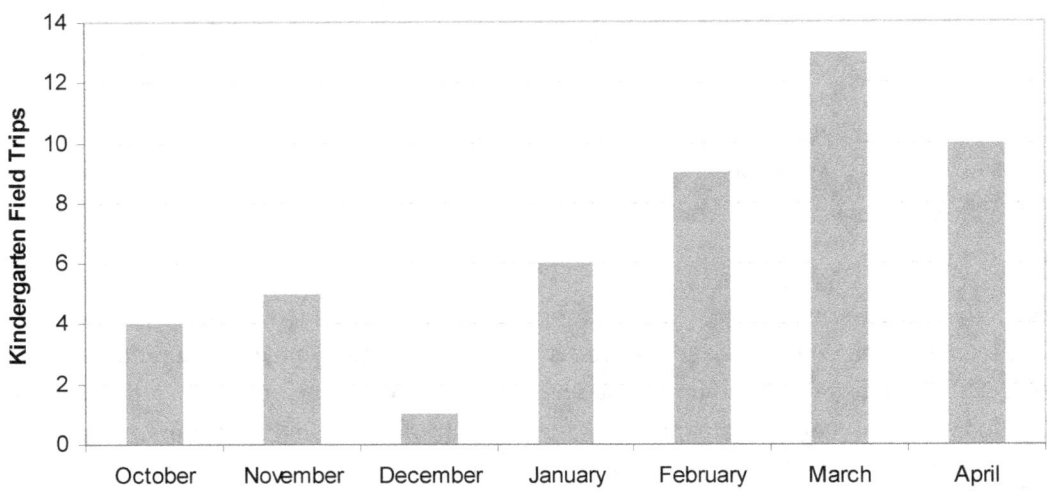

Figure 38 – SCVN kindergarten fieldtrips for the 2008-2009 school year

SCVN runs an elementary school program that operates from October to the end of April. SCVN hosts child summer programs each Wednesday morning in June and July. SCVN provides public interpretation events for all ages on topics such as predator/prey relationships, canyon information, plants and birds, the Hohokam peoples, and geology. These events recur on a weekly schedule during the months of January to April. For less interpretation and more hiking, the group leads hikes every Friday at 8:30 a.m. throughout the canyon.

Organized student groups currently arrive at Gun Club Road in buses or private vehicles and enter through the rear entrance of the recreation area. Since other transportation options haven't been identified, these private vehicles are allowed to travel to the teaching sites. A volunteer meets the vehicles and/or buses and leads them into the canyon. Private vehicles present a specific challenge for kindergarten groups because each child needs to be in a car seat. About once a month, a single class may occupy up to 13 or 14 private vehicles. Private vehicle usage has not been increasing, but SCVN is watching for a trend as spending for field trips is cut and school buses cost $150/hr. Buses and/or private vehicles are led to Cactus Picnic Area for the kindergarten program and to Sabino Dam for the elementary school program. Designated parking exists for only seven vehicles at Cactus Picnic Area, but there is technically room for more. Pedestrians are disturbed by private vehicle convoys and drivers can get lost or go to the wrong area when kindergarten and elementary programs are run simultaneously on Tuesdays, Wednesdays, and Thursdays.

Security, safety, and rescue personnel
Security, safety, and rescue personnel consist of the Pima County Sheriff's Department Parks Enforcement Unit with the support of Southern Arizona Rescue Association (SARA), Sheriff's Auxiliary Volunteers, the Sheriff's Mounted Posse, the Sabino Volunteer Patrol, and the Coronado Mounted Assistance Unit. The frequency and occurrence of rescue operations are highly correlated with canyon usage. There are roughly two rescues a week. Roughly one-third of rescues occur near Catalina highway,

one-third occur in the foothills of the Catalina mountains, and one-third occur in other places that border Sabino Canyon. SARA responds to roughly 30 search and rescue missions in and around Sabino Canyon each year. In the last 10 years, there were four major flash floods in Sabino and Bear Canyons. One event precipitated the evacuation of over 50 people and 60 in another. Despite the severity of flood events, most rescues involve people being injured or hurt under normal conditions. Rescue operations include search, rescue, recovery, first-aid, and evacuation. Cell phones and GPS devices are increasingly facilitating rescues. Responsibilities of the Sheriff's Department also include traffic and parking enforcement on the road network outside Sabino Canyon Recreation Area.

The rescue community has expressed desire for a flash flood warning system that predicts flood events and provides early warning to allow people to exit the canyon. It has also noted a lack of shelter locations and rendezvous points that would allow stranded visitors to congregate and support one another. Rescuers can better assist and rescue groups rather than individuals. There are currently no 'connector' trails that would allow people to reach such rendezvous points, and there may be a need for pedestrian bridges that allow people to evacuate the canyon. Rescuer access to the recreation area is not an issue.

III.   Existing condition themes

A review of existing conditions at Sabino Canyon Recreation Area reveals complex and interrelated natural environments, built improvements, and strongly held personal values and beliefs. Taken together, these conditions explain the current popular usage of the recreation area and its existing transportation system. The existing conditions also represent a set of five fundamental themes that may guide planning of the future transportation system at Sabino Canyon: public safety; infrastructure preservation and management; mobility, accessibility, and connectivity; visitor experience; environmental stewardship.

Theme 1 – Public safety

Several safety concerns have been identified in Sabino Canyon. Many visitors arrive unaware of the hazards recreating in the Sabino Canyon Recreation Area or any wildland area poses. Visitors ignore, fail to recognize the seriousness, or fail to see posted warnings concerning wildlife, heat exhaustion, steep drop-offs, thunderstorms, and flooding. The gap between the Forest Service efforts to inform visitors and resulting visitor awareness results in a small fraction of visitors injured in minor accidents or temporarily stranded by high water at the creek crossings every year.

The most serious safety concern impacting the transportation system is that of flooding. Severe flooding can potentially injure or kill visitors who have traveled up Sabino or Bear Creek Canyons. More moderate flooding, a frequent occurrence in these canyons, may injure or trap visitors where roads and trails cross creeks. Specially trained rescue personnel are often required to extract or recover victims of flood events. There are procedures in place for tram operations and posting public access advisories, but there is no simple exit from Sabino or Bear Creek Canyons for stranded pedestrians and bicyclists once water levels rise.

Upper Sabino Canyon Road is used by pedestrians, cyclists, service vehicles, and motorized trams. There have been conflicts among these users in the past and opportunity for future conflicts exist, particularly near the bridges. The bridges are the interfaces between the built environment (the road) and a desirable feature of the natural environment (the creek). The bridges are popular areas at which visitors congregate, and because they are the narrowest points along the road, the bridges create bottlenecks and conflict points. Vehicles (private cars and buses) that transport kindergarten and elementary school children create additional potential hazards for pedestrians and trams for a variety of reasons.

Outside the recreation area boundary, nearby elementary and middle schools create periods of peak congestion on weekday mornings. These coincide with popular visitation hours and create potential safety issues for drivers leaving the recreation area and making a left-hand turn out of the parking lot on to North Sabino Canyon Road, and for pedestrians wishing to cross North Sabino Canyon Road.

After hours, law enforcement is minimal in the parking lot and within the canyons.

Theme 2 – Infrastructure preservation, maintenance, and management

Preservation, maintenance, and management of transportation infrastructure within Sabino Canyon is challenging given the history and likelihood of flooding. Past road and bridge repairs have been expensive due to the extent of damage, the sensitive nature of the natural environment, and the difficulty in transporting standard construction equipment across the bridges. Preventative and planned pavement maintenance is also costly, estimated at an average of $80,000 annually.

The bridges, which technically are vented low-water crossings, present preservation and management complexities. The narrow width of the bridges and bridge approaches constrain vehicle dimensions and operating characteristics of potential tram vehicles. As previously mentioned, the bridges also hinder the approach of normal construction vehicles to work sites in the upper canyon. The bridges disturb the normal flow of the creek and collect silt both on their upstream sides and on their decks after flooding events.

The bridges themselves have withstood numerous flooding events but the roadway approaches to them are very expensive to repair and require specialized labor. While the bridges create operational and maintenance challenges, they are a popular feature of the canyon and are potentially eligible for inclusion in the National Register of Historic Places.

The parking lot and associated main entrance station also provide maintenance and management challenges. The current parking lot is unable to meet peak parking demands on weekends and holiday periods from December through April. The parking lot, like the road, requires expensive preventative and planned maintenance. The main entrance station is staffed only during normal visitor hours.

The tram system, while not owned by the Forest Service, operates under a special use permit issued by the agency. The tram vehicles have been in operation since the mid 1980s. They are aging, and numerous visitors have complained about the tram's exhaust and the high-decibel volume of the interpretive narration provided by the driver. Overall, however, the tram ride into Sabino Canyon is very popular with visitors and generates relatively few complaints from users compared to the number of riders. Complaints about the tram tend to come from other users of the recreation area.

Theme 3 – Mobility, accessibility, and connectivity

Mobility, accessibility, and connectivity challenges exist both internally and externally to the recreation area.

Internal issues

The presence of pedestrians, bicycles, trams, service vehicles, and vehicles associated with field trips create opportunities for conflicts along the road. Bicyclists have expressed interest in reviewing the bicycle usage times in the recreation area, citing limited daylight hours and cold weather during winter mornings as well as equity for bicyclists among other user types. Others have expressed a desire to alter the potentially confusing access of field trip groups or possibly prohibit all motorized visitor access.

The tram provides the only access for visitors with limited mobility.

The physical construction of the bridges and the approaches to the bridges constrain the characteristics of potential tram vehicles. The narrowness of the bridges and tight turning radii at the approaches limits tram length, width, clearance, and turning radius.

The current network of roads and trails does not allow visitors to exit the canyon when the bridges are flooded. In the past, visitors have frequently become trapped during flood events, but more recently the Forest Service has partnered with the National Weather Service (NWS) to sponsor Monsoon Safety Awareness Week, increased its monitoring of flash flood conditions, and has actively restricted access to roads and stream crossings. These active management techniques have reduced the need for rescues caused by high water in Sabino Canyon from 126 in 2007 to 1 in 2008.

During peak visitation periods on weekends during winter months, December through April, there is inadequate parking to meet demand. Parking space turnover is frequent and correlates with the return of the trams to the visitor center. Some recreation area patrons, however, do not like to wait for parking spaces and sometimes park illegally on North Sabino Canyon Road.

External issues

The predominant mode of access to Sabino Canyon is private automobile. SunTran, Tucson's public transit provider, does not directly serve the northeast foothills outside the city of Tucson where Sabino Canyon Recreation Area is located. The closest bus stop is 3.5 miles away. Transit service that facilitates access to Sabino Canyon may be important for environmental, as well as equity reasons.

Recent shoulder widening and striping has improved bicycle accessibility near Sabino Canyon, but many recreational cyclists who frequent Sabino Canyon are unwilling to ride in traffic to access the recreation area.

Automobile congestion caused by parents dropping children off at the nearby elementary and middle schools has created ingress and egress challenges for visitors to the recreation area. Anecdotal comments indicate that visitors must wait a long time in order to make a left-hand turn south on North Sabino Canyon Road.

Theme 4 – Visitor experience

The visitor experience at Sabino Canyon begins prior to entering the recreation area. Access issues contribute to how visitors perceive their time in the canyon. Several challenges previously discussed including inability to find parking, congestion resulting from nearby schools, limited after-hours information resources, bicycle and transit connectivity, and lack of services contribute to the overall visitor experience.

Within Sabino Canyon, a primary cause of many use conflicts is the differing and sometimes competing values of diverse user groups and stakeholders. As mentioned previously, pedestrians, bicyclists, tram passengers, and field trip groups share the road and hikers and equestrians share the trail network. Each group generally has differing ideas regarding the following:

- How road and trail usage rights are shared among users;

- How many users can enjoy the canyon at a given time (from perspectives of safety, comfort, and environmental responsibility); and
- Whether additional improvements should be made to increase the number of users that can visit at a given time.

The tram service has an impact on visitor experience regardless of mode of travel within the canyon. Some visitors who do not use the tram service have expressed interest in reducing or ceasing tram service altogether. On the other hand, the tram itself has become a popular attraction, and some riders may not be able to reach the upper canyon without motorized assistance. A wide cross-section of visitors, both riders and non-riders, have made suggestions regarding the tram service and tram vehicles, including acquiring quieter, less-polluting vehicles, and providing narrative interpretation that cannot be heard by non-tram visitors. The tram concessionaire does not currently accept credit cards for ticket payments and there is no ATM at the recreation area. Visitors who do not have cash must leave Sabino Canyon and travel several miles to a shopping center for ATM services.

Theme 5 – Environmental stewardship

A significant determinant of how all challenges at Sabino Canyon are addressed is that of carrying capacity; that is, the recognition that there is a limit to the amount of human interaction with the natural environment beyond which the environment can no longer sustain itself. Daily visitation and introduction of infrastructure contribute to the impact humans have on the natural environment. For example, increased visitation by humans over time can alter animal behavior, trample vegetation, and introduce non-native species. Carrying capacity is not currently used to guide policy in Sabino Canyon Recreation Area.

The vented low-water crossings impede the natural flow of Sabino Creek which results in siltation, and adversely affects native endangered fish and downstream water flows.

Tram engine noise and exhaust and the noise from tram loudspeakers potentially affect the environment.

Service vehicles potentially cause disturbances similar to the tram and can also transport non-native plant seeds into the recreation area.

IV. Goals and criteria

The existing conditions and themes identify and clarify transportation problems at Sabino Canyon. Defining goals focus transportation planning efforts based on shared values and beliefs. Defining criteria ensures objective and transparent analysis of potential solutions.

Creating the goals

Transportation planning goals were determined by reviewing the existing conditions themes, reviewing the project scope of work, reviewing the goals of the 1993 Sabino Canyon Recreation Concept Plan, and obtaining input from Coronado National Forest staff members. These ideas were integrated into the five transportation planning goals as shown in Figure 39.

Existing conditions themes

The five themes identified by the existing conditions were used as the foundation for goal identification. Each theme represents a category of identified issues at Sabino Canyon, and at a minimum the goals should encompass these themes. The themes are as follows:

- Theme 1 – Public safety;
- Theme 2 – Infrastructure preservation, maintenance, and management;
- Theme 3 – Mobility, accessibility, and connectivity;
- Theme 4 – Visitor experience; and
- Theme 5 – Environmental stewardship.

Volpe Center scope of work

At the beginning of this study effort, the Forest Service and Volpe Center included focus areas in the project scope of work that would inform the study. These foci are:

- Improve visitor education, recreation, and health benefits; and
- Enhance visitor mobility, accessibility, and safety.
- Reduce traffic congestion

1993 Sabino Canyon Recreation Concept Plan goals

The 1993 Sabino Canyon Recreation Concept Plan explicitly states goals that remain relevant and inform the goals for transportation planning. The goals and associated objectives are as follows:

- Emphasize environmental education at Sabino Canyon;
- Maintain the natural character of Sabino Canyon;
- Provide for a spectrum of compatible activities for people to enjoy the canyon;
- Maintain ecosystem integrity;
- Preserve and interpret cultural resources; and
- Encourage visitors to feel a sense of ownership and responsibility for resources on public lands.

Transportation planning goals

Coronado National Forest staff members worked iteratively with project staff to develop and fine tune transportation planning goals based on the precedents above as well as first-hand knowledge of the recreation area and the visitors. The refined list of transportation goals and their justifications are below. The relationships between the transportation goals and their inputs are shown in Figure 39.

Financial sustainability (FS) – Maintain assets and operate systems in a cost-effective and financially sustainable way.

Justification: The U.S. Forest Service, as a federal agency has both a stewardship and fiduciary responsibility to the American public to manage public lands, including its assets and facilities, and to operate systems in a non-wasteful and cost-effective manner.

Public safety (PS) – Improve public safety and reduce visitor risk with respect to natural disasters and user conflicts.

Justification: User and use conflicts not only impair the visitor experience but are also unsafe and potentially hazardous to users. Stakeholder input provides additional supporting evidence in the existing conditions that public safety with respect to natural disasters and user conflicts is an area of concern.

Historical and cultural sites (HCS) – Preserve, protect, and restore unique historical and cultural sites within Sabino Canyon.

Justification: Federal actions must comply with Section 106 of the Historic Preservation Act. Other federal legislation (e.g., the Antiquities Act, and legislation protecting tribal sacred sites) also mandate a preservation, protection, and restoration policy. Stakeholder input to the existing conditions supports preservation and restoration of the historic vented low-water crossings.

Natural and ecological resources (NER) – Preserve, protect, and restore the natural and ecological resources within Sabino Canyon.

Justification: Both the National Forest System Land Management Planning rule (FR/ Vol. 70, No. 3/Wednesday January 5, 2005), and Forest Service directives and federal legislation (e.g., Clean Air and Clean Water Acts) require the Forest Service to manage its public lands to ensure clean air, clean water, and abundant wildlife for future generations.

Access and circulation (AC) – Provide access to and circulation within Sabino Canyon for all visitors as the basis for an enjoyable experience.

Justification: Forest Service directives and federal legislation guarantees a right for the public to access public lands, but also imposes on the Land Management Agency (in this case, the Forest Service) a duty to manage that access in a way which is environmentally benign and sustainable. The Americans with Disabilities Act of 1990 extends that right to persons with disabilities. Current regulations (36 CFR) prohibit trail construction (§261.10(a)) and operation of vehicles in a manner damaging to the land, wildlife, or vegetation (§ 261.13(h)). Stakeholder input to the existing conditions also indicated a strong desire to maintain access to and through the canyon. This includes a substantial educational component through field trips associated with local schools. Disbursed visitor activities at multiple sites require a well-functioning circulation system.

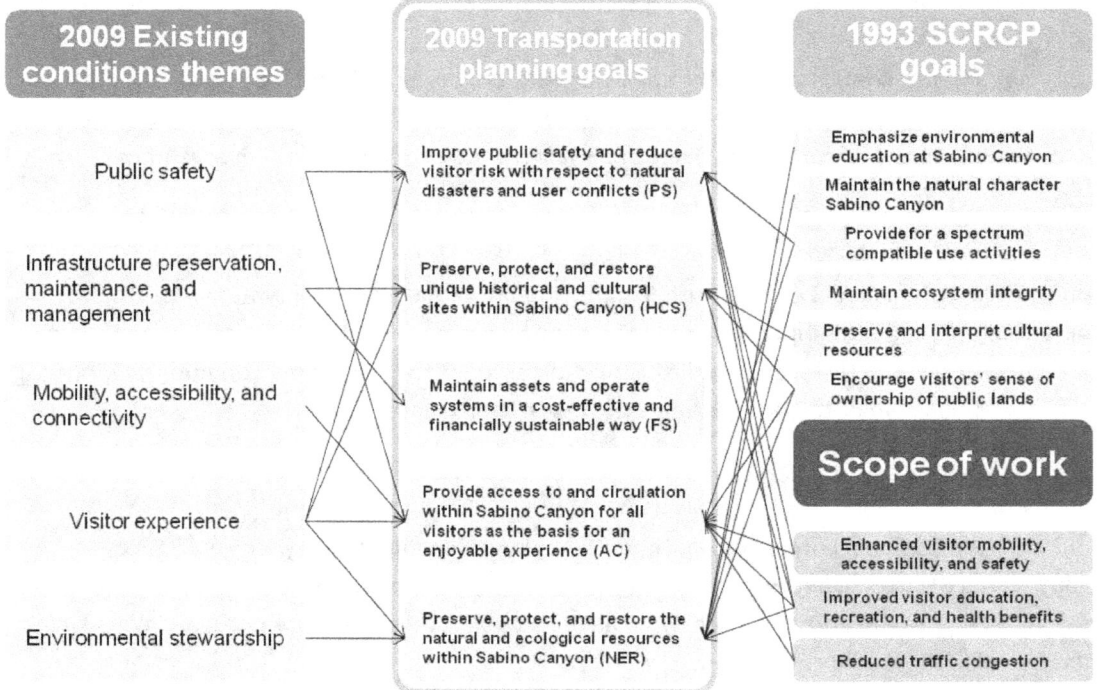

Figure 39 - Transportation planning goals and related goals and themes.

Criteria

Objective criteria used to compare possible transportation solutions, or elements, were based on the transportation planning goals. Criteria were identified from best practices from similar transportation planning efforts and adapted for Sabino Canyon. The criteria are shown in Table 7.

Table 7 – Best practices criterion adapted for Sabino Canyon

Goal	Criterion	Threshold	Value
Financial sustainability (FS)	Capital cost	<= $5,000 $5,001 - $100,000 > $100,000	Low Med High
	Annual operations and maintenance costs	<= $5,000 $5,001 - $100,000 > $100,000	Low Med High
	Technical difficulty	Minimal difficulty Moderate difficulty Unknown difficulty	1 0 -1
Public safety (PS)	Safety – Risk of flooding	Reduces risk No change Increases risk	1 0 -1
	Safety – Flood evacuation	Improves evacuation No change Hinders evacuation	1 0 -1
	Safety – User conflicts	Decreases conflicts No change Increases conflicts	1 0 -1
Historical and cultural sites (HCS)	Cultural landscape	Improves cultural landscape No change Degrades cultural landscape	1 0 -1
	Historic resources	Improves historic resources No change Degrades historic resources	1 0 -1
Natural and ecological resources (NER)	Natural environment	Improves natural environment No change Degrades natural environment	1 0 -1
Access and circulation (AC)	Pedestrians	Improves experience No change Degrades experience	1 0 -1
	Cyclists	Improves experience No change Degrades experience	1 0 -1
	Tram riders	Improves experience No change Degrades experience	1 0 -1
	Equestrians	Improves experience No change Degrades experience	1 0 -1
	Student groups	Improves experience No change Degrades experience	1 0 -1
All	Anticipated public acceptance	Strong public support Public indifference Strong public outcry	1 0 -1

V.   Elements

Following completion of the goals and criteria, a list of 80 transportation solutions or elements, was compiled. Each element specifically addressed one or more issues identified in the review of existing conditions. During the course of the project, the transportation solutions became referred to as elements because they would later be combined as elements of more comprehensive transportation alternatives.

The elements were collectively determined by the Volpe Center and the Forest Service. Each element is categorized as one of the following issue areas:

- AM – Access Management Elements;
- BPE – Bicycle, Pedestrian, and Equestrian Elements;
- COM – Communications Elements;
- INF – Infrastructure Elements;
- MGMT – Management Elements;
- MOT – Motorized Elements; and
- SCH – School Elements.

To ensure a complete list, the elements were presented to a broad group of Sabino Canyon stakeholders in August 2009. During the meeting, stakeholders were given the opportunity to suggest new elements, and each stakeholder was asked to vote for five elements he or she preferred and five elements he or she disliked. Forest Service staff members were also given the opportunity to comment and vote.

The Volpe Center team and the Forest Service analyzed each element according to the criteria defined in the previous section. Stakeholder preferences were considered as part of the "anticipated public acceptance" criterion. This analysis was used to filter out those elements that were hugely unpopular or unrealistic. The filtered list of elements is shown in Table 8, while those that were removed from consideration are shown in Table 9. A table showing the elements ranked by the criteria in the filtered list is shown in Appendix C, which is provided as a separate document due to its size and format.

Table 8 – Filtered list of transportation elements

Element ID	Element description
AM 01	Create a new internal road connecting the current and future parking areas or redevelop the existing interior access road for public access to the new overflow lot.
AM 02	Institute 24-hour access control.
AM 03	Develop south-side access-egress from lot to avoid conflicts with school.
AM 04	Install a traffic signal at the recreation area entrance.
AM 05	Expand public transit service to Sabino Canyon Recreation Area.
AM 06	Stripe and widen shoulders of roads to improve bicycle access.
AM 07	Create off-road path connecting to greenway for bikes and pedestrians.
AM 08	Encourage walking or cycling to the recreation area from nearby neighborhoods.
AM 09	Improve Bear Canyon access point.

Element ID	Element description
AM 10	Dedicated right-turn lane into Sabino Canyon parking lot.
AM 11	Create new broad walking path from new parking lot directly to Cactus Picnic Area.
AM 12	Install a southbound right-turn lane from Sabino Canyon Road to Skyline.
BPE 01	Initiate bicycle guided tours of Sabino Canyon.
BPE 02	Create a grade-separated bike and/or pedestrian trail.
BPE 03	Stripe an at-grade bike and/or pedestrian trail using the existing road width, widening where possible.
BPE 04	Provide bicycle parking at trail-heads.
BPE 05	Develop equestrian tours.
BPE 06	Create additional or improve infrastructure for equestrian users.
COM 01	Install mile markers and directory kiosks with distances to infrastructure and amenities.
COM 02	Advertise that the tram runs on bio-diesel fuel.
COM 03	Improve the frequency and accuracy of visitor communications via the website.
COM 04	Expand information delivery methods to include new distribution channels.
COM 05	Use variable message signs for disseminating parking and safety messages.
COM 06	Collect parking lot utilization and disseminate in real-time via the web and/or variable message signs on approach roads.
INF 01	Create alternate trail network that avoids stream crossings and facilitates evacuation.
INF 02	Relocate the visitor center farther up the canyon and shuttle between it and the parking lots.
INF 03	Widen road to reduce user conflicts.
INF 04	Widen the bridges and bridge approaches.
INF 05	Redesign bridges to improve flow and reduce sedimentation issues; keep historic look but change engineering.
INF 06	Regularly maintain culverts to maintain desired (conceptualized at the creation of the bridges) water flow.
INF 07	Develop new bridges for pedestrians (or tram) off of the existing roadway network.
INF 08	Eliminate planned overflow parking.
MGMT 01	Create and disseminate a disaster evacuation, rescue, and communication plan.
MGMT 02	Develop aggregation points to shelter-in-place or facilitate evacuation for visitors within Sabino Canyon up to the end of Sabino Canyon Road.
MGMT 03	Develop flood detection and early warning system.
MGMT 04	Update and enforce time-separation strategies for different user types.
MGMT 05	Require the tram vehicles to conform to specified noise and air quality requirements.
MGMT 06	Include/enforce shuttle service requirements in special-use permit.
MGMT 07	Transfer ownership of the tram vehicles to USFS and continue operation by a contractor.
MGMT 08	Provide the tram as a fare-free service for visitors.
MGMT 09	Charge an expanded amenity recreation fee to pay for fare-free shuttle service.
MGMT 10	Institute a frequent rider pass.
MGMT 11	Develop a parking reservation system.
MGMT 12	Charge entry fee for all users, per person.
MGMT 13	Maintain existing tram operation and service concept.
MOT 01	Use trams for evacuation.
MOT 02	Remove the tram.
MOT 03	Develop aerial tram service.
MOT 04	Electric carts could be provided for mobility-impaired visitors by reservation.
MOT 05	Rent electric bicycles to assist people to get up canyon.
MOT 06	Create an on-demand and/or reservation system for the mobility-impaired.
MOT 07	Replace with in-kind vehicle of same size/function.
MOT 08	Replace vehicles with larger or smaller vehicles but run at equivalent capacity.
MOT 09	Replace trams with an enclosed vehicle design.

Element ID	Element description
MOT 10	Upgrade interpretation method/technology.
MOT 11	Add passenger safety equipment.
MOT 12	Limit hours/days/seasons of tram.
MOT 13	Limit tram route to lower canyon only.
MOT 14	Connect new parking lot to visitor center via tram.
MOT 15	Replace Sabino Canyon shuttle with more developed shuttle service in Bear Canyon.
MOT 16	Develop separate shuttle options and/or routes within CNF (to Mt. Lemmon and/or additional parking areas).
SCH 01	Provide free tram shuttle to transport student groups within the canyon.
SCH 02	Relocate educational facilities or build trails so that students can walk from the parking lot.
SCH 03	Purchase vehicle specifically for student group travel.

Table 9 – Elements removed from consideration

Reason for removing from consideration	Element description
Considered as part of MGMT 03	Develop flood detection and early warning system.
Considered as part of MGMT 07	Provide tram services for free.
Considered as part of MGMT 10	Implement parking reservation system for main lot.
Considered as part of MGMT 10	Develop a tram reservation system.
Considered as part of MGMT 9	Institute a frequent rider pass.
Considered as part of MOT 15	Shuttle from satellite parking.
Considered as part of SCH 01 and SCH 03	Prohibit private automobiles (supporting field trips) from entering the canyon.
Infeasible	Regularly dredge culverts to maintain desired (conceptualized at creation of the bridges) water flow.
No identified need	Sign equestrian trails with shared use message.
No identified need; counterproductive to discouraging shared parking	Improve pedestrian crossing between canyon and schools.
Significantly unpopular	Build more flood-resistant new roadway.
Significantly unpopular	Build multi-story parking garage.
Significantly unpopular	Sell food and other convenience items (water, sunscreen) from a pushcart.
Significantly unpopular	Develop cable railway service.
Significantly unpopular	Develop funicular railway service.
Significantly unpopular	Allow private vehicles on all days.
Significantly unpopular	Allow private vehicles on specific days.

The Volpe Center performed a detailed analysis of each element in the filtered list. These elements were analyzed on the following bases:

- **Description** of the element.
- Identified **costs** including capital and operations and maintenance.
- **Safety** issues particularly related to flooding and user conflicts.
- Impacts and **disruptions** to the **cultural landscape**, **natural environment**, and **historic resources** from constructing and operating the element.
- **Technical feasibility** of implementing the element and **anticipated response** from park users.

- **Next steps** required to move forward with element. Often include further study or obtaining public feedback on the concept.

The final analysis of elements is provided in Appendix D.

VI. Alternatives

Based on independent analysis, insight from Forest Service and stakeholders, and knowledge of alternative transportation systems on other recreational and public lands, the Volpe project team considered the costs and benefits of individual transportation elements and their potential interactions. The Volpe project team then constructed five logical groupings of elements into transportation alternatives. A sixth grouping describes long-range operations and management elements that would likely be compatible with each of the proposed alternatives.

The six groupings identified by the Volpe project team are as follows:

- Long-range operations and management elements;
- Alternative 0 – No Action;
- Alternative 1 – Parking management and capacity control;
- Alternative 2 – Expanded non-motorized use;
- Alternative 3 – Fare-free shuttle; and
- Alternative 4 – Infrastructure improvements.

Major elements of each alternative are described in the text in terms of how they may interact with one another and address transportation issues at Sabino Canyon. Following each alternative is a table of included elements as well as another table of elements that relate but are not included in the alternative concept. Each alternative concludes with an evaluation based on the transportation goals identified earlier during the project:

- Financial sustainability (FS) – Maintain assets and operate systems in a cost-effective and financially sustainable way;
- Public safety (PS) – Improve public safety and reduce visitor risk with respect to natural disasters and user conflicts;
- Historical and cultural sites (HCS) – Preserve, protect, and restore unique historical and cultural sites within Sabino Canyon;
- Natural and ecological resources (NER) – Preserve, protect, and restore the natural and ecological resources within Sabino Canyon; and
- Access and circulation (AC) – Provide access to and circulation within Sabino Canyon for all visitors as the basis for an enjoyable experience.

The alternatives outlined below are meant to provide a basis for focused and continued discussion among the Forest Service and its community of stakeholders, especially as Sabino Canyon revises its recreation plan. Although several alternatives may be in direct competition with one another, they need not be considered in isolation or as mutually exclusive options. Rather, in on-going discussions, components of one alternative may be combined with one another as the basis for additional ideas, or sets of elements may be combined with one another to create alternatives not covered by this document. For this reason, tables of related elements are provided for each alternative, and a list of elements not contained in any of the alternatives is included in 0.

Furthermore, there may be other ways of organizing the elements besides recreational concept or visitation experience. Alternatives may be created that align with Forest Service program or management functions, such as information technology or civil engineering. Other alternatives may contain elements that deal specifically with outreach to external agencies and departments.

Thus, in addition for suggesting possible alternatives, this section is a model for how to combine elements into logical alternatives and how to analyze and compare those alternatives with one another. Values and beliefs solidified by the recreation area's pending recreation plan process will provide the Forest Service and its stakeholders further direction considering and selecting alternatives.

Long-range operations and management elements

Long-range operations and management elements description

The long-range operations and management elements are those elements that are so universal that they may apply to any of the alternatives. These elements tend to have low cost to the Forest Service and high benefits to the visiting public. They may be considered in concert with broader alternatives or independently of one another.

Safety is often a subject of concern in all public places, but the potential for fatal flooding and debris flows at Sabino Canyon renders safety-related elements applicable to all future scenarios there. The Forest Service, in concert with SARA and Pima County Sheriff office, may consider creating and disseminating a disaster evacuation, rescue, and communication plan; developing safe, intuitive aggregation points to shelter-in-place or facilitate evacuation; and developing a flood detection and early warning system. For the latter, the Forest Service may add two new rain gauges, partner with weather specialists to obtain and analyze real-time data, and set up flashing lights/alarms on restrooms and other key locations to alert visitors to an impending flood.

Noise created by the current shuttle's interpretation system is a common complaint of visitors and one that may be addressed technologically. The Forest Service may work with the concessionaire to upgrade the interpretation technology. A variety of inexpensive tour audio technologies is on the market and may be integrated into the current tour concept, with or without new vehicles.

All transportation-related improvements at Sabino Canyon will require accurate and timely communications. The Forest Service may improve the frequency and accuracy of visitor communications at Sabino Canyon by reorganizing its website, keeping the website updated, and exploring new communications techniques related to the web and mobile devices.

Some visitors have noted a lack of information regarding distances and locations of amenities along the canyon road. The Forest Service may improve visitor wayfinding and trip planning by installing mile markers, maps, and signs with distances to points of interest and amenities.

Several elements focus on decreasing the number of automobile trips made to the canyon by visitors. The Forest Service may work with partners to provide transit or non-motorized access to Sabino Canyon Recreation area and thus reinforce societal goals to reduce greenhouse gas emissions. Specifically, the Forest Service can work with SunTran to expand public transit access to Sabino Canyon, with Pima County and city of Tucson to create an off-road path connecting to a greenway for bikes and pedestrians, and with visitors and nearby neighborhood associations to encourage walking from nearby neighborhoods. Table 10 provides some long-range operations and management elements that may be used for all transportation alternatives.

Table 10 – Long-range operations and management elements, common to all transportation alternatives

Element ID	Element Description
AM 05	Expand public transit service to Sabino Canyon Recreation Area.
AM 07	Create off-road path connecting to greenway for bikes and pedestrians.
AM 08	Encourage walking or cycling to the recreation area from nearby neighborhoods.
COM 01	Install mile markers and directory kiosks with distances to infrastructure and amenities.
COM 03	Improve the frequency and accuracy of visitor communications via the website.
MGMT 01	Create and disseminate a disaster evacuation, rescue, and communication plan.
MGMT 02	Develop aggregation points to shelter-in-place or facilitate evacuation for visitors within Sabino Canyon up to the end of Sabino Canyon Road.
MGMT 03	Develop flood detection and early warning system.
MOT 10	Upgrade interpretation method/technology.

Long-range operations and management elements evaluation

Evaluation criterion FS: Maintain assets and operate systems in a cost-effective and financially sustainable way

In a strict financial sense, none of these elements seek to directly increase revenue and all will require at least a marginal increase in spending. However, each of these elements provides for other non-monetary benefits which may well outweigh the financial costs, and this may indirectly generate additional revenue by making Sabino Canyon a more attractive destination for visitors. These elements do tend to have reasonable costs, especially when compared to the costs of building infrastructure such as roads, trails, buildings, or parking facilities. It is likely much of the funding for these management and operations elements will come from the recreation area's operating budget. There may be opportunities for both operating and funding partnerships for the safety and access initiatives, but these opportunities will be explored when these initiatives are formally addressed.

Evaluation criterion PS: Improve public safety and reduce visitor risk with respect to natural disasters and user conflicts

Several of the elements specifically seek to improve visitor safety from natural disasters. Creating and disseminating a disaster evacuation and rescue will provide vital preventative and corrective safety information to visitors and will formalize many of the rescue practices that are already in place.

Developing aggregation points for visitors to shelter-in-place will allow rescuers to reach more people more quickly during disaster events. Developing a flood detection and early warning system will provide advanced warning to visitors and allow them to evacuate Sabino Canyon prior to flood events. None of the elements specifically address user conflicts in the recreation area, although this issue is specifically addressed by other alternatives.

Evaluation criterion HCS: Preserve, protect, and restore unique historical and cultural sites within Sabino Canyon

Each management and operations element would leave existing historical and cultural sites unchanged. None of the management and operations elements would specifically protect historical and cultural sites. None of the elements specifically restore historical and cultural sites.

Evaluation criterion NER: Preserve, protect, and restore the natural and ecological resources within Sabino Canyon

Though each management and operations element would not infringe upon natural and ecological resources, none specifically protects or restores these resources.

Evaluation criterion AC: Provide access to and circulation within Sabino Canyon for all visitors as the basis for an enjoyable experience

Several of the elements deal specifically with improving access to Sabino Canyon for cyclists, pedestrians, transit riders, and residents from nearby neighborhoods. None of the elements specifically improve access and circulation within the canyon. This issue is addressed by other alternatives. None of the elements specifically improve access for elderly visitors and persons with disabilities. This issue is specifically addressed by Alternative 2. Finally, several of the elements seek to improve the visitor experience. Installing mile markers and providing location and distance information to visitors regarding infrastructure and amenities would allow visitors to explore the canyon more comfortably. Upgrading the interpretation technology would significantly reduce noise emanating from the shuttle and would improve non-riders' perception that they are in a relatively natural setting. Several elements seek to improve visitor safety, and visitors who are safe and healthy will always have a better experience than those who are not.

Alternative 0 – No action

Alternative 0 Description

The no action alternative preserves the status quo related to the existing shuttle service and operation and how visitors use the canyon road. This alternative serves as the baseline against which other alternatives are evaluated. There are no changes under this alternative to the existing road, bridge, trail, and parking infrastructure, and existing level-of-service including route length, number and location of stops, frequency of service, operating season, and hours of service per day, would be maintained.

Nothing, however, remains completely static, and some actions related to contract language and enforcement of environmental and service performance attributes are anticipated even under the no action alternative. These actions may result in vehicle improvements including a modernized version of the existing shuttle set (with equivalent passenger carrying capacity and geometric envelope), expanded use of biodiesel and/or alternative fuel sources, and added safety equipment for passengers. The shuttle would also continue serving as a motorized mechanism to evacuate stranded visitors up the Canyon when it is safe and feasible to operate the shuttle in this capacity. Table 11 lists the elements that make up Alternative 0 – No Action.

Table 11 – Elements comprising Alternative 0 – No Action

Element ID	Element Description
COM 02	Advertise that the tram runs on bio-diesel fuel.
MGMT 05	Require the tram vehicles to conform to specified noise and air quality requirements.
MGMT 06	Include/enforce shuttle service requirements in special-use permit.
MGMT 13	Maintain existing tram operation and service concept.
MOT 01	Use trams for evacuation.
MOT 07	Replace with in-kind vehicle of same size/function.
MOT 11	Add passenger safety equipment.

Alternative 0 evaluation

Evaluation criterion FS: Maintain assets and operate systems in a cost-effective and financially sustainable way

As with the current baseline, fares are set at a level to at least sustain the operation. It is not clear whether the fares can be set at a level to also recapitalize the tram fleet. The concessionaire, as is the current situation, under the No Action alternative would also pay the Forest Service for the exclusive right to operate within the canyon, and to allow the Forest Service to recover incremental maintenance costs for repair of the road infrastructure due to "wear and tear" from the tram operations. Capital costs and fleet size would essentially be equivalent to the current operation. A modernized version of the existing tram fleet is likely to be more expensive though may have lower maintenance costs.

Evaluation criterion PS: Improve public safety and reduce visitor risk with respect to natural disasters and user conflicts

This alternative will have no effect on the level of visitor risk due to natural disaster events. Similarly, because there is no change in the scope of operations and level-of-service offered relative to the current situation, user conflicts remain and are unchanged from the current baseline.

Evaluation criterion HCS: Preserve, protect, and restore unique historical and cultural sites within Sabino Canyon

Because this alternative maintains the current status quo, historical and cultural sites and artifacts are neither improved nor made substantially worse. That said, over time there could be some minor deterioration due to that fact that this alternative enables a sustained high level of visitor use, and the continued presence of the corrosive effects of air toxic emissions given continued use of fossil fuels.

Evaluation criterion NER: Preserve, protect, and restore the natural and ecological resources within Sabino Canyon

As with historic and cultural resources, the No Action alternative neither substantially improves nor substantially impairs beyond current conditions natural and ecological resources. Assuming that environmental performance specifications in the concessionaire's contract are now enforced, there may be slight improvement to the ecology of the area from reductions in noise and air toxic emissions.

Evaluation criterion AC: Provide access to and circulation within Sabino Canyon for all visitors as the basis for an enjoyable experience

No changes are anticipated under this alternative to access modes or level-of-service to reach Sabino Canyon. Service within the canyon is set at current or baseline levels. Because this alternative maintains the same type of equipment (within the same geometric envelope), it is unlikely that access for elderly and persons with disabilities will be improved. Visitor experience should be moderately improved with a modernized version of the tram that is likely to reduce noise and toxic emissions.

Alternative 1 – Parking management and capacity control

Alternative 1 description

The parking management and capacity control alternative seeks to address inadequate parking during peak visitation periods without expanding parking capacity beyond environmental limits. The recreation area is currently building additional parking adjacent to SARA's new headquarters. There have been some concerns that the environment at Sabino Canyon is being negatively impacted by having too many visitors, and creating additional parking may exacerbate this.

This alternative presumes that only a single, main parking lot is active and that during peak periods, all spaces could be full. If the visitor center is moved farther up the fore-range, the lot near the SARA headquarters may be better as a main lot. Alternatively, that lot could be used by SARA, Forest Service staff, and volunteers only, with visitors constrained to use the existing lot.

During peak periods, it is important to provide information to visitors about the availability of parking. Having an electronic system that tracks vehicles in and out of the parking lot would provide data on the number of available spaces at a given time. The recreation area already has an inductive loop traffic counter at the entrance to the parking area. If a second traffic counter were added to the exit lane, software could be set up to track the number of vehicles in the parking lot and therefore the number of spaces available. After collecting data for some time, it may be possible to estimate the amount of time before a space opens up (i.e., someone leaves approximately every 10 minutes therefore "expect a 10 minute wait"; there are a number of people who leave every half hour when the shuttle returns therefore "expect parking to be available at 0:10 or 0:40").

Number of spaces or approximate wait times can then be transmitted to visitors via multiple distribution channels. Variable Message Signs (VMS) could be set up either at the parking lot entrance or along East Sunrise Drive and North Sabino Canyon Road. Messages such as "lot full, expect X minute delay" would inform visitors of the current parking availability and estimates of when parking may be available. Information may also be transmitted to the Arizona 511 system which is accessible by phone. Up-to-date information for over 50 state and national parks within Arizona are currently available through the 511 system. Visitors could call en-route to determine the current parking situation.

Parking availability could be posted on the Coronado National Forest website. If the information changes more frequently than the half hour it takes the average visitor to travel to the recreation area, this information may be confusing, but as there are more and more people who have web-enabled telephones, having real-time parking information online could be useful. Table 12 provides a list of the elements that comprise Alternative 1. Table 13 provides a list of the elements related to Alternative 1.

Table 12 – Elements comprising Alternative 1 – Parking management and capacity control

Element ID	Element Description
COM 04	Expand information delivery methods to include new distribution channels.
COM 05	Use variable message signs for disseminating parking and safety messages.
COM 06	Collect parking lot utilization and disseminate in real-time via the web and/or variable message signs on approach roads.
INF 08	Eliminate planned overflow parking.

Table 13 – Elements related to Alternative 1 – Parking management and capacity control

Element ID	Element Description
MGMT 11	Develop a parking reservation system.

Alternative 1 evaluation

Evaluation criterion FS: Maintain assets and operate systems in a cost-effective and financially sustainable way

The capital and operations and maintenance costs for a parking management system would be minimal. An additional loop detector and controller would need to be added to the parking lot exit and both loop detectors would need to be networked into a computer. A connection, either wireline or wireless, would then need to be made to a (number of) VMS. Approximately 10 percent of the capital costs should be expected for annual maintenance. There is no expectation that the parking management system would produce revenue or be self-supporting.

Evaluation criterion PS: Improve public safety and reduce visitor risk with respect to natural disasters and user conflicts

As this alternative does not change the use of the canyon itself, the public safety implications are relatively minor. The most important public safety feature of this alternative is the communication system that is developed, which could alert approaching visitors of potential safety hazards such as wild animal sightings or potential adverse weather conditions.

Evaluation criterion HCS: Preserve, protect, and restore unique historical and cultural sites within Sabino Canyon

The current uses of the canyon would continue and have the same impacts on the cultural and historical resources in the canyon as they now do. The key provision of this alternative that impacts these resources is that the number of visitors is limited to current parking capacities instead of having visitors also use a new secondary lot that is planned.

Evaluation criterion NER: Preserve, protect, and restore the natural and ecological resources within Sabino Canyon

Limiting the number of parking spaces to a single lot would maintain visitation at current levels instead of allowing it to increase with the extra parking available at a second parking area. This would limit additional damage caused by allowing more people into the recreation area but would have no direct impact on the recreation area's natural resources.

Evaluation criterion AC: Provide access to and circulation within Sabino Canyon for all visitors as the basis for an enjoyable experience

The concept of this alternative is to maintain or limit the number of visitors at Sabino Canyon. Presuming most visitors will be limited to the current parking area and access to the site would not change, there would be no change in access and circulation as compared to the current conditions. Since additional parking information will be provided to visitors before they arrive, they will be better prepared for the conditions at the recreation area and can choose to alter their plans if the conditions are not desirable.

Alternative 2 – Expanded non-motorized use

Alternative 2 description

The expanded, non-motorized use alternative removes general shuttle service from the canyon road. To continue accommodating visitors with mobility impairments, a small electric van or mini-bus as shown in Figure 40 would be offered on a reservation basis for mobility impaired visitors. The van would operate a limited number of scheduled trips per day (e.g., two in the morning, and two in the afternoon).

Several of the existing shuttle stops would be removed from service and reconfigured to provide pedestrian/bicyclist amenities and enhanced wayside interpretative markers, possibly featuring smart-phone based systems. These amenities would also be provided at trailheads.

A technical advisory committee consisting of non-motorized user groups including cyclists, pedestrians, naturalists, and hikers would be convened under Forest Service auspices to develop a mutually-acceptable partial time-separation strategy to help manage remaining user conflicts. The advisory committee would allocate three blocks of time to the road:

1. Time wherein the Sabino Canyon Road is the exclusive domain for use by bicyclists;
2. Time wherein Sabino Canyon Road is the exclusive domain for use by pedestrians; and
3. Time wherein all non-motorized users share the road (with agreed-upon operating speeds for bicyclists).

Both bicyclists and pedestrians would now have the option to be free from a conflicting use on the narrow road alignment if they wish. Because this alternative emphasizes experiencing Sabino Canyon Road via non-motorized modes, the Forest Service may allow a concessionaire to provide bicycle rentals for visitors in the vicinity of the visitor's center.

Signage imploring all users to share the road would be installed at regular intervals along the road alignment in both directions. The road would neither be widened nor striped, though the existing road surface would be improved to a high-quality smooth road surface with uniform edges. At locations along the road at which sight lines are currently limited, clearing of vegetation would improve sight distance and road safety. The road would be subject to an updated maintenance schedule to keep it free from debris.

The Forest Service may initiate a public education campaign to inform the public of the new operating regime for the canyon road and update its website accordingly. Signage at the beginning of the road would explain the new rules, and handout cards and perhaps a 10-minute movie would be available at the visitor's center. Table 14 provides a list of elements that comprise Alternative 2. Table 15 provides a list of elements that are related to Alternative 2.

Figure 40 – Electro Transport Buddy (14-passenger capacity)[94]

Table 14 – Elements comprising Alternative 2 – Expanded non-motorized use

Element ID	Element Description
BPE 01	Initiate bicycle guided tours of Sabino Canyon.
BPE 04	Provide bicycle parking at trail-heads.
MGMT 04	Update and enforce time-separation strategies for different user types.
MOT 02	Remove the tram.
MOT 12	Limit hours/days/seasons of tram.

---

[94] "Electro Transport Buddy 15p LE" Gatormodo. http://www.gatormoto.com/index.cfm?action=ViewDetails&ItemID=63 (1/14/2010)

Table 15 – Elements related to Alternative 2 – Expanded non-motorized use

Element ID	Element Description
MOT 04	Electric carts could be provided for mobility-impaired visitors by reservation.
MOT 05	Rent electric bicycles to assist people to get up canyon.
MOT 06	Create an on-demand and/or reservation system for the mobility-impaired.
MOT 15	Replace Sabino Canyon shuttle with more developed shuttle service in Bear Canyon.
SCH 03	Purchase vehicle specifically for student group travel.

Alternative 2 evaluation

Evaluation criterion FS: Maintain assets and operate systems in a cost-effective and financially sustainable way

The proposed electric vehicle to service elderly and disabled visitors is substantially less expensive than the existing tram units, but will not bring in revenue for either the tram operator or the Forest Service that the current operation provides. The operating and maintenance costs of the electric vehicle as well as signage, information, and software reservation costs currently born by the tram operator will become the responsibility of the Forest Service. Revenue to offset these costs (capital costs, and the cost of facilitating access by elderly and disabled visitors) is an issue. The proposed bicycle concession would be on a financially-sustainable basis (i.e., rental rates covering the cost of the operation) and not born by the Forest Service.

Evaluation criterion PS: Improve public safety and reduce visitor risk with respect to natural disasters and user conflicts

While the risk of accident or injury due to the reduction in user conflicts is substantial, the inherent risk from natural disasters is unchanged. To the extent that this alternative induces greater visitation and numbers of visitors on-site at a time, the consequences for evacuation could be adverse in the absence of aggregation points and a robust shelter-in-place strategy with supportive facilities and infrastructure (e.g., new trail system to these aggregation points). This alternative also limits the possibility of using the tram as a motorized means of evacuation, although the ability to use the tram to negotiate the water and debris swept road during flood events is quite small.

Evaluation criterion HCS: Preserve, protect, and restore unique historical and cultural sites within Sabino Canyon

This alternative will help to preserve and restore historical and cultural sites primarily by reducing the environmental damages induced from continued operation of the existing tram service. This alternative does not actively protect these resources.

Evaluation criterion NER: Preserve, protect and restore the natural and ecological resources within Sabino Canyon

As with historic and cultural resources, the effect of this alternative on natural and ecological resources is minimal. Any impact should be marginally beneficial due to the removal of the existing tram service operation and associated environmental externalities (e.g., emissions and noise).

Evaluation criterion AC: Provide access to and circulation within Sabino Canyon for all visitors as the basis for an enjoyable experience

No change in access to Sabino Canyon is affected by this alternative. User conflicts for visitors traveling up Sabino Canyon will be reduced. Visitor experience should improve for pedestrians who will no longer have to be monitoring for regular tram service. Cyclists may also see an improvement to access due to increased hours of when bicycle use in the canyon is permitted. Visitors who enjoy the canyon by tram will see their current experience basically eliminated except for limited motorized service for the elderly and the disabled.

Alternative 3 – Fare-free shuttle

Alternative 3 description

Constraints of stamina, time, and climate prevent most pedestrians from reaching the end of the 4-mile road on a regular basis. Furthermore, ticket prices of $8 for adults and $4 for children render the shuttle cost prohibitive for some visitors to use as point-to-point transportation on a regular basis. This alternative seeks to alter the shuttle concept from an interpretive tour to a fare-free, hop-on-hop-off transportation service.

To implement this fare-free shuttle alternative, the Forest Service would allow the concessionaire agreement to expire. It would then purchase cleaner, quieter, and safer vehicles (perhaps through the Federal Transit Administration's Transit in the Parks (TRIP) grant program) and contract operations and maintenance to a private vendor. Potential vendors would not be burdened with the capital cost of the vehicles, thus more vendors would be able to compete and introduce operational and maintenance efficiencies.

To pay for operations and maintenance of the fare-free shuttles, the Forest Service may levy an expanded amenity recreation fee on all visitors (for example, $3 for day pass, $4 for week pass, and $5 for annual pass[95]). Operations and maintenance of the shuttle by the vendor would be covered by this fee. The Forest Service and vendor may consent to a concessionaire agreement to operate an interpretative tour using wireless tour guide audio system. Visitors who wish would pay an additional fee for this service and could listen to interpretation via a personal audio device as they ride the shuttle.

To remain economically feasible, shuttle service in Bear Canyon would be terminated. The Forest Service may thus consider allowing bicycles at all times in Bear Canyon.

This alternative is compatible with several of the elements in Alternative 4, namely those that would build walking paths from the overflow parking lot to Cactus Picnic Area and to the road. The former would remove parent drivers and buses from the canyon road as kindergarteners could walk to their educational site, and a dedicated shuttle could take elementary school children to their site at Sabino Dam. Furthermore, the shuttle could transport visitors who parked in the overflow lot either up into the

---

[95] These funding levels are provided as a realistic example of what might be needed to run the current level of shuttle service. Further study will be needed to estimate the change in demand and therefore service provided if the shuttle were to become fare free.

canyon or down to the visitor center. Table 16 provides a list of elements that comprise Alternative 3. Table 17 provides a list of elements that are related to Alternative 3.

Table 16 – Elements comprising Alternative 3 – Fare-free shuttle

Element ID	Element Description
AM 11	Create new broad walking path from new parking lot directly to Cactus Picnic Area.
MGMT 08	Provide the tram as a fare-free service for visitors.
MGMT 09	Charge an expanded amenity recreation fee to pay for fare-free shuttle service.
SCH 01	Provide free tram shuttle to transport student groups within the canyon.

Table 17 – Elements related to Alternative 3 – Fare-free shuttle

Element ID	Element Description
MGMT 10	Institute a frequent rider pass.
MOT 14	Connect new parking lot to visitor center via tram.

Alternative 3 evaluation

Evaluation criterion FS: Maintain assets and operate systems in a cost-effective and financially sustainable way

The Forest Service could explore purchasing vehicles through the Federal Transit Administration's Transit in the Parks (TRIP) grant program, which is specifically designed to help fund capital expenditures for alternative transportation systems on public lands. Grant money distributed by the program would require a local match, possibly generated from the Forest Service or the FOSC organization.

There are options for replacement of rolling stock, particularly electric, gasoline, diesel, or propane trams. Minimum vehicle requirements of the canyon road include minimum turning radius of 30 feet, a maximum grade of 14 percent, and maximum width of 8 feet and 6 inches. Several tram vehicles from vendors such as Trams International[96] and Maritime Applied Physics Corporation[97] meet these criteria, while more traditional bus vehicles are either too wide to cross the vented low-water crossings or too long to accommodate some of the hills and sags. The Forest Service may be able to find newer, safer, cleaner, and quieter replacement vehicles for a reasonable cost. Costs may be higher for state-of-the-art technology including powertrains driven by alternative fuel sources. A fleet of four shuttles may cost as little as $250,000 and as much as $1,000,000.

The operating costs would likely be less than the operating costs of the current system for two reasons. First, new vehicles would in theory require less maintenance than the old vehicles. Second, because the operations and maintenance contractor would not be burdened by ownership of the vehicles themselves, more contractors could compete for the contract and would thus have incentives to improve operations and drive operating costs down.

---

[96] http://www.tramfactory.com/
[97] http://www.mapcorp.com/

Evaluation criterion PS: Improve public safety and reduce visitor risk with respect to natural disasters and user conflicts

This alternative does not specifically reduce visitor risk with respect to natural disasters, but by removing shuttle service on Bear Canyon Road, it may be possible for cyclists and pedestrians to share that road at all times on all days.

Evaluation criterion HCS: Preserve, protect, and restore unique historical and cultural sites within Sabino Canyon

The fare-free shuttle alternative does not actively seek to alter historical or cultural sites within Sabino Canyon. The fare-free shuttle alternative does not directly seek to protect or restore unique historical and cultural sites within Sabino Canyon.

Evaluation criterion NER: Preserve, protect, and restore the natural and ecological resources within Sabino Canyon

While the fare-free shuttle alternative does nothing to harm the natural and ecological resources beyond current conditions, it does nothing to directly protect or restore these resources. Reduced emissions from a new vehicle would reduce air pollutants.

Evaluation criterion AC: Provide access to and circulation within Sabino Canyon for all visitors as the basis for an enjoyable experience

The fare-free shuttle seeks to improve access for all visitors within Sabino Canyon by reducing financial barriers to riding the shuttle and thus allowing visitors to reach interior parts of the canyon that previously could not reached on foot. The fare-fare free shuttle will particularly improve access for elderly persons and persons with disabilities and allow them to reach interior destinations within the canyon on a repeat basis. This alternative will likely improve the visitor experience for many visitors, recognizing that all visitors to Sabino Canyon have different expectations that they use as benchmarks against which they gauge the quality of their experiences. Although some visitors would prefer complete removal of the shuttle, many other visitors are either indifferent or enjoy the shuttle experience. It is likely that if the shuttle becomes fare-free, the number of visitors who ride will increase significantly. It is also possible that some of the visitors who currently want to remove the shuttle may find value in a hop-on-hop-off service that takes them to their favorite spots in the canyon quickly and easily. Furthermore, the fare-free alternative would likely remove shuttle service on Bear Canyon Road, thus possibly freeing the road for bicycle use at all times of day on all days of week.

Alternative 4 – Infrastructure improvements

Alternative 4 description

The current configuration of Sabino Canyon's roads and trails leaves visitors and the infrastructure vulnerable to flooding. In addition, the narrowness of the bridges limits the types of vehicles that can be driven up the canyon. This alternative seeks to improve visitor mobility and safety and to provide additional options for shuttle vehicle designs. These ideas would improve visitor egress during flooding events and reduce conflicts between vehicles and pedestrians along the canyon road.

The Forest Service may move the main entrance station to what is now the northern service entrance and thus emphasize the new parking area which many regular visitors may prefer due to its proximity to the canyon. Moving the entry north of the schools also reduces conflicts between canyon visitors and parents dropping their children off at the two schools on North Sabino Canyon Road. Canyon visitors may still have to wait in school traffic, but they will not have difficulty making a left-hand turn when exiting the recreation area. The Forest Service may also build a new access road parallel to North Sabino Canyon Road to connect the new main entrance to the existing parking lot. This will force all vehicles to enter through a single entrance and allows the Forest Service to monitor and greet all vehicles entering the recreation area. In addition, the visitor center may be moved closer to the new parking area by the Cactus Ramada and Rattlesnake Creek drainage.

To accommodate a wider range of shuttle vehicles and to decrease the potential for visitors to be stranded by flooding, the Forest Service should consider developing new bridges adjacent to vented low-water crossings 1-4. New bridges, as shown in Figure 41, may be located in the following locations:

- Downstream of vented low-water crossing 1.
- Downstream of crossing 3.
- Upstream of crossing 4.

The Forest Service may develop additional trails that bypass the vented low-water crossings and allow visitors to get to shelter-in-place locations. The following trails would be required on the east side of the creek:

- From before crossing 6 to after crossing 7.

The following trails would be required on the west side of the creek:

- From before crossing 7 to after crossing 8.
- Trails providing access to the new bridges for evacuation.

The Forest Service may further develop rescue locations at the two east-side restrooms and one of the west side restrooms to provide shelter to visitors waiting for the weather to improve.

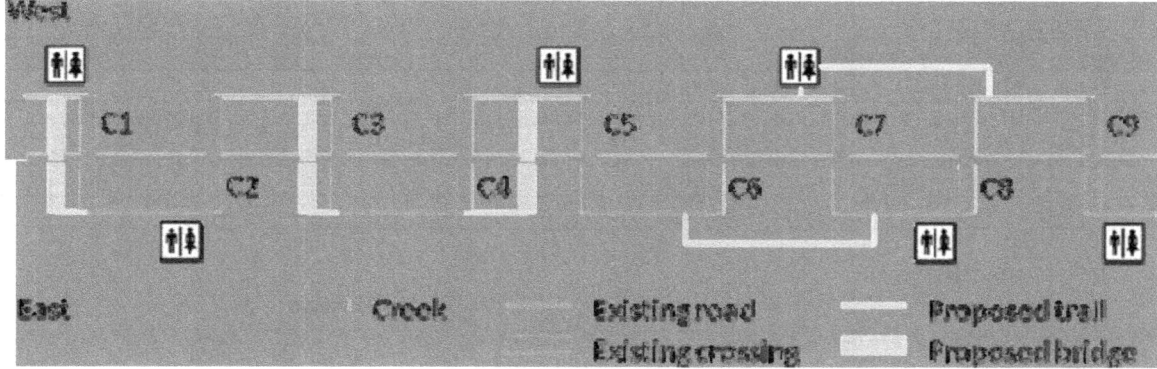

Figure 41 - Proposed trail and bridge infrastructure improvements

The Forest Service may purchase new shuttle vehicles to meet the needs of visitors, either with interpretation technology or not. If new bridges are installed, the vehicles may be wider, heavier, and have wider turning radii than the current trams. The shuttle vehicles would provide service up to Stop 4 in order to allow the upper portion of the canyon road to remain a remote, pedestrian experience. Doing so would also allow the Forest Service to focus its maintenance on the fore-range and the lower canyon.

The Forest Service may build a road or path from the new parking lot to Cactus Picnic Area. School groups may either walk from the new parking lot to the picnic area or ride the shuttle to the picnic area access road or the picnic area itself. Elementary school children would ride the shuttle to their educational site at Sabino Dam. Table 18 provides a list of the elements that comprise Alternative 4. Table 19 provides a list of the elements that are related to Alternative 4.

Table 18 – Elements comprising Alternative 4 – Infrastructure improvements

Element ID	Element Description
AM 01	Create a new internal road connecting the current and future parking areas or redevelop the existing interior access road for public access to the new overflow lot.
AM 11	Create new broad walking path from new parking lot directly to Cactus Picnic Area.
INF 01	Create alternate trail network that avoids stream crossings and facilitates evacuation.
INF 02	Relocate the visitor center farther up the canyon and shuttle between it and the parking lots.
INF 07	Develop new bridges for pedestrians (or tram) off of the existing roadway network.
MOT 13	Limit tram route to lower canyon only.
SCH 01	Provide free tram shuttle to transport student groups within the canyon.

Table 19 – Elements related to Alternative 4 – Infrastructure improvements

Element ID	Element Description
BPE 02	Create a grade-separated bike and/or pedestrian trail.
BPE 03	Stripe an at-grade bike and/or pedestrian trail using the existing road width, widening where possible.
INF 03	Widen road to reduce user conflicts.
INF 04	Widen the bridges and bridge approaches.

Alternative 4 evaluation

Evaluation criterion FS: Maintain assets and operate systems in a cost-effective and financially sustainable way

It is not expected that this alternative will have a direct impact on revenue either for the Forest Service or for a shuttle service operator. While the new facilities will have additional ongoing maintenance costs, it is possible that there will be some reductions in operating costs due to the ability to buy potentially less expensive shuttle vehicles and the potential for heavier duty vehicles/machinery to be brought into the canyon for maintenance of the road, bathrooms, and other facilities.

The capital costs of developing new bridges and trails would be high, at approximately $750,000 per bridge and $200,000 per mile for trails. The costs for a new visitor center would start in the low two-digit millions and increase based on size and design features.

Evaluation criterion PS: Improve public safety and reduce visitor risk with respect to natural disasters and user conflicts

Public safety is one of the key reasons for the infrastructure improvements suggested in this alternative. As described above, the additional bridges and trails would reduce pedestrian-vehicle conflicts and increase visitor mobility during high-water events.

Evaluation criterion HCS: Preserve, protect, and restore unique historical and cultural sites within Sabino Canyon

This alternative would have a significant impact on the current look and feel of the Canyon. While it would preserve the historically important vented low-water crossings, there would be new infrastructure that would add "clutter" within the canyon.

Evaluation criterion NER: Preserve, protect, and restore the natural and ecological resources within Sabino Canyon

This alternative would create significant changes to the current natural environment due to the new infrastructure that is proposed. Stabilized cuts into the hillside may be required to create flat sections for new bridges and trails. This may create more issues with landslides.

Evaluation criterion AC: Provide access to and circulation within Sabino Canyon for all visitors as the basis for an enjoyable experience

There are significant benefits to access to and circulation within Sabino Canyon due to infrastructure improvements. The new single point of entry is located beyond the local schools allowing visitors to turn on/from North Sabino Canyon Road before/after the heavy traffic created by the schools when the schools open and let out for the day.

Access within Sabino Canyon is improved in two ways. New bridges at Crossing 1, 3, and 4 would reduce the tight curves that limit the type of vehicles that can be used in the lower portion of the canyon. The new bridges and additional pedestrian trail segments should provide options for pedestrians to segregate themselves from vehicles and provide increased mobility throughout the canyon during high-water events.

Little change is expected for elderly visitors or those with mobility impairments. Fewer conflicts between the shuttle service and pedestrians may improve the shuttle service which may be used by a higher proportion of visitors in these categories.

VII. Financial opportunities

There are a number of funding sources for transportation through the Forest Service, U.S. DOT Federal Highway Administration and Federal Transit Administration, and through private sources. Many of the programs are oversubscribed compared to the current need, making the programs highly competitive.

Forest Service

Forest Service Discretionary Funds for Capital Improvements and Maintenance

The primary source of funding for forest service roads is the through Forest Service Discretionary Funds for Capital Improvements and Maintenance. Approximately $230 million is set aside annually for road maintenance. Capital improvements funds are distributed through a competitive process and are rarely designated for transportation projects. Maintenance funds are allocated annually based on a standardized formula. It is recognized that the need for these funds far exceeds the availability.

Legacy Roads and Trails Program

The Legacy Roads and Trails Program is a forest-service wide program set up to reduce or eliminate risks to water quality and aquatic habitats from roads and trails. The program is funded for approximately $50 million dollars annually and appropriate projects include road/trail decommissioning, stream crossing improvements and maintenance projects. Work on the bridges and the approaches could be funded through this program, particularly if the focus is on restoring the natural stream flow.

Recreation Fee

The Federal Lands Recreation Enhancement Act permits Public Lands to collect fees to maintain facilities and programs in developed areas of public land, such as Sabino Canyon. At least 95 percent of recreation fees are expected to stay at the unit to maintain the visitor facilities. Up to five percent of funds can be used by the region. Three types of fees can be collected: Standard Amenity Fees, Expanded Amenity Fees and Special Recreation Permits.

Standard Amenity Fees are generally paid by the general visitor population to specific area where significant visitor infrastructure such as parking, toilets, interpretation and other amenities have been provided, such as the current entrance fee at Sabino.

Expanded Amenity Fees are used when only a subset of visitors benefit from investments such as a developed campgrounds, monitored and maintained swimming areas, and both optional and mandatory transportation systems. Often reservation systems or limited entry to the facilities allow fees to be collected from users of the system. An expanded amenity fee could be collected for a forest-service run transportation service. Fees for the current concessionaire-run transportation system are not covered through this program, but overseen by the concession office.

The Special Recreation Permit focuses on limiting visitation to environmentally sensitive areas and does not apply to Sabino Canyon.

Federal Highway Administration

The Federal Highway Administration (FHWA) makes funds available for highway and other transportation improvements through a number of programs, including the Federal-Aid Highway Program, the Forest Highways Program, Coordinated Technology Implementation Program (CTIP), and the Scenic Byways Program. Since Sabino Canyon Road is entirely within the Forest Service boundaries, FHWA programs that are administered through states or local governments, such as the Federal-Aid and Forest Highways funding sources, typically are ineligible or a viewed as a lesser priority by the primary recipients.

Federal Lands Highway Program – Discretionary Funding

Federal Lands Highway Discretionary program is a program available for a wide variety of project types. The funding for this program increased significantly during SAFETEA-LU to $102 million in 2009, but due to the broad eligibility requirements and the limited funding available after funds earmarked for specific projects are set aside, competition for discretionary funding is high.

Recreational Trails Program

The Recreational Trails Program provides funding for capital and maintenance of both motorized and non-motorized trail use. In Arizona, funding is distributed by Arizona State Parks.[98]

Surface Transportation Program Set Aside for Transportation Enhancements

As described on the FHWA website,[99] Transportation Enhancement funding is designed to "expand transportation choices and enhance the transportation experience." There are 12 specific eligible activities focusing on surface transportation including "pedestrian and bicycle infrastructure and safety programs, scenic and historic highway programs, landscaping and scenic beautification, historic preservation, and environmental mitigation." ADOT manages the program in the State of Arizona.[100]

Coordinated Technology Implementation Program (CTIP)

Federal Highways also has funding for technology-based projects through the Coordinated Technology Implementation Program (CTIP). With an open and rolling call, projects must meet the following criteria:

- Innovative, unique, or underused transportation technology
- Doesn't require research
- Adds Value
- Meets a specific need
- Supports public roads or facilities
- Costs less than $200,000
- Time frame less than three (3) years

More information can be found at http://www.ctiponline.org/submit_proposal/. Parking management or interpretation may be particularly appropriate for this funding source.

---

[98] Arizona State Parks Grant Programs website, http://www.azparks.gov/grants/.
[99] FHWA Environment Transportation Enhancement Activities website, http://www.fhwa.dot.gov/environment/te/.
[100] ADOT Transportation Enhancement website, http://www.azdot.gov/highways/SWProjMgmt/enhancement_scenic/enhancement/Index.asp.

Federal Transit Administration

Paul S. Sarbanes Transit in Parks Program (TRIP)

TRIP provides funds for planning and capital projects for alternative transportation systems including shuttle buses and bicycle trails in or connecting to public lands. Projects can be proposed by the public lands agency or local governments or other partners.[101] New vehicles, trails connecting to the new parking area, bicycle or pedestrian trails accessing Sabino Canyon or additional planning studies are all eligible for TRIP funding.

Sponsorship or partnership with local private business

Another opportunity for funding would be to look toward private sector sponsorship. Major companies or other local businesses (e.g., Canyon Ranch, VisionQuest, Raytheon, Summit Hut), may be potential sponsors of shuttle services. One potential model for such sponsorship is the Island Explorer bus service at Acadia National Park in Bar Harbor, Maine, which is funded in part by L.L. Bean. As there are federal funding opportunities for capital improvements and maintenance, sponsorships and partnerships that support ongoing operating costs such as shuttle services or interpretive programming are most valuable.

---

[101] This project was funded in FY 2007 by the precursor to TRIP, the Alternative Transportation in Parks and Public Lands Program.

VIII. Next Steps

By summarizing the natural environment of Sabino Canyon, its history, surroundings and the people who use the canyon, key themes and goals for Sabino Canyon became apparent. This document provides the background for current and future planning for Sabino Canyon, particularly focusing on the transportation systems surrounding and within the canyon.

Though various user and stakeholder groups may place more or less emphasis on specific issues, two commonalities exist among all:

- Sabino Canyon is a popular and respected attraction by all visitors; and
- All users and stakeholder groups desire what is best for Sabino Canyon.

By describing current conditions and potential conflict points, this document provides a basis on which all stakeholders may collectively determine the best use of the canyon and the feasible transportation alternatives that will support this vision.

This document is not designed to provide a specific plan of action for transportation at Sabino Canyon, but instead provide solutions to specific transportation issues that were identified. It is expected that as the preferred alternative is developed for the Sabino Canyon Recreation Concept Plan, transportation elements from this study can be combined to develop the appropriate transportation system to meet the future desired goals for Sabino Canyon and its visitors.

Chapter VI provides an example of how a number of elements can be combined to create very different experiences within the canyon and how these alternatives can be analyzed and compared to each other. There are a number of long-range operations and management elements that the project team feels could benefit Sabino Canyon regardless of direction defined by the Recreation Concept Plan.

IX. Appendices

Appendix A. Hourly Tram Ridership Estimation Methodology

Hourly tram ridership was not available, thus Figure 29 shows estimated hourly tram ridership based on arrivals rates of private automobiles, adjusted for monthly tram ticket sales. The methodology used for the estimation is described below. Example calculations are provided in italics.

Assumptions

- Assume tram riders arrive predominantly by private automobile.
- Assume three riders per car on average during hours which the shuttle is running, 9:00 AM to 4:30 PM.

Methodology

1. Calculate the sum of the total tram ticket sales for a given period. The 2008 peak season, December through April, resulted in 86,615 tram tickets sold.
2. Divide the total ticket sales by 3 to calculate the estimated number of cars required to bring those riders to SCRA. 28,872 cars would have been required to generate 86,615 tram tickets sold.
3. Calculate the sum of cars that arrive during the given period but only during hours that will generate ticket sales. Though the tram operates from 9:00 AM to 4:30 PM, some cars may arrive as early as 8:00 AM to catch the first tram. Car counts are hourly, so to capture arrivals from 4:00 PM to 4:30 PM, all the cars from 8:00 PM to 5:00 PM are counted. During the hours of 8:00 AM to 5:00 PM, December 2008 to April 2009, 124,474 cars entered the parking lot.
4. Divide the result from (2) by the result from (3). This is the percentage of car arrivals during daytime hours that utilize the tram. During the hours of 8:00 AM to 5:00 PM, December 2008 to April 2009, 23.2% of cars would have contained on average three riders of the tram.
5. Calculate the average hourly car arrivals during a given period during hours of tram operation. This can be done for both weeks and weekends. For example, on an average weekday during December 2008 and April 200, between 8:00 AM and 9:00 AM, 107 cars enter the parking lot.
6. Multiply the percentage calculated in (4) by the hourly car arrivals calculated in (5). Multiply by 3 to calculate number of tram rider arrivals per hour. This result is shown in Figure 29. For example, on an average weekday during December 2008 and April 200, between 8:00 AM and 9:00 AM, 25 cars contain an average of three tram riders, or a total of 75 tram riders.
7. Repeat steps 1-6 for the other period (May-November).

Appendix B.Planning document overview

Regional planning, transportation planning, and public lands planning documents were reviewed while compiling the existing conditions of Sabino Canyon Recreation Area. An overview of these documents is provided in this appendix.

2030 Regional Transportation Plan (June 29, 2006)

The Regional Transportation Plan is a long-range vision of transportation addressing challenges created by current travel demand and continuing growth. It identifies a set of potential multimodal projects, policies, and strategies that will help move people and goods efficiently in the future. The plan does not explicitly address but does note "fixed-route community circulators" are planned for the Catalina Foothills and Bear Canyon areas. Pima Association of Governments (PAG) is currently updating the plan which will become the 2040 Long Range Transportation Plan. During one of the public participation workshops for the plan update, interest was expressed in extending circulator routes and expanding current bus routes to key locations at the base of the Catalina Mountains including Sabino, Pima, and Ventana Canyons.

Forest Level Roads Analysis Report, Coronado National Forest (January 2003)

This report analyzes roughly 800 miles of road within Coronado National Forest and makes recommendations as how to best manage the transportation system within existing and anticipated funding levels. It contains i) a report that identifies opportunities and sets priorities for the future National Forest road system, ii) maps displaying the main road system, and iii) tables listing priorities and recommended changes in the road system. The report provides qualitative descriptions of roads, a summary of road operation/maintenance funding and costs, and assessments of road infrastructure values related to facilities, resources, recreation, and safety and road effects related to human-caused wildfires, watershed conditions, wildlife, cultural resources, and air quality. Analysis results are presented as maintenance needs, reducing maintenance needs, mitigating undesirable effects, right-of-way needs and priorities, ecological, social, and economic considerations, and additional roads analyses.

National Visitor Use Monitoring Results (2002)

This study of the Coronado National Forest reports demographic statistics of visitors and descriptions of visits. It reports on visitor activities, economics, satisfaction, and crowding. It does not consider discretely aggregate statistics for Sabino Canyon Recreation Area.

National Visitor Use Monitoring Results (2008)

This is an update to the 2002 study. This study is more comprehensive than its predecessor and contains comparisons with the 2001 data. It expands significantly on the 2002 study by providing tables, charts, and graphs of detailed visitor and visit information and includes a 40-page appendix of tables. However, it still does not consider discretely aggregate statistics for Sabino Canyon Recreation Area.

Pima County Multi-Species Conservation Plan Draft Version 5 (2008)

This plan provides the framework for Endangered Species Act compliance for federal and non-federal participants throughout Pima County. Regarding Sabino Canyon, the plan notes that Sabino Canyon provides critical habitat for the Gila chub. It also notes that Sabino Canyon is being invaded by arundo, a perennial grass, and that the county is attempting to restrict its commercial use and use in new development. Pima County is implementing monitoring controls and monitoring efforts.

Sabino Canyon, Coronado National Forest, Planning Project Proposal (2007)

This proposal is a funding request from the Coronado National Forest for a transportation analysis and feasibility study. It demonstrates need by outlining the current issues, suggesting a methodology for assessing visitor mobility and experience, proposing a methodology for assessing environmental benefits, and recommending a methodology for assessing operational efficiency and financial sustainability.

Sabino Canyon Interpretive Plan (1991)

This plan describes the state of interpretive services and facilities at Sabino Canyon Recreation Area, provides detailed interpretations of the recreation area itself, and outlines plans for how to accurately disseminate this information to visitors.

Sabino Canyon Recreation Concept Plan (1993)

This plan responds to previous findings that existing facilities are deteriorated, few facilities are accessible to disabled visitors, and some facilities are not located where visitors need or want them. It recommends restoration or rehabilitation of many recreation sites, removal of incompatible facilities, and enhancement or addition of other facilities. The plan is not a decision document and does not consider National Environmental Policy Act provisions, recognizing many of the recommendations will require public involvement.

Southern Arizona Rescue Association Annual Report (2006)

The annual report contains a history of the organization, a description of its operations, and statistics and descriptions of the previous year's activities. It provides some geographical statistics regarding mission areas and shows that in 2005 and 2006, 30 percent of rescue missions began or ended in Sabino Canyon.

Appendix C. Element criteria

Management Costs and Benefits

1 = improves experience
0 = no change
-1 = degrades experience

Element	Capital Cost	Annual O&M Cost	Safety, Risk of Fatality	Safety, Risk of Crashes	Safety, User Conflicts	Cultural Landscape	Technical Difficulty	Civic Anticipated Public Acceptance	Natural Environment	Historic Resources	Dispersion	Pedestrians	Cyclists	Tram Riders	Equestrians	Site management

Cat.	#	Description		
AM	2	Institute 24-hour access control with an electronic pass system through the main entrance	High	Low
AM	3	Develop south-side access-egress from lot to avoid conflicts with school	High	Low
AM	4	Install a traffic signal at the recreation area entrance	Med	Low
AM	5	Expand public transit service to Sabino	Med	High
AM	6	Stripe & widen shoulders of road to improve bicycle access	Med/High	Med
AM	7	Create off-road path connecting to greenway for bikes and pedestrians	Med/High	Med
AM	8	Encourage walking from nearby neighborhoods	Low	Low
AM	9	Improve Bear Canyon access point	Med	Med
AM	10	Dedicated right-turn lane into Sabino Canyon parking lot	High	Med
AM	11	Create new walking path from new parking lot directly to Cactus	Med	Low
COM	1	Install mile markers and distances to infrastructure and amenities	Low	Low
COM	2	Advertise the tram runs on biodiesel	Low	Low
COM	3	Improve frequency and accuracy of visitor communications	Med	Low
COM	4	Expand information delivery methods to include telephone, highway advisory radio, email, RSS, SMS, and web/mobile web.	High	Low
COM	5	Use variable message signs for disseminating parking and safety messages.	Med	Low
COM	6	Collect parking lot utilization and disseminate in real-time via the web and/or variable message signs on approach roads	High	Med
BPE	1	Initiate bicycle guided tours of Sabino Canyon	Med	Med
BPE	2	Create a grade-separated bike and/or pedestrian trail	High	Med
BPE	3	Create an at-grade bike and/or pedestrian trail	Med	Low
BPE	4	Provide bicycle parking at trail-heads	Low	Low
BPE	5	Develop equestrian tours	Med	Med
BPE	6	Create additional or improve existing infrastructure for equestrian users	Med	Low
INF	1	Create alternate trail network that avoids stream crossings and facilitates evacuation	High	Med
INF	2	Relocate the visitor center farther up the canyon and shuttle between it and the parking lots	High	Med
INF	3	Widen road to reduce user conflicts	High	Med
INF	4	Widen the bridges and bridge approaches	High	Med
INF	5	Redesign bridges to improve flow under to reduce sedimentation	High	Med

Cat	#	Description		
		issues; keep historic look but change engineering		
INF	6	Regularly dredge culverts to maintain desired	High	Med
INF	7	Develop new bridges for pedestrians (or the tram) off of the existing roadway network (conceptualized at creation of the bridges) water flow	High	Med
INF	8	Eliminate planned overflow parking	Low	Low
MGMT	1	Create and disseminate a disaster evacuation, rescue, and communication plan	Med	Low
MGMT	2	Develop safe, intuitive aggregation points to shelter-in-place or facilitate evacuation	Med	Med
MGMT	3	Develop flood detection and early warning system	Med	Med
MGMT	4	Update and enforce time-separation strategies for different user types	Med	Med
MGMT	5	Include/enforce environmental requirements (noise, air quality) in special use permit	Low	Med
MGMT	6	Include/enforce shuttle service requirements in special use permit	Low	Low
MGMT	7	Transfer ownership of the tram vehicles to USFS and continue operation by concessionaire	High	Med
MGMT	8	Provide tram as a free service for visitors	Low	Low
MGMT	9	Charge an expanded amenity recreation fee to pay for shuttle service		
MGMT	10	Institute a frequent rider pass	Med	Med
MGMT	11	Develop a parking reservation system	Med	Low
MGMT	12	Charge entry fee for all users, per person	Low	Low
MGMT	13	Maintain existing tram operation and service concept	Low	Low
MOT	1	Allow tram use and use vehicles for evacuation	Low	Med
MOT	2	Remove the tram	Low	Low
MOT	3	Develop aerial tram service	High	High
MOT	4	Provide electric carts for mobility impaired visitors	Med	Med
MOT	5	Rent electric bicycles to assist people to get up canyon	Med	Med
MOT	5a	Rent bicycles		
MOT	6	Create an on-demand and/or reservation system for the mobility-impaired	Med	Med
MOT	7	Replace with in-kind vehicle of same size/function	High	Med
MOT	8	Replace vehicles with larger or smaller vehicles but run at equivalent capacity (fewer or more trips)	High	Med
MOT	9	Replace with enclosed vehicle design	High	Med
MOT	10	Upgrade interpretation method/technology (headphones)	Med	Low
MOT	11	Add passenger safety equipment	Med	Low
MOT	12	Limit hours/days/seasons	Low	Low

		Description		C1	C2	C3	C4	C5	C6	C7	C8	C9	C10	C11	C12	C13	C14	C15	C16	C17	C18	C19	C20	C21	C22
MOT	13	Limit tram route to lower canyon only	Low	0	0	1	1	1	-1	1	0	0	1	1	-1	0	0	2	2	2	0	1	1	1	0
MOT	14	Connect new parking lot to visitor center via tram	Low	0	0	0	0	-1	1	1	0	1	0	0	1	0	0	2	2	0	1	1	1	0	0
MOT	15	Replace Sabino Canyon shuttle with more developed shuttle service in Bear Canyon	Low	0	0	0	0	0	-1	1	0	1	1	1	-1	-1	0	0	0	1	0	1	1	0	0
MOT	16	Develop additional shuttles and/or routes within CNF (to Mt. Lemmon and/or additional parking areas)	High	0	0	0	-1	1	0	0	0	1	0	0	1	0	0	2	1	0	0	1	0	0	0
SCH	1	Require shuttle to transport student groups within the canyon for free	Low	0	0	1	1	0	0	1	1	1	1	1	0	0	1	4	0	0	1	1	1	0	0
SCH	2	Relocate educational facilities or build trails so that students can walk from the parking lot	Med	0	1	1	0	1	0	1	1	-1	1	1	1	0	1	-	-	-	0	1	1	0	0
SCH	3	Purchase vehicle specifically for student group travel	High	0	0	0	1	1	1	0	1	1	0	0	1	0	1	0	1	6	0	1	1	0	0

Appendix D. Elements analysis

Sixty-four transportation solutions, or elements, were analyzed with respect to their efficacy at Sabino Canyon. An overview of the element generation and analysis process is found in Section V. This appendix contains the detailed analysis for each element.

Element ID	Element description
AM 01	Create a new internal road connecting the current and future parking areas or redevelop the existing interior access road for public access to the new overflow lot.
AM 02	Institute 24-hour access control.
AM 03	Develop south-side access-egress from lot to avoid conflicts with school.
AM 04	Install a traffic signal at the recreation area entrance.
AM 05	Expand public transit service to Sabino Canyon Recreation Area.
AM 06	Stripe and widen shoulders of roads to improve bicycle access.
AM 07	Create off-road path connecting to greenway for bikes and pedestrians.
AM 08	Encourage walking or cycling to the recreation area from nearby neighborhoods.
AM 09	Improve Bear Canyon access point.
AM 10	Dedicated right-turn lane into Sabino Canyon parking lot.
AM 11	Create new broad walking path from new parking lot directly to Cactus Picnic Area.
AM 12	Install a southbound right-turn lane from Sabino Canyon Road to Skyline.
BPE 01	Initiate bicycle guided tours of Sabino Canyon.
BPE 02	Create a grade-separated bike and/or pedestrian trail.
BPE 03	Stripe an at-grade bike and/or pedestrian trail using the existing road width, widening where possible.
BPE 04	Provide bicycle parking at trail-heads.
BPE 05	Develop equestrian tours.
BPE 06	Create additional or improve infrastructure for equestrian users.
COM 01	Install mile markers and directory kiosks with distances to infrastructure and amenities.
COM 02	Advertise that the tram runs on bio-diesel fuel.
COM 03	Improve the frequency and accuracy of visitor communications via the website.
COM 04	Expand information delivery methods to include new distribution channels.
COM 05	Use variable message signs for disseminating parking and safety messages.
COM 06	Collect parking lot utilization and disseminate in real-time via the web and/or variable message signs on approach roads.
INF 01	Create alternate trail network that avoids stream crossings and facilitates evacuation.
INF 02	Relocate the visitor center farther up the canyon and shuttle between it and the parking lots.
INF 03	Widen road to reduce user conflicts.
INF 04	Widen the bridges and bridge approaches.
INF 05	Redesign bridges to improve flow and reduce sedimentation issues; keep historic look but change engineering.
INF 06	Regularly maintain culverts to maintain desired (conceptualized at the creation of the bridges) water flow.
INF 07	Develop new bridges for pedestrians (or tram) off of the existing roadway network.
INF 08	Eliminate planned overflow parking.
MGMT 01	Create and disseminate a disaster evacuation, rescue, and communication plan.
MGMT 02	Develop aggregation points to shelter-in-place or facilitate evacuation for visitors within Sabino Canyon up to the end of Sabino Canyon Road.
MGMT 03	Develop flood detection and early warning system.
MGMT 04	Update and enforce time-separation strategies for different user types.
MGMT 05	Require the tram vehicles to conform to specified noise and air quality requirements.
MGMT 06	Include/enforce shuttle service requirements in special-use permit.

Element ID	Element description
MGMT 07	Transfer ownership of the tram vehicles to USFS and continue operation by a contractor.
MGMT 08	Provide the tram as a fare-free service for visitors.
MGMT 09	Charge an expanded amenity recreation fee to pay for fare-free shuttle service.
MGMT 10	Institute a frequent rider pass.
MGMT 11	Develop a parking reservation system.
MGMT 12	Charge entry fee for all users, per person.
MGMT 13	Maintain existing tram operation and service concept.
MOT 01	Use trams for evacuation.
MOT 02	Remove the tram.
MOT 03	Develop aerial tram service.
MOT 04	Electric carts could be provided for mobility-impaired visitors by reservation.
MOT 05	Rent electric bicycles to assist people to get up canyon.
MOT 06	Create an on-demand and/or reservation system for the mobility-impaired.
MOT 07	Replace with in-kind vehicle of same size/function.
MOT 08	Replace vehicles with larger or smaller vehicles but run at equivalent capacity.
MOT 09	Replace trams with an enclosed vehicle design.
MOT 10	Upgrade interpretation method/technology.
MOT 11	Add passenger safety equipment.
MOT 12	Limit hours/days/seasons of tram.
MOT 13	Limit tram route to lower canyon only.
MOT 14	Connect new parking lot to visitor center via tram.
MOT 15	Replace Sabino Canyon shuttle with more developed shuttle service in Bear Canyon.
MOT 16	Develop separate shuttle options and/or routes within CNF (to Mt. Lemmon and/or additional parking areas).
SCH 01	Provide free tram shuttle to transport student groups within the canyon.
SCH 02	Relocate educational facilities or build trails so that students can walk from the parking lot.

AM 01 – Create a new internal road connecting the current and future parking areas or redevelop the existing interior access road for public access to the new overflow lot.

Description: If the overflow parking lot is built, managing a second entrance to the recreation area would be a significant challenge for USFS. Enforcing fee payment may be difficult or costly and maintaining visitor safety may be more difficult. Visitors to the main parking lot can receive safety and visitation information from signs and personnel in both the entrance booth and at the visitor center, neither of which would be visited by those entering a separate entrance to the overflow lot. By providing an internal access road between both parking areas, USFS could enforce fee payment and disseminate safety and visitation information at the entrance booth. Drivers could easily drop off group members at the visitor center before parking their cars in the overflow lot.

Two options include redeveloping the current internal road network to be used by private vehicles or developing a new access road parallel to North Sabino Canyon Road between the two parking areas. There may be some archaeological or environmental issues with developing a new road on undisturbed lands.

If the current entry and internal roadway were to be used, pedestrian and bicycle use could be moved to one of several trails that run adjacent to the interior access road, up to the point where motor vehicle use leaves the main road. This would maintain a physical separation from motor vehicles for both safety and aesthetics. The original public motor vehicle route travels from the visitor center to the four-way junction, past the warehouse to the warehouse gate, and to the county's Sabino Canyon Road (which then connects to the overflow parking lot in the other direction). There are archaeological challenges to be considered with this option.

Costs: An access road built parallel to North Sabino Canyon Road would be roughly ¾ miles and would cost roughly $2.5 million per mile.[102] Such a road would also require annual maintenance similar to other paved infrastructure at the recreation area. It would be less expensive and more archaeologically-sensitive to reuse the existing interior roads, with some realignment at junctions and curves to smooth public motor vehicle flow and remove "decision points" (obvious intersections) for public drivers regarding the side roads, on which they should not drive.

Safety: An interior access road would increase visitor safety by encouraging interaction with USFS staff members who may be able to warn visitors of flood conditions, heat conditions, user conflicts, and the necessity for proper gear and water.

Cultural Landscape, Natural Environment, Historic Resources, Disruption: An internal access road would have substantial archaeological effects on the cultural landscape. If the road were built close and parallel to the existing North Sabino Canyon Road, from a distance recreation visitors may not be able to

---

[102] "Generic Cost Per Mile Models" Florida DOT. ftp://ftp.dot.state.fl.us/LTS/CO/Estimates/CPM/summary.pdf (could not find local data; cost estimate for undivided two-lane rural road with 5' paved shoulders)

differentiate between traffic on the main road and the access road. Development of an interior access road will result in loss of desert habitat. Development of an interior access road would not affect historic resources, nor would it disrupt users or precipitate closures.

Technical Feasibility and Anticipated Response: Developing an interior access road is technically feasible. Anticipated public response is not expected to be strong either for or against an internal access road.

Next Steps: To develop an interior access road, the Forest Service would have to conduct preliminary engineering, environmental assessment, final design, and identify a funding source.

AM 02 – Institute 24-hour access control.

Description: The entrance booth is staffed during daytime hours between 6 am and 6pm (although exact start and end times within this period may vary). Though there is an honor-system fee tube to collect fees after hours (during which times there may be significant numbers of visitors taking advantage of cooler temperatures), not everyone pays or knows to pay.

Furthermore, if the overflow parking lot is built with a second entrance, managing fee collection may be a costly challenge for the Forest Service, and fee evasion may increase. Depending on the future management and funding mechanisms for the tram system, it may be in the Forest Service's best interest to maximize collection of entrance fees.

A 24-hour access control system would allow visitors to pay fees or verify payment in the case of long-term pass holders. It would provide parkers proof of payment they may leave in their cars and would be implemented at either the main entrance, the entrance to the overflow parking lot, or both. A 24-hour access control system may also be integrated with information systems to provide parking utilization to potential visitors via the web, and it could include security cameras to improve visitor safety and law enforcement.

Rocky Mountain National Park has a Vehicle Access Control System (VACS) that allows Rocky Mountain National Park annual pass holders to enter through an unstaffed, gated lane. Rocky Mountain National Park is very pleased with its system. The system has worked very well since 2003 and has cost a small amount to operate and maintain. The biggest benefit for the park has been positive public relations with park visitors, especially locals who use the park frequently.

Figure 42 - Automatic vehicle access control[103]

---

[103] CampusSafetyMagazine.com. SepOct 2006. /http://www.campussafetymagazine.com/Articles/?ArticleID=55

Costs: The cost for planning, acquiring, and installing a 24-hour access control system is roughly $15,000 to $70,000.[104] Depending on complexity, annual operations and maintenance may be as little as $500 per year[105].

Safety: A 24-hour access control system could improve visitor safety and law enforcement with the inclusion of cameras to record license plates.

Cultural Landscape, Natural Environment, Historic Resources, Disruption: A 24-hour access control system would have minimal impact on the cultural landscape, natural environment, or historic resources of Sabino Canyon. User disruption could be minimized by installing the system in the off-peak season.

Technical Feasibility and Anticipated Response: Implementing a 24-hour access control system is technically feasible. Public response will depend largely on the reliability and user-friendliness of the system. The system should be intuitive for visitors to use and for the Forest Service to manage and operate.

Next Steps: The Forest Service should first determine its financial needs with respect to entrance fees and conduct a period of monitoring fee payment compliance. A recent, short monitoring effort reported 93 percent payment compliance, but the results do not include visits for all hours of the day. The Forest Service should also investigate parking management at other high-intensity use public lands and identify best practice management techniques or systems.

AM 03 – Develop south-side access-egress from lot to avoid conflicts with school.

Description: In the mornings (7:00 am to 8:00 am) during the school year (September through May), traffic resulting from parents dropping children off at the elementary and middle schools hinders egress from Sabino Canyon Recreation Area. To avoid this conflict, this element seeks to create a southern access point to the main parking lot which would connect to the east side of the signalized intersection of North Sabino Canyon Road and East Sunrise Drive / East Remount Place.

Costs: Costs for this element include partial or fee simple acquisition of land south of the main parking lot and soft and hard construction costs. Costs would depend on many factors, including the cooperation of the current land owner and the design of the new entrance. Additional costs might include reconfiguration of the traffic signal at the main intersection to accommodate the reconstructed road, in addition to the potential need for a right turn lane to be built northbound on Sabino Canyon Road.

Safety: Flood safety and evacuation would be unaffected by this element. This element would not affect user conflicts within the canyon, though it would reduce conflicts between parents of school children and visitors exiting the recreation area during school-year weekday mornings.

---

[104] "Pay and display parking stations costing approximately $15,000 each are recommended for the City of Bellingham, Washington" RITA. http://www.itscosts.its.dot.gov/its/benecost.nsf/0/228CAF6FAB8F52B98525732400472018?OpenDocument&Query=Home
[105] Email communication with John Hannon, Rocky Mountain National Park (October 5, 2009). "RE: From NPS.gov: Vehicle Access Control System at Beaver Meadows Entrance Station."

Cultural Landscape, Natural Environment, Historic Resources, Disruption: The cultural landscape, natural environment, and historic resources in the canyon would be unaffected. Canyon visitors could continue to use the existing entrance and would be minimally affected during construction.

Technical Feasibility and Anticipated Response: Though technically feasible, there may be significant barriers to this element. First, USFS does not own the land directly south of the main parking lot and would have to acquire all or partial rights. This land may contain artifacts or elements of cultural significance and may not be appropriate for paving.

Second, current USFS policy is to deny private access off of USFS roads if the property also borders a public road. Thus south-side ingress/egress would require negotiation with the current landowners for the road facility as well as negotiations with the landowners and Pima County to relocate their access as well. This could substantially add to the cost of this element or make it completely out of the realm of feasibility, depending on the landowners' response. One potential solution is for USFS to purchase the south-side access-egress road and design, develop/pave the road segment and then convey it to Pima County as a public road. This would ensure legal and adequate access to the roadway for private and public uses. A remote-controlled access gate could be provided for the private use beyond the new road segment.

Third, a traffic study of the intersection would have to be completed to ensure the change would not adversely impact congestion in the area. Traffic control and congestion issues could be more easily dealt with at this location than anywhere else in the study area since the intersection is already signalized. If the land does not contain elements of cultural significance, and if the change would not adversely affect overall congestion in the area, popular response is expected to be positive.

Next Steps: Next steps include researching the land south of the main parking lot (particularly ownership and existence of easements) and working with Pima County to conduct a traffic study of the intersection. If the rights to the land may be acquired and traffic may not be adversely affected, the Forest Service may move forward with initial design, environmental study, and implementation.

AM 04 – Install a traffic signal at the recreation area entrance.

Description: In the mornings (7:00 am to 8:00 am) during the school year, traffic resulting from parents dropping children off at the elementary and middle schools hinders egress from Sabino Canyon Recreation Area. To avoid this conflict, this element seeks to install a traffic light on North Sabino Canyon Road at the entrance of the main parking lot. This would promote egress from the parking lot of the recreation area during highly congested hours.

Costs: Costs of this element would include staff time to attend community meetings and planning events, engineering and design studies as well as construction and installation costs. These costs would most likely be borne by Pima County.

Safety: Flood safety and evacuation would be unaffected by this element. This element would not affect user conflicts within the canyon; however it would reduce conflicts between parents of school children and visitors exiting the recreation area during weekday mornings.

Cultural Landscape, Natural Environment, Historic Resources, Disruption: The cultural landscape, natural environment, and historic resources in the canyon would be unaffected. Canyon visitors would be minimally affected during installation of a new traffic signal.

Technical Feasibility and Anticipated Response: Although it is technically feasible to install a traffic light at the main entrance to Sabino Canyon, a traffic study would have to be conducted to verify the benefits that would outweigh the costs. The county may find the proposed signal is too close to the existing signal and traffic would likely be exacerbated. But if a traffic light eases egress from Sabino Canyon without greatly hindering access to the schools or backing up traffic into the intersection of North Sabino Canyon Road and East Sunrise Drive, public response would be expected to be positive.

Next Steps: Next steps include working with Pima County to conduct a traffic study of the intersection.

AM 05 – Expand public transit service to Sabino Canyon Recreation Area.

Description: SunTran, the local transit provider, has one commuter route that stops within 1.5 miles of Sabino Canyon. This location is served by only three round-trips daily. The nearest all-day SunTran bus stop, part of Route 37, which runs every half-hour, is located at the intersection of North Sabino Canyon Road and East Cloud Road, nearly three miles away from the recreation area. Providing bus service to Sabino Canyon Recreation Area, either by extending an existing line or creating dedicated loop service within the foothills northeast of Tucson, would expand access to low-income and carless individuals and provide an environmentally friendly alternative to private automobiles.

Several examples of partnerships between public lands and municipal transit agencies my provide a template for partnership. White River National Forest partners with Roaring Fork Transportation Authority (RFTA) to provide access to the forest as well as eight local cities, and towns including Aspen and Aspen Highlands.[106] Zion National Park's transit system connects to the gateway town of Springdale, UT.[107] Grand Canyon National Park began providing shuttle access to Tusayan, AZ, in 2008.[108]

Costs: Costs of this element would include Forest Service staff time to attend community meetings and planning events. Implementation costs, including one additional vehicle and driver would be borne by SunTran, although the vehicle might be purchased by the Forest Service through the Paul S. Sarbanes Transit in Parks (TRIP) program.

Safety: Flood safety and evacuation would be unaffected by this element. This element would not affect user conflicts within the canyon.

Cultural Landscape, Natural Environment, Historic Resources, Disruption: The cultural landscape, natural environment, and historic resources in the canyon would be unaffected.

---

[106] Roaring Fork Transportation Authority (2009). RFTA – Roaring Fork Transportation Authority. Last accessed on October 5, 2009 from http://www.rfta.com/.
[107] National park Service (2009). Zion National Park – Green Transit – The Zion Shuttle (U.S. National Park Service). Last accessed from http://www.nps.gov/zion/naturescience/green-transit-the-zion-shuttle.htm.
[108] National Park Service (2009). Grand Canyon National Park – South Rim Shuttle Bus Routes 2009 (U.S. National Park Service). Last accessed October 5, 2009 from http://www.nps.gov/grca/planyourvisit/shuttle-buses.htm.

Technical Feasibility and Anticipated Response: Though it is technically feasible to extend bus service to Sabino Canyon Recreation Area, the Forest Service will likely have to make the case that demand for such a service exists and that the benefits would outweigh the additional operations and maintenance costs. If service is to be expanded, SunTran has stated its preference for a dedicated loop service within the northeast foothills with a stop near Sabino Canyon at North Sabino Canyon Road and East Sunrise Drive rather than extending an existing bus line.

Response of most visitors is likely to be ambivalent as most visitors currently arrive by automobile. Response of transit riders may be positive, although the number of these riders wishing to visit the canyon is unclear without further study.

Next Steps: It is expected that detouring the Route 37 bus to Sabino Canyon would take approximately 21 minutes round trip. If the route were to terminate at Sabino Canyon and not serve Cloud and Pantano, the route would add only 6 minutes round trip. Still, since buses on this route often continue on to another route, significant schedule adjustments would be required. Next steps include characterizing transit demand to Sabino Canyon and working with SunTran on operational concepts for extended service.

AM 06 – Stripe and widen shoulders of roads to improve bicycle access.

Description: Although road shoulders have been widened on roads leading to Sabino Canyon including East Sunrise Drive and North Sabino Canyon Road, some recreational riders may continue to be intimidated by riding with traffic on other key roads. This element seeks to construct additional bicycle improvements within the road network surrounding Sabino Canyon Recreation Area.

Costs: Costs of this element would include staff time to attend community meetings and planning events. Planning, design, and construction costs for this element would be borne by Pima County and/or the city of Tucson.

Safety: This element would not affect flood safety or evacuation capability, nor would it affect potential for conflict between various users of the canyon. It may, however, reduce conflicts between automobiles and cyclists in the area surrounding Sabino Canyon.

Cultural Landscape, Natural Environment, Historic Resources, Disruption: The cultural landscape, natural environment, and historic resources in the canyon would be unaffected by this element. Bicycle improvements would not hinder or reduce access to the recreation area. It is possible that more visitors would chose to bike to Sabino Canyon if a safer route were developed. This could reduce vehicle emissions.

Technical Feasibility and Anticipated Response: Bicycle improvements to the surrounding road network are technically feasible. Response within the bicycle community is expected to be positive. Response outside this community is expected to be ambivalent.

Next Steps: Next steps include participating in bicycle planning and long- and short-term transportation planning efforts in Pima County and the city of Tucson. The Forest Service may wish to emphasize in these forums that it wishes to encourage the use of bicycles to access Sabino Canyon.

AM 07 – Create off-road path connecting to greenway for bikes and pedestrians.

Description: Although road shoulders have been widened on roads leading to Sabino Canyon including East Sunrise Drive and North Sabino Canyon Road, some recreational riders may continue to be intimidated by riding with traffic on other key roads. Recreational riders may seek to visit Sabino Canyon in addition to other city, county, state, and federal parks accessible by greenway bicycle trails. This element seeks to work with Pima County to construct a path to a grade-separated greenway connecting other parks and destinations in Pima County and city of Tucson. Connection to a countywide bicycle network will enable cyclists to more easily reach Sabino Canyon by bicycle.

The Pima Regional Trail System Master Plan includes a grade separated greenway facility connecting Sabino Canyon Recreation Area to a future extension of the River Park Trail along the Tanque Verde River. The River Park Trail is part of a much larger trail network that will connect throughout Pima County.[109] Pima County Department of Natural Resources, Parks & Recreation has stated that although the River Park Trail is not included in the region's 2009–2013 TIP, the River Park Trail is a priority.[110] The greenway connection to Sabino Canyon would be a planned future addition.

Examples from other locations include Ocala National Forest which provides access to the Wekiva-Ocala Greenway, the Grand Canyon Greenway which was developed to provide multimodal access to the park,[111] the Grand Canyon Connector, which connects Zion National Park to Grand Canyon, continuing to Phoenix,[112] and the Great Smoky Mountains Regional Greenway Council was formed to connect the park to surrounding communities.[113]

Costs: Costs of this element would include time to attend community meetings and planning events. Planning, design, and construction costs would be borne by Pima County and the city of Tucson.

Safety: This element would not affect flood safety or evacuation capability, nor would it affect potential for conflict between various users of the canyon.

Cultural Landscape, Natural Environment, Historic Resources, Disruption: The cultural landscape, natural environment, and historic resources in the canyon would be unaffected.

Technical Feasibility and Anticipated Response: Creation of a path to the greenway is technically feasible, although implementation of such a greenway may depend on factors including land ownership and alignment, cost, connections to other origins and destinations, and recreational demand in Tucson.

---

[109] "Pima Regional Trail System Master Plan" Pima County Natural Resources, Parks & Recreation. http://www.pima.gov/nrpr/pdfs/Trails_MP_map_DRAFT_2009_10_28.pdf (1/13/2010)
[110] Telephone conversation with Steve Anderson, Pima County Natural Resources, Parks & Recreation (1/13/2010)
[111] "Grand Canyon Gateway" National Park Service. http://www.nps.gov/grca/parkmgmt/upload/greenway.pdf (10/6/2009)
[112] "Grand Canyon Connector" Adventure Bicycling Association. http://www.adventurecycling.org/routes/grandcanyon.cfm (10/6/2009)
[113] "Interlocal Agreement Creating the Great Smoky Mountains Regional Greenway Council" Knoxville Regional Transportation Planning Organization. http://www.knoxtrans.org/meetings/agendas/exec/aug09/att6.pdf (10/6/2009)

Response within the pedestrian and bicycle community is expected to be high. Response outside this community may be ambivalent.

Next Steps: Next steps include participating in bicycle planning and long- and short-term transportation planning efforts in Pima County and the city of Tucson. The Forest Service may wish to emphasize in these forums that it wishes to encourage the use of bicycles to access Sabino Canyon.

AM 08 – Encourage walking or cycling to the recreation area from nearby neighborhoods.
Description: Congestion created by school drop-offs in the mornings during the school year and full utilization of the parking lot during peak weekends in the winter can make accessing Sabino Canyon by automobile difficult and even stressful. Furthermore, accessing Sabino Canyon by private automobile is comparatively less environmentally friendly than by an alternative mode such as biking or walking. Thus, this element seeks to encourage visitors who live within walking or biking distance to use one of these modes, thereby minimizing frustration, decreasing parking demand, and decreasing automobile emissions.

The Tucson Metro Bike Map[114] and the Pima Regional Trail System Master Plan[115] show the current inventory of bicycle-friendly roads and future plans for multi-use paths, respectively. The Forest Service can continue to work with Pima County and nearby residential communities to expand and advertise access routes to facilitate bicycle and pedestrian connectivity. Outreach and marketing materials made available online and at the recreation area may encourage visitors from surrounding neighborhoods to walk and cycle to the canyon.

Costs: The costs for this element include staff time to attend community and county meetings and development of marketing and outreach materials. Since entry fees are only paid by cars, if visitors who currently arrive via car were to bike or walk, it is possible that total revenues would decrease. Entry fees, regardless of arrival mode should be considered, especially if the number of pedestrians and cyclists were to increase. There is currently little information on how many visitors uses these non-motorized modes to travel to Sabino Canyon.

Safety: This element would not affect flood safety or evacuation capability, nor would it affect potential for conflict between various users of the canyon.

Cultural Landscape, Natural Environment, Historic Resources, Disruption: The cultural landscape, natural environment, and historic resources in the canyon would be unaffected by this element. This element would neither hinder nor reduce visitor access to the recreation area.

Technical Feasibility and Anticipated Response: Improving bicycle and pedestrian connections to Sabino Canyon is technically feasible, though success depends largely on land owners ceding land rights to create paths and individuals' inclination to use those paths. Response is anticipated to be moderate, neither strongly for nor against.

---

[114] "Tucson Metro Bike Map" Pima County Bicycle and Pedestrian Program.
http://www.bikeped.pima.gov/Pubs/MetroBikeMap609INTERIORdave.pdf (1/13/2010)
[115] "Pima Regional Trail System Master Plan" Pima County Natural Resources, Parks & Recreation.
http://www.pima.gov/nrpr/pdfs/Trails_MP_map_DRAFT_2009_10_28.pdf (1/13/2010)

Next Steps: Next steps include taking inventory of existing bicycle and pedestrian connections to the recreation area, identifying additional potential connections, engaging neighborhood associations and Pima County, and creating marketing and outreach materials to be made available online and at the recreation area.

AM 09 – Improve Bear Canyon access point.

Description: Congestion created by school drop-offs in the mornings during the school year and full utilization of the parking lot during peak weekends in the winter can make accessing Sabino Canyon by automobile difficult and even stressful. This element seeks to improve the Bear Canyon access point so that visitors may avoid congestion or lessen parking demand in the main parking lot during peak times. This element could be targeted toward frequent, repeat visitors who are already familiar with the recreation area and the visitor center. Potential improvements include building a ramada, adding restrooms and a source of potable water, adding a large information board, and potentially adding a paved parking area.

Costs: The cost for this element depends on what improvements are made. A ramada built to provide shade will cost $2000.[116] Complete composting toilet units including the building cost approximately $16,000 per toilet.[117] A variable information board may cost $35,000-$55,000;[118] a static information board would be considerably less expensive. A parking lot generally costs $5,000[119] per space.

Safety: This element would not affect flood safety or evacuation capability, nor would it affect potential for conflict between various users of the canyon.

Cultural Landscape, Natural Environment, Historic Resources, Disruption: The cultural landscape and natural environment would be marginally impacted at the Bear Canyon access point; however improvements would be invisible from Bear Canyon Road and largely invisible from most other points within the recreation area. Historic resources in the canyon would be unaffected by this element. This element would neither hinder nor reduce visitor access to the recreation area.

Technical Feasibility and Anticipated Response: This element is straightforward and technically feasible, although the Bear Canyon parking area is owned and managed by Pima County and is not under the control of the Forest Service. Changes could be recommended to the County by the Forest but would be made by the County. Response is anticipated to be moderate, neither strongly for nor against.

Next Steps: Next steps include design, conducting an environmental study, and construction of improvements, as well as marketing and outreach to repeat visitors.

---

[116] "TIMPA History" Tucson International Modelplex Park Association. http://www.timpa.org/History/timpahst.htm
[117] "M54W Trailhead integrated building structure and complete composting toilet system" purchased through GSA. https://www.gsaadvantage.gov/advgsa/advantage/catalog/product_detail.do?contractNumber=GS-07F-0361V&BV_UseBVCookie=Yes&itemNumber=M54W+TRAILHEAD
[118] "TMC central hardware costs can exceed $200,000 if regional communications and system integration are required." RITA. http://www.itscosts.its.dot.gov/its/benecost.nsf/ID/47C7F45CDAF371EA852573E90068CF64?OpenDocument&Query=CApp (2004)
[119] "The Business Case for Commuter Benefits at Colleges and Universities." Best Workplaces for Commuters. http://www.bestworkplaces.org/pdf/college_university%20case_FINAL_508.pdf

AM 10 – Dedicated right-turn lane into Sabino Canyon parking lot.

Description: During peak visitation periods, traffic from cars lined up waiting to enter the main parking lot extends out of the parking lot into the north-bound lane of North Sabino Canyon Road. This congestion is a hindrance to through traffic and could be alleviated by the addition of a dedicated right-turn lane into the recreation area.

Costs: Costs to the Forest Service would include staff time to attend transportation planning meetings with Pima County DOT. Other costs include engineering and design studies as well as construction and installation costs would most likely be borne by Pima County.

Safety: Flood safety and evacuation would be unaffected by this element. This element would not affect user conflicts within the canyon. This element would reduce conflicts between visitors and non-visitors traveling on North Sabino Canyon Road.

Cultural Landscape, Natural Environment, Historic Resources, Disruption: The cultural landscape, natural environment, and historic resources in the canyon would be unaffected by this element. This element would only slightly hinder visitor access to the recreation area during a period of construction which could last between two and four weeks.

Technical Feasibility and Anticipated Response: Though it is technically feasible to install a right-turn lane at the main entrance to Sabino Canyon, a traffic study would have to be conducted to verify that the benefits would outweigh the costs. If a right-turn lane eases congestion on North Sabino Canyon Road during peak visitation periods, response is anticipated to be positive, especially by non-visitors.

Next Steps: Next steps include working with Pima County DOT to conduct a traffic study of the main entrance to the recreation area.

AM 11 – Create new broad walking path from new parking lot directly to Cactus Picnic Area.

Description: Private automobiles and buses are currently used to transport kindergarten children to the education site at Cactus Picnic Area. These vehicles create added potential for pedestrian conflicts on the canyon road. This element seeks to provide reasonable pedestrian access from the new overflow parking lot to the Cactus Picnic area by constructing a ¼ mile path. This path would normally be walked but could be designed to be driven on for maintenance or school programs needs. Such use by vehicles would reduce the same amount of use on the main USFS Sabino Canyon Road. This would be a substantial benefit. It is also less expensive to maintain a trail as a road rather than an often-used hardened trail (paved) due to the efficiencies of road construction techniques and equipment.

Costs: A ¼ mile path from the new overflow parking lot to the Cactus Picnic Area could be expected to cost $200,000 per mile, or $50,000.[120]

---

[120] *Trail and Path Planning: A Guide for Municipalities,* County of Chester, Pennsylvania (http://dsf.chesco.org/planning/lib/planning/trailguide/trailguideappc.pdf), using the average of a $106,700 estimate for a 10-ft wide non-motorized asphalt surface in Iowa and a $300,000 estimate for a 12-ft wide multi-purpose asphalt trail in Asheville, NC

Safety: The proposed pedestrian path would have no effect on flood safety or evacuation. It may reduce potential for user conflicts, particularly those between motorized field-trip vehicles and pedestrians on the canyon road (see SCH 02).

Cultural Landscape, Natural Environment, Historic Resources, Disruption: This element will improve the cultural landscape and natural environment by removing field trip vehicles from Sabino Canyon (see SCH 02). It will have little impact on historic resources and may cause minor noise disruptions during construction.

Technical Feasibility and Anticipated Response: This element is technically feasible. Response is anticipated to be positive because it provides additional access for picnickers and students and removes additional motorized vehicles from the canyon road.

Next Steps: Next steps include initial design, conducting an environmental study, and construction.

AM 12 – Install a southbound right-turn lane from Sabino Canyon Road to Skyline.

Description: In the mornings (7:00 am to 8:00 am) during the school year, traffic resulting from parents dropping children off at the elementary and middle schools hinders egress from Sabino Canyon Recreation Area. To avoid this conflict, this element seeks to install a southbound right-turn lane at the intersection of North Sabino Canyon Road and East Sunrise Drive in order to reduce the southbound backup that extends past the entrance to the parking lot.

Costs: Costs to the Forest Service would include staff time to attend transportation planning meetings with Pima County DOT. Other costs include engineering and design studies as well as construction and installation costs would most likely be borne by Pima County.

Safety: Flood safety and evacuation would be unaffected by this element. This element would not affect user conflicts within the canyon. This element would reduce conflicts between visitors and non-visitors traveling on North Sabino Canyon Road.

Cultural Landscape, Natural Environment, Historic Resources, Disruption: The cultural landscape, natural environment, and historic resources in the canyon would be unaffected by this element. This element would only slightly hinder visitor access to the recreation area during a period of construction which could last between two and four weeks.

Technical Feasibility and Anticipated Response: Though it is technically feasible to install a right-turn lane at this intersection, a traffic study would have to be conducted to verify that the benefits would outweigh the costs. If a right-turn lane eases congestion on North Sabino Canyon Road during morning periods during the school year, response is anticipated to be positive, especially by non-visitors.

Next Steps: Next steps include working with Pima County DOT to conduct a traffic study of the intersection.

BPE 01 – Initiate bicycle guided tours of Sabino Canyon.

Description: A common complaint-about the tram is that its engine noise and exhaust are dissonant with the serenity of the natural environment. One possible way to provide quieter access to points deep in the canyon is to provide organized bicycle tours of Sabino Canyon. Tours could be provided by USFS staff, volunteers, or a concessionaire under a special-use permit could operate the tours as a commercial business.

Costs: Costs would depend on whether the bike tours were provided by Forest Service staff or volunteers with visitors' own bikes, or if bikes and guides were provided by a concessionaire. Labor costs would be the primary costs for a Forest Service-led tour. For a commercial outfitter, costs would include the tour leader, administrative staff and capital costs for developing the administrative system, purchasing bikes, and building/renting operations space. Rugged basic bicycles could be purchased for approximately $400 each. Power assisted bicycles, costing approximately $1,200 would facilitate riding up the hills.[121] A secure facility for storing and administering the project is expected to cost between $10,000 and $150,000, depending on the complexity of the facility.

Safety: No impact on flood risk is anticipated, since tours would not operate during times when a flood evacuation capability is needed by first responders. It might be possible to minimize user conflicts by operating a time separation strategy which would restrict use of the canyon road by pedestrians and the tram when the tours operate. Alternatively, the guide or first rider would need to warn other road users of a large group of cyclists arriving. Tram service would need to be suspended during bicycle tours to prevent conflicts since there large group of cyclists would not have room to move out of the trams' way.

Cultural Landscape, Natural Environment, Historic Resources, Disruption: Bicycle tours are not particularly compatible with interpretive cultural themes focused on either pre-historic Native American use of the canyon or the Civilian Conservation Corps (CCC)-developed bridge structures and road. The tours would have no adverse impact however on the natural environment or the historic resources (e.g., the bridges), but would disrupt other visitors.

Technical Feasibility and Anticipated Response: There is no technical difficulty to implementing the tours. Public response is likely to be neutral at best, but probably negative. Pedestrians and tram users will not like the restricted use during the operating times when the tours are provided. Bicycle users are likely to prefer going at their own pace, though some might enjoy an organized and interpretive tour.

Next Steps: Next steps would involve conducting a market study for such a service, analyzing the benefits/costs of a public versus private provision of the service, and analyzing optimal times to conduct the tours and limit other uses. Any ability to adjust the operational days of the tram is not likely before 2014 when the existing permit expires. Alteration of operation times and days during normal operating hours by the current tram operator is not likely.

---

[121] "E-Bikes" Tucson Electric Bikes. http://www.tucsonelectricbikes.com/store/categories/E%252dBikes/

BPE 02 – Create a grade-separated bike and/or pedestrian trail.

Description: To address user conflicts between the tram and bicyclists and pedestrians, this element would create a shared-use path for bicycles and pedestrians separate from the canyon road. Connections between the exiting canyon road and the bike and pedestrian path would need to be made at trams stops.

In the fore canyon, the existing unpaved trail that parallels the road could be upgraded to encourage more use by bicycles and larger pedestrian groups. Once in the Canyon proper, finding level surfaces to build a new segregated trail may be difficult.

Costs: A grade-separated shared-use path would have high capital expense. The cost of recreational bike and pedestrian trails range considerably depending on the stability of the terrain, the number of stream crossings, and the ability to choose an alignment without excessive grades. Research conducted for local trails estimate approximately $203,350 per mile[122], although estimates varied from as low as $92,000[123] to as high as $835,000.[124] Many of these projects did not have the steep grades of Sabino Canyon so costs here would be significantly higher. Maintenance costs are also apt to be moderate as a result of substantial erosion and damage due to flash flooding on Sabino Canyon Road.

Safety: If properly sited and designed, there should be minimal risk related to flooding. As a paved path, there would be some increase in the amount of impervious surface leading to greater runoff. If properly sited, the shared-use path could also be used for evacuation. For minimizing conflicts between users, the cross section should be a minimum of 10 feet, preferably 12 feet. The benefit would be substantial to both bicyclists and pedestrians since they would no longer have to share the same road space with the tram. Similarly, the tram benefits from exclusive use of the canyon road.

Cultural Landscape, Natural Environment, Historic Resources: A shared-use path would be a new man-made structure, thus the impact to the historic and cultural resources is adverse. Significant environmental impact is expected in the relatively steep canyon.

Technical Feasibility, Anticipated Response, Disruption: The technical feasibility is unknown but likely to be challenging due to the steep, narrow nature of the Canyon. User disruption during construction would be high as a result of shutdowns during construction. Once the trail is complete, user conflicts should be lessened. Anticipated response by pedestrians and particularly bicyclists is likely to be very positive.

Next Steps: Next steps include conducting a survey and geotechnical study to confirm technical feasibility and identify potential alignments, and develop a preliminary design and cost estimate.

---

[122] *Trail and Path Planning: A Guide for Municipalities,* County of Chester, Pennsylvania (http://dsf.chesco.org/planning/lib/planning/trailguide/trailguideappc.pdf), averaging a $106,700 estimate for 10-ft non-motorized asphalt surface in Iowa & $300,000 estimate for 12-ft multi-purpose trail in NC
[123] *CHART 2025 Planning Update: Recommended Pedestrian and Bicycle Projects,* Thomas Jefferson Planning District Commission (http://www.tjpdc.org/pdf/unJam/rep_tran_bikeProjects.pdf)
[124] *CMAQ Process Improvement Team: Final Recommendations and Summary Report,* Idaho Transportation Department (http://www.itd.idaho.gov/planning/cmaq/CMAQ_PIT_Items.PDF)

BPE 03 – Stripe an at-grade bike and/or pedestrian trail using the existing road width, widening where possible.

Description: To address user conflicts between the tram and bicyclists and pedestrians, this element would widen and/or stripe the current road to define space for bicyclists and pedestrians.

These types of paths work well for those visitors that are already familiar with them. For many first-time visitors, the striped pathway may be confusing and could result in poor compliance. Poor compliance lessens the value of such striped routes and could create potential head-on conflicts between first-time visitors to the canyon and cyclists. Additional liability rests on the USFS to properly maintain signage, striping, and other pavement markings, as well as managing the accident data and taking action on that basis.

Costs: Striping alone would have little capital or maintenance cost. Widening the existing road would have high capital expense, but less than a completely segregated bike/pedestrian trail. The capital and maintenance costs of recreational bike and pedestrian trails range considerably depending on the stability of the terrain, the number of stream crossings, and the ability to find an alignment without excessive grades (see BPE 02).

Safety: Effects of striping are unclear. Forest Service representatives have suggested striping may be ineffective. Pedestrians and cyclists tend to ignore striping; those visitors who ignore striping and area listening to personal audio devices may cause greater opportunity for conflicts and collisions. To minimizing conflicts and increase the probability of success, the amount of room granted to pedestrians and cyclists only (and not shared with the tram), should be a minimum of 10 to 12 feet wide (i.e., "a road") (see BPE 02).

Cultural Landscape, Natural Environment, Historic Resources: Striping the existing road would have little effect on the cultural landscape, natural environment, or historic resources. Construction of an at-grade shared-use path would introduce a new man-made structure, thus the impact to the historic and cultural resources would be adverse. Significant environmental impact is expected in the relatively steep canyon.

Technical Feasibility, Anticipated Response, Disruption: On its own, striping is technically feasible, would result in little disruption. Existing users would likely be ambivalent about such a change, with some liking the idea and others ignoring the striping all together. The technical feasibility of widening the road to create a shared-use path is unknown but likely to be challenging. User disruption during construction would be high as a result of shutdowns during construction. Once the trail is complete, user conflicts should be lessened. Anticipated response by pedestrians and particularly bicyclists is likely to be very positive.

Next Steps: Next steps include conducting a survey and geotechnical study to confirm technical feasibility and identify potential alignments, and develop a preliminary design and cost estimate.

BPE 04 – Provide bicycle parking at trail-heads.

Description: This element would allow bicyclists to park their bicycles at trailheads, such as at the trailheads to Bear Canyon or Sabino Canyon Trail, in order to hike as opposed to taking the tram or walking up the roads. Currently, bicycle racks are available only at the visitor center. In order to make full use of the added parking, bicycles would need greater access to the canyon road.

Costs: Bike racks can be well under $500 each. For example, a Rolling Rack Mini, from Dero Bike Rack Co., holds 5-7 bikes and costs $177[125], or approximately $25-$35 per bike. Cost would depend on the number of locations and attachments per location.

Safety: There would be no impacts on flood risk, or the capability to evacuate visitors. User conflicts at the trailheads may lessen since the haphazard storing of bicycles at the trailheads would now be avoided.

Cultural Landscape, Natural Environment, Historic Resources, Disruption: If properly sited, and with good design of the bicycle racks, there should be minimal adverse impact on the cultural landscape or on historic resources. There should be no negative impact on the natural environment. Disruption would be minimal since the construction at the trailheads would be minor.

Technical Feasibility and Anticipated Response: There are no technical difficulties. Public response is anticipated to be mildly positive to this concept. If coordinated with increased biking hours, bicyclists would be more supportive, although pedestrians would likely be unhappy.

Next Steps: It is recommended that bike parking be piloted at a key trailhead to see if they are used and how well received they are. An appropriate rack design would need to be identified.

BPE 05 – Develop equestrian tours.

Description: Equestrian tours of the canyon would provide an alternative means of accessing and enjoying the canyon. It is expected that horses would be used on trails already available to equestrians, and not on the paved roads.

Costs: An equestrian tour operation would likely be owned and operated privately by an existing local stable through a special-use permit. It is expected that horses would be housed off-site, although the forest could provide space to set up a barn on-site if demand warranted. It is expected that costs, which would include the horses and their feeding, care and housing, and administrative costs would be shared between other business activities conducted by the concessionaire. An additional cost would be required to move the horses to and from Sabino Canyon.

Safety: There should be no impact on the risk of flooding. Horseback riding, like any activity, has risks to participants. It is expected that any concessionaire would do their best to minimize these risks.

Cultural Landscape, Natural Environment, Historic Resources, Disruption: Equestrian tours would be compatible with the cultural landscape, although the natural environment would be impacted by the

---

[125] Dero Bike Rack Co, Rolling Rack Mini, http://www.dero.com/products/rolling_rack_mini/rolling_rack_mini.html

horses compacting the trails, accelerated trail erosion from increased horse traffic, eating trailside vegetations, deposition of manure, potential for dispersal of certain invasive plant species through manure, as well as the possibility of endangering the water quality in Sabino Canyon from runoff containing manure. No impact would be anticipated on historic resources. Increased equestrian use may create some disruption for other trail users although the trails that the riders would be on are already open to equestrians.

Technical Feasibility and Anticipated Response: There are no inherent technical difficulties, but finding a suitable site for a stable within the Coronado National Forest could be difficult. Public response is likely to be minimal, except for a small minority who would like the visitor experience of riding the canyon road on horseback. The local resorts who currently use the trails may be displeased by additional competition

Next Steps: Next steps would be to develop a request for proposals for interested concessionaires.

BPE 06 – Create additional or improve infrastructure for equestrian users.

Description: Equestrian use of Sabino Canyon, though allowed on trails, is relatively limited. Improvements such as watering sites, pull-offs for resting or standing, more shared use signs or additional trails could be constructed to encourage equestrian use. Alternatively additional trails designed specifically for equestrian use.

Costs: Costs are dependent on the number and type of infrastructure improvements. New equestrian trails would cost roughly $30,000 per mile (at a cost of $0.58 per square foot),[126] pull-outs cost about the same per-square-foot, and the cost of watering holes is dependent on whether piping needs to be constructed.

Safety: Improved equestrian infrastructure would not increase or decrease risk damage due to flooding. More horses on the trail could cause more pedestrian – equine interactions, but additional pull-offs would facilitate riders passing pedestrians.

Cultural Landscape, Natural Environment, Historic Resources, Disruption: Equestrian users would not harm the cultural landscape or adversely impact historic resources. The waste product (i.e., horse manure) is an adverse impact on the natural environment but could be dealt with using fanny bags and off-site disposal. User disruption would depend on the extent and location of where infrastructure improvements are made.

Technical Feasibility and Anticipated Response: There is no technical difficulty in implementing these or similar equestrian improvements, except that access to water for the horses is limited to areas with existing plumbing. It is expected that other users would not be highly affected by the changes and have little reaction. Equestrians would likely think positively of such changes, though there does not appear to be significant pressure from this community.

---

[126] Average from $10,775 estimate from Iowa DOT (http://www.iowadot.gov/iowabikes/trails/CHPT05.HTML) for 10-foot width snowmobile or equestrian trail and $50,000 from *Asheville Greenways Master Plan*, Asheville, NC (http://www.ashevillenc.gov/uploadedFiles/Residents/Parks_and_Recreation/Greenways/Estimates_of_Cost_and_Return.pdf) for 8-foot width bare earth equestrian trail

Next Steps: It is recommended that the Forest Service work with local commercial equestrian facilities or private equestrian organizations to solicit their feedback regarding increased equestrian use of the Recreation Area. No equestrians have participated in stakeholder meetings to date. Initial steps would include identification of the specific types of infrastructure improvements and their locations and cost estimates.

Communications Elements

COM 01 – Install mile markers and directory kiosks with distances to infrastructure and amenities.

Description: Visitors have logged complaints that availability and location of infrastructure and amenities such as drinking water and toilets is unclear. Lack of distance information may foster unsafe hiking conditions in the hot canyon environment. Mile markers and distance information to amenities would provide increased safety and comfort to visitors. Directory kiosks could provide a shaded relief map of Sabino Canyon with details and locations of the various amenities and park infrastructure.

Costs: Mileage and distance markers would cost around $18 each.[127] With proper materials and graffiti-resistant surfaces, maintenance would be low. Directory kiosks are likely to cost several thousand dollars to install, plus several hundred dollars per directory to produce the artwork.[128]

Safety: Mile and distance markers would increase general safety and comfort of visitors by allowing them to make sound decisions based on knowledge of the canyon environment and their individual strengths and weaknesses. Mile and distance markers would also allow visitors to make more educated decisions about whether to attempt evacuation during a flood event or seek shelter nearby.

Cultural Landscape, Natural Environment, Historic Resources, Disruption: Additional signage including mileage and distance markers would affect the natural view shed and therefore should be implemented in a manner that provides information but does not visually litter the cultural landscape. Adding a directory to a potty assemblage will not materially degrade the viewshed. Additional signage would not adversely affect the natural environment, historic resources, or unduly disrupt or distract visitors.

Technical Feasibility and Anticipated Response: Installing mile and distance markers is technically feasible and is not expected to engender negative public response.

Next Steps: The locations of necessary additional mileage and distance signage should be compared with locations of current signage as documented in the 2008 Sabino Canyon Recreation Area Sign Inventory. Gaps between what is needed and what exists should be documented and programmed for installation by the Forest Service.

COM 02 – Advertise that the tram runs on bio-diesel fuel.

Description: A common complaint of Sabino Canyon visitors is the odor and visible smoke plumes resulting from the diesel engines of the trams, and several comment cards have suggested the tram

---

[127] "Cost of Traffic Signs" Manual of Traffic Signs. http://www.trafficsign.us/signcost.html
[128] "Re: Batch 1 Transportation Elements Comments," email from Walter Keyes, 12/4/2009.

should be powered by an alternative fuel. Unbeknownst to most visitors is that the tram operator currently uses B30, a diesel mix consisting of 30 percent bio-diesel. Visitor perceptions of the tram may be improved if the use of B30 in the trams is actively communicated to them. As a point of reference, Zion National Park owns 30 propane-powered buses and advertises the benefits of propane as well as other tips and suggestions for "green travel" on its website.[129] Grand Canyon National Park notes on its website that many of its shuttle buses use compressed or liquefied natural gas and that this fuel is "cleaner burning."[130]

Costs: Minimal efforts could spread the message among visitors effectively, thus advertising costs could be kept very small. A simple bio-diesel logo on the trams, a sign at the visitor center, and a note on the websites of Sabino Canyon Recreation Area and the tour operator would probably suffice.

Safety: This element has no effect on safety.

Cultural Landscape, Natural Environment, Historic Resources, Disruption: This element has no effect on the landscape, environment, or historic resources and does not threaten to disturb or disrupt visitor use of the canyon.

Technical Feasibility and Anticipated Response: Advertising that the tram runs on bio-diesel is technically feasible and could be done by the tram provider on their website and in the loading area. Because visitor comment cards have requested the use of alternative fuels, public response is likely to be favorable. Friends of Sabino Canyon and SCVN may be less willing to share due to many of their members dislike of the tram.

Next Steps: The Forest Service and tram operator may together disseminate information regarding the use of bio-diesel in the tram. Several advertising distribution channels include the information boards inside and outside at the visitor center, signage along the canyon road, the operator's website, the Sabino Canyon Recreation Area website, and newsletters and websites of both the Friends of Sabino Canyon and SCVN. The visitor center may install an educational component to explain to visitors what bio-diesel is, where it comes from, and how its use affects emissions levels.

COM 03 – Improve the frequency and accuracy of visitor communications via the website.
Description: The way visitors use transportation infrastructure may be influenced by the information to which they have access. The greater the quantity and quality of information, the better the visitor experience will be. Increased usage of the Internet by desktop and laptop computers and mobile devices means visitors expect frequent and accurate communications via the web. Sabino Canyon can improve visitor communications and influence the way they use the transportation system by considering the following suggestions:

- **Improve visitor perception that the information online is accurate and timely.** Updating the website daily or even weekly will improve visitor confidence regarding communications. The last

---

[129] National Park Service (2009). Zion National Park – Green Travel – The Zion Shuttle (U.S. National Park Service). Last accessed October 5, 2009 from http://www.nps.gov/zion/naturescience/green-transit-the-zion-shuttle.htm.
[130] National Park Service (2009). Grand Canyon National Park – South Rim Shuttle Bus Routes 2009 (U.S. National Park Service). Last accessed October 5, 2009 from http://www.nps.gov/grca/planyourvisit/shuttle-buses.htm.

update date should be prominently displayed on the first web page that a user navigates. Sections that have not been updated in a while (e.g., the news section) do not inspire confidence and cause visitors to question the accuracy of all information they receive.

- **Reorganize information so that it is location specific.** Currently, information about Sabino Canyon Recreation Area is found in topical sections of the Coronado National Forest website. Navigating this site and extracting useful information may be tedious for users who are only interested in visiting Sabino Canyon. Improving and highlighting the existing section specific to Sabino Canyon may increase the likelihood visitors will find information regarding weather, monsoons, safety, parking, transit, and congestion.

- **Integrate website communications with daily operations.** There are opportunities to provide visitors accurate and current logistical information before they even arrive at the recreation area. For example, information regarding weather, rainfall, and stream flow taken directly from meteorological and hydrological sensors can provide visitors a snapshot of current conditions in the canyon. A webcam of the parking lot or count of cars currently in the parking lot can give visitors an idea of parking availability, and hopefully induce them to schedule their visit earlier or later in the day when parking demand is not as high. Another webcam could show conditions on North Sabino Canyon Road and allow visitors to plan their trips for periods of low demand.

- **Advertise the website as a single source of information.** By keeping the Sabino Canyon website as up-to-date and accurate as possible and suggesting the website as a primary source of recreation area information, the Forest Service can reduce the number of individual marketing efforts or information campaigns. Tour books in particular should reference the website as printed material quickly becomes outdated.

Costs: Updating the Sabino Canyon website could cost $10,000[131,132] and could be expected to cost between $6,000-$35,000[133] annually for regular updating and annual maintenance. Savings could be expected as the demand for printed materials and marketing campaigns lessen. Automatic integration with daily operations could cost additionally and would depend on other project expenditures.

Safety: Providing more accurate and trustworthy information could increase visitor awareness of flood safety, mountain lion activity, and user and transportation conflicts. Visitors could be warned of extreme weather conditions before they leave home, allowing them to postpone their visit to a future time.

Cultural Landscape, Natural Environment, Historic Resources, Disruption: Improving frequency and accuracy of visitor communications would not affect the physical environment nor disrupt the visitor experience.

Technical Feasibility and Anticipated Response: Improving frequency and accuracy of visitor communications is technically feasible. Anticipated response by the public is anticipated to be very positive. People generally approve of having more and better information on which to base decisions, and have come to depend on web-based information.

---

[131] "The Cost of Building a Website" AllBusiness. http://www.allbusiness.com/technology/internet-web-development/479-1.html
[132] "The cost of building a website" Webriver. http://www.toddturner.com/cost-of-a-website.asp
[133] "How Much Should a Website Cost?" WebpageFX. http://www.webpagefx.com/How-much-should-web-site-cost.html

Next Steps: The Coronado National Forest could begin by assessing the online presence of other National Forest units and public lands organizations. It could identify best practices and conduct a gap analysis between its communication efforts and those of similar organizations. It could investigate the use of technologies such as Twitter and text messages (SMS), RSS feeds, and email lists to disseminate information (see COM 04). The Forest Service may also reach out to tour book companies and recommend they list the web address of Sabino Canyon so that non-local and foreign visitors may always have the most up-to-date information regarding access to the recreation area. A staffing requirements plan to effect these changes will be required.

COM 04 – Expand information delivery methods to include new distribution channels.

Description: While print, telephone, and radio communications continue to be important delivery channels for information, more and more people are turning toward the Internet and mobile communications for up-to-the-minute access to accurate information.

The Forest Service could take advantage of information technology and novel distribution channels to communicate with visitors, improve safety, and manage visitor demand. Possibilities include posting Sabino Canyon updates in a really-simple-syndicate (RSS) feed so that individuals may subscribe to information, integrating recreation area information systems (for example, a parking management system) with online communications, and creating a mobile website for people to quickly obtain parking, weather, and other information on their mobile devices.

Costs: The costs of creating and maintaining such distribution channels vary based on complexity. RSS feeds have become state of the practice in website design and would be a function of the Sabino Canyon website. The feed would have to be updated regularly (at least 15-20 minutes of staff time once every few days) to remain useful and relevant. As described in COM 03, this could be expected to cost between $6,000-$35,000[134] annually in regular updating and annual maintenance.

Safety: Disseminating more accurate and timely information to visitors will improve visitor awareness and safety with respect to flooding, wildlife awareness, and weather and climate.

Cultural Landscape, Natural Environment, Historic Resources, Disruption: Disseminating more accurate and timely information to visitors will not alter the cultural landscape, natural environment, or historic resources, nor will doing so disrupt users.

Technical Feasibility and Anticipated Response: Disseminating more accurate and timely information to visitors is technically feasible though may require some additional training of Forest Service staff members. It is anticipated that the public will respond positively to dissemination of more accurate and timely information. Forest Service policies will need to be investigated to determine whether some of the newer social media tools have been authorized for use by Forest Service staff.

Next Steps: Sabino Canyon should ensure all information on its website is up-to-date and establish processes for updating it in a timely and accurate manner. It should establish a staffing requirements plan to effect these changes. It should research Forest Service capability with respect to RSS feeds and

---

[134] "How Much Should a Website Cost?" WebpageFX. http://www.webpagefx.com/How-much-should-web-site-cost.html

mobile websites, and consider the information technology and communications components of additional systems installed in the recreation area.

COM 05 – Use variable message signs for disseminating parking and safety messages.

Description: Despite the presence of information on the radio, on television, or online, some visitors may not utilize the Internet or other 'networked' methods of communication. To communicate with visitors who have already left home, variable message signs (VMS) may be placed at strategic locations on the road to communicate parking availability, weather and climate conditions, and alternative routes or activities (if Sabino Canyon is closed or inaccessible). Banks have been using variable message signs for years to display the time and temperature, while highways have been using them for 10 to 15 years to communicate with drivers. Sabino Canyon may want consider placing using some existing VMS signs owned by Arizona Department of Transportation (ADOT) or Pima County or may want to purchase new signs to place on local roads for visitors as they approach the canyon.

Costs: Variable message signs on highways cost $35,000-$55,000 per sign for arterial roads, with overhead support systems ranging from $25,000-$115,000. Annual operations and maintenance costs for a freeway VMS range from $5,000-$16,500.[135] They must be updated in a timely fashion so that users may be confident that the information is accurate and up-to-date.

Safety: Installing variable message signs on the road network will facilitate dissemination of accurate and timely information to visitors and will improve visitor awareness and safety with respect to flooding, wildlife awareness, and weather and climate.

Cultural Landscape, Natural Environment, Historic Resources, Disruption: Installing variable message signs on the road network outside the boundaries of the USFS Recreational Area will not alter the cultural landscape, natural environment, or historic resources, nor will doing so disrupt visitors to the canyon.

Technical Feasibility and Anticipated Response: Installing variable message signs on the road network is technically feasible though maintaining up-to-date messages may require additional training of Forest Service staff members. Proper site locations and adequate space is a necessary requirement and will need to be worked out with Pima County. The signs also need to comply with ADOT standards. It is anticipated that the public will respond positively to the dissemination of more accurate and timely information via VMS.

Next Steps: The Forest Service must work with city of Tucson and Pima County to identify appropriate points at which to install VMS. Where signs are already installed on highways in Tucson, the Forest Service will need to negotiate with the existing signs' operators to display its message. Furthermore, great care must be made when writing the message to be displayed. The Forest Service must define specific message protocols for various conditions at Sabino Canyon. The Forest Service may wish to coordinate with nearby public lands and cultural recreational attractions such as Saguaro National Park and the Arizona-Sonora Desert Museum.

---

[135] "TMC central hardware costs can exceed $200,000 if regional communications and system integration are required." RITA. http://www.itscosts.its.dot.gov/its/benecost.nsf/ID/47C7F45CDAF371EA852573E90068CF64?OpenDocument&Query=CApp (2004)

COM 06 – Collect parking lot utilization and disseminate in real-time via the web and/or variable message signs on approach roads.

Description: Parking demand is exceeding lot capacity on peak weekends during the winter months between December and April. Although there are plans to build an overflow lot, this may be a relatively short term solution. In 5-10 years the overflow lot may fill up at peak times as well. An alternative to increasing parking supply is to manage parking demand by tracking the number of cars in the parking lot and making this information available to visitors before they leave home or to visitors en route. This allows visitors to make more informed decisions about when to visit. Visitors who understand when the lot is full may schedule their trip for times when the canyon is less crowded, thus shifting demand from peak to non-peak hours.

This element can be implemented in phases. Loop counters that report parking lot occupancy to the canyon entrance station would be very useful at present. Being able to integrate this information with VMS or electronic means of communication to visitors arriving at Sabino Canyon would be a second useful stage.

Sandy Hook, a beach at Gateway National Recreation Area, located 16 miles south of Manhattan, uses such a parking management system.[136] Before implementing the system, on peak summer weekend days, nearly 17,000 motor vehicles competed for 4,100 parking spots. When Sandy Hook parking areas filled, traffic backed up for miles on state and local highways. Sandy Hook now uses VMS and highway radio advisories to let visitors know when its nine parking areas are full or nearly full. Accessing real-time parking information via a central computer database, park rangers direct visitors to bus and ferry options or to alternative parking areas.

Costs: The cost to collect parking lot utilization and disseminate this data in real-time will depend on the approach used. Advanced parking information systems such as those found in parking garages at airports and malls will likely count cars and keep track of the results on web server that may be queried by web-services. Such systems general cost $250-$800 per spot[137], and $17,000-$38,000 for a complete system.[138] A far less expensive but potentially less reliable method would be to have Forest Service staff at the entrance booth keep track of cars and manually update a webpage or webserver.

Safety: Managing visitor demand with parking lot information would not affect safety related to floods or evacuation, but could potentially reduce conflicts within the recreation area by spreading visitation demand from peak to non-peak hours.

Cultural Landscape, Natural Environment, Historic Resources, Disruption: Managing visitor demand with parking lot information would not affect the cultural landscape, the natural environment, or the historic resources, nor would it disrupt users.

---

[136] National Park Service (2003). "Fact Sheet: Intelligent Transportation Systems (ITS) in National Park Units. Last accessed 9/29/2009 from http://www.nps.gov/transportation/tmp/documents/Factsheets/finalitsfactsheet.pdf.
[137] "Advanced Parking Management Systems: A Cross-Cutting Strategy" FHWA. http://www.its.dot.gov/jpodocs/repts_te/14318_files/14318.pdf
[138] "Equipment Costs for Parking Management" RITA. http://www.itscosts.its.dot.gov/its/benecost.nsf/SubsystemCostsAdjusted?ReadForm&Subsystem=Parking+Management+(PM)

Technical Feasibility and Anticipated Response: Managing visitor demand with parking lot information is technically feasible. Public response is anticipated to be positive. Off-property signs would need to be negotiated with Pima County DOT, the city of Tucson, and private landowners.

Next Steps: The Forest Service would need to add traffic detectors at the current parking area's exit and at the entrance and exit to the new parking area. Monitoring software could then be developed and hard-wired into the entry station. Future efforts would include connecting this information to visitor information services.

Infrastructure Elements

INF 01 – Create alternate trail network that avoids stream crossings and facilitates evacuation.

Description: Since the main road loops back and forth across Sabino Creek, it would be necessary to construct two trails—one on each side of the canyon above the flood grade, with connections to the canyon road at frequent intervals to allow easy access. These trails could serve all areas and would need to be made accessible for people with mobility impairments in order to assist those with mobility issues. Total length of the trails would be approximately eight miles.

Costs: Trails may cost around $200,000 per mile.[139] With two trails paralleling the existing four-mile canyon, costs would be roughly $1.6 million. Construction of this trail, however, would be particularly costly due to the steep grades of the canyon walls. Ongoing maintenance costs would be significant due to run-off, erosion, and debris flows during the rainy seasons.

Safety: If feasible, having two ADA accessible trails along each of the canyon walls would conceptually improve safety and evacuation. In order to develop an appropriate trail, some carving into the canyon wall may be necessary. This may undermine the slope and increase mass movement of the slope above (i.e. landslides).

Cultural Landscape, Natural Environment, Historic Resources, Disruption: Because the alternate path would constitute an addition to the built environment in a location likely observable from many points in the canyon, this element would adversely impact the cultural landscape. It may also further disturb the natural environment by redirecting natural paths of water and debris down the canyon walls. An alternate trail network would have little effect on the historic resources and cause minor disruption during construction. Although construction efforts would be visible, they would not affect visitor access within the canyon.

Technical Feasibility and Anticipated Response: It is unclear that this element is technically feasible. The canyon walls may be too steep to facilitate construction of a useable path. Furthermore, visitors would require education about the existence, purpose, and function of the trail, and signage would have to be created to facilitate wayfinding in the event of an emergency. Public response is likely to be ambivalent.

Next Steps: A consultation with geo-technical engineers to provide an initial assessment as to technical engineering feasibility and approach should be the next step.

INF 02 – Relocate the visitor center farther up the canyon and shuttle between it and the parking lots.

Description: This element proposes to move the visitor center from its current location to a site on the slight rise between the Cactus Ramada and Rattlesnake Creek drainage. This is where the upper canyon

---

[139] *Trail and Path Planning: A Guide for Municipalities,* County of Chester, Pennsylvania (http://dsf.chesco.org/planning/lib/planning/trailguide/trailguideappc.pdf), using the average of a $106,700 estimate for a 10-ft wide non-motorized asphalt surface in Iowa and a $300,000 estimate for a 12-ft wide multi-purpose asphalt trail in Asheville, NC

begins, approximately ½ mile up Sabino Canyon Road from the current location. This location would provide visitor amenities closer to the key features of the canyon, namely Sabino Creek and the impressive canyon walls.

The overflow parking area would likely become the primary desired parking area for visitors and expansion of this area may be desired. Alternatively, parking could remain at the current location with a free shuttle transferring people from the parking area to the visitor center. Paid tours could then be run from the visitor center up the remainder of the canyon. A limited number of parking spots for disabled visitors, volunteers, and employees could be built at the visitor center itself.

The existing visitor center and administrative buildings could be used solely for administration and volunteer office space.

Costs: Costs for a new building would be significant and depend on the scope of the building. Mount Rainier National Park built a new 18,000 square foot visitor center in 2008 for $21.2 million,[140] while a $103 million, 139,000 square foot building and museum was built at Gettysburg National Military Park the same year.[141] The visitor center at Mount Saint Helens National Volcanic Monument was opened in 1993, costing $12 million for 17,000 square feet.[142]

Safety: A new visitor center is not expected to impact visitor safety directly.

Cultural Landscape, Natural Environment, Historic resources, Disruption: Moving the visitor center would have a significant impact on the cultural landscape and natural environment. Views of Sabino Canyon from the adjacent public roadways would include a new man-made structure, while the current visitor center blends in to the adjacent development. Current undeveloped land would be disturbed. It is expected that the location of the visitor center would be selected so as to minimize its impact on historic resources. Though water and sewer lines already exist near the Cactus Picnic Area, installation of a visitor center near this location would require extension of electric power, telecommunications and potentially other utilities to the site.

It is expected that construction of the site would not directly impact visitors use of Sabino Canyon. The physical construction and associated noise would not fit the character of the natural environment and therefore be seen as a disturbance. The construction noise may negatively impact the local animal population.

Moving the visitor center would significantly impact how people use the canyon. Visitors desiring a short relatively flat walk may have to compete with more frequent shuttles if they are provided free to the visitor center. Alternatively, more people may use the upper canyon since they would be able to get closer without having to pay a fee.

---

[140] http://seattletimes.nwsource.com/html/localnews/2008246817_rainiervc10m.html
[141] http://www.nps.gov/partnerships/gettysburg.htm
[142] http://www.fs.fed.us/gpnf/msh25/facts/documents/final-crvc-fact-sheet-jan-2005_000.doc

Technical Feasibility and Anticipated Response: Building a new visitor center is technically feasible. During meetings, the response from Forest Service staff was relatively positive although the response from other stakeholders was decidedly negative.

Next Steps: The next steps would be to discuss the concept with stakeholders and develop a more comprehensive concept of operations for the facility. If the response is positive, preliminary architectural drawings would be needed to estimate the total cost. Finding funding, either from the Forest Service capital funding sources, or private donations would likely need to follow.

INF 03 – Widen road to reduce user conflicts.

Description: This element would widen Sabino Canyon Road to facilitate better shared use of the road by both motorized and non-motorized users.

Costs: Costs are highly dependent on soil condition, materials used and desired durability, and terrain. The isolation of the work site also tends to increase costs of construction. For low-volume roads, Louisiana has developed a stone-interlayer pavement to reduce premature failure from reflective cracking due to differential shrinkage of the cement-stabilized base[143]. The design consists of a stone interlayer base of 4 inches of limestone placed over 6 inches of cement-stabilized soil, and topped with a 4 inch surface treatment of asphalt concrete. Costs are on the order of $118,000 per lane-mile.

Safety: Widening the road increases the acreage of impervious surface and can potentially increase the risk of flooding and due to the geology of loose sediment, would require significant reinforcement of additional cuts made into the canyon wall, which themselves may cause future mass movement of the slope above. To the extent that a widened road decreases the inconvenience and discomfort arising from user conflicts, it could induce more pedestrians and bicyclists to use the road. This would increase the risk due to evacuation since more users are apt to be present and stranded from flooding events.

A widened road would decrease user conflicts and facilitate a better level-of-service from shared use of the road.

Cultural Landscape, Natural Environment, Historic resources, Disruption: This element would change the road prism from its original design. It therefore would have a negative impact on the cultural landscape. A widened road increases storm water runoff. This would have a slightly negative impact on the receiving soils and water, mitigated by the fact that there are only a few motorized vehicles (i.e., tram trips, and USFS vehicles) using the road. Provided that the additional width does not impinge on archeological sites or sites thought to be significant, and the bridges are not widened, this element would have no impact on historic resources. Disruption would be larger since it would require road closure. However, construction phasing by segmenting the project into smaller limits of construction could greatly reduce user impacts and facilitate some use of the road and trails.

Technical Feasibility and Anticipated Response: Barring unknown subsurface conditions (which would be revealed by soil borings and underground soil mapping) that would prohibit or make prohibitively

---

[143] See Masood Rasoulian, *Research Pays Off: Stone Interlayer Pavement System – Extending the Service Life of Low-Volume Roads*, at http://onlinepubs.trb.org/onlinepubs/trnews/rpo/rpo.trn233.pdf

expensive a widening of the road's cross section, this element is technically feasible. Public response is likely to be mixed. Those who desire preservation of the road as originally designed and built would oppose this action. Pedestrians would have fewer conflicts with vehicles on the road but would still encounter conflicts at the bridges as widening these are not part of this element.

Next Steps: A detailed preliminary engineering assessment should be undertaken (which is likely to also include some soil borings).

INF 04 – Widen the bridges and bridge approaches.

Description: This element proposes to widen the cross-section of the existing bridges to permit shared use and passage by trams and non-motorized users. The approaches to the bridges would also have to be widened. The design would replicate the current design but have a wider span in order to maintain the historic feel while meeting the current need for a wider crossing. It is possible that such projects could be done when major reconstruction of the bridge is needed due to damage from a flooding event or other major maintenance overhaul activities.

Costs: Costs would be highly dependent on how the bridges are widened. It could require labor-intensive dismantling and reassembling of the "dragon tooth" stone sidings, and cantilevering of the added lane width. A reinforced concrete flat slab simple span using Florida cost estimation parameters runs as high as $160 per square yard.[144]

Safety: This action is unlikely to change the baseline risk of flooding except to the extent that widening the bridge also addresses sedimentation issues for the stream flow through the bridge. The frequency of evacuation due to flood events should also hold constant.

A widened bridge would marginally reduce user conflicts at these choke points.

Cultural Landscape, Natural Environment, Historic resources, Disruption: This action would have severe adverse impacts on the historic integrity of the existing bridges. It would add a new man-made engineered structure to the cultural landscape era that is being interpreted (CCC built bridges c. 1935). Disruption would be complete and of long duration since the bridges would have to be shut during construction. However, some of this would be mitigated by construction phasing of the bridges so that users would have access to the road, bridges, and trailheads below the bridge subject to construction.

Technical Feasibility and Anticipated Response: Pending a bridge structural and engineering assessment, it is probably unlikely that this element is technically feasible at an acceptable cost. Public response will be quite negative.

Next Steps: The next step would be to conduct a preliminary structural and engineering assessment and conduct a cultural analysis to determine the feasibility of changing the historic structures.

---

[144] See http://www.dot.state.fl.us/planning/policy/costs/Bridges.pdf

INF 05 – Redesign bridges to improve flow and reduce sedimentation issues; keep historic look but change engineering.

Description: This element proposes to change the profile of the existing bridges to increase the volume of water flowing underneath.

Costs: Cost estimates are highly dependent on the particular bridge, but due to the nature of the intervention, will be significant. This element would probably require complete jacking of the existing bridge structure and re-grading the vertical profile of the approach road at both ends. Additionally, it may require dredging, and additional drainage structures including rip rap and river barbs (i.e., drainage structure that re-directs the flow to a desired channel).

Safety: This element would substantially reduce the risk of flooding because the normal stream flow and drainage could be maintained. The low water vented crossings would operate as designed, not acting as a 'dam' leading to overflows across the road surface with a rise in water level. With lowered risk of routine flooding, the frequency of requiring evacuation should also fall. The only impact on user conflicts is that the re-engineering of the bridges would require significant road closures.

Cultural Landscape, Natural Environment, Historic Resources, Disruption: This action is likely to have an adverse impact on the cultural environment despite the intent to retain the "historic look." Historic resources are also likely to be adversely impacted. Disruption will be significant. Assuming technical feasibility, the impact on the natural environment is likely to improve because the normal stream flow is maintained.

Technical Feasibility and Anticipated Response: It is unclear whether this element is technically feasible. The required vertical profile of the road approaches may be too great. It may not be possible to jack the existing bridges. It may require dismantling the bridges stone-by-stone, then reconstructing them. Public response is likely to be extremely negative.

Next Steps: A consultation with bridge and geo-technical engineers to provide an initial assessment as to technical engineering feasibility and approach.

INF 06 – Regularly maintain culverts to maintain desired (conceptualized at the creation of the bridges) water flow.

Description: This element proposes to regularly clean the culverts integral to the low water crossing vent bridge design to maintain proper water flow function and reduce flooding. This solution may represent difficulties for wildlife, particularly the endangered gila chub, but may have collateral benefits of reducing flood damage to bridge approaches.

Costs: Costs are dependent on whether specialized core-boring machinery is needed.[145] Costs associated with maintaining and cleaning typical roadside ditches and culverts can run $300 per mile.[146] However, specialized circumstances (e.g., submerged culverts under a narrow bridge with difficult access via

---

[145] See http://www.cimcor.net/index_files/Page400.html
[146] USFS Mt. Baker - Snoqualmie N.F. Road Maintenance Plan, at
http://www.fs.fed.us/r6/mbs/projects/documents/MBS_RTE_RMPSUM_07202009.pdf

vehicles and specialized cleaning equipment) could require a substantial investment in both equipment and labor. Costs would also be dependent on the rate of siltation and therefore the required frequency of cleaning.

Safety: This element would substantially reduce the risk of flooding because the normal stream flow and drainage would be maintained. The low water vented crossings would operate as designed, instead of acting as 'dams' leading to overflows across the road surface with a rise in water level. With lowered risk of routine flooding, the frequency of requiring evacuation should also fall. The only impact on user conflicts is that the cleaning operation may require closing the road completely.

Cultural Landscape, Natural Environment, Historic Resources, Disruption: The cultural landscape is unlikely to be impaired by this maintenance activity. There should be improvement to the natural ecology of the area due to restoration of the hydrological stream flows, and the ability to sustain higher dissolved oxygen levels. Assuming the bridges are not damaged in the process of gaining access to the underlying culverts, there should be no serious impact to these historic resources. User disruption would depend on whether the road or segments of the road (depending on staging) require closure.

Technical Feasibility and Anticipated Response: An intensive culvert cleaning operation is technically feasible, but as mentioned, could require the procurement of specialized equipment. The public, properly educated as to the reason and benefits of an intensive culvert cleaning maintenance operation, should be supportive. Some may object if frequent road closures are necessary.

Next Steps: USFS may consult with ecologists and hydrologists to develop a culvert cleaning plan that includes specification of equipment, operational staging, cleanout protocols, debris disposal, frequency, and detailed cost estimate. Specialized knowledge in this area may be needed to develop this plan.

INF 07 – Develop new bridges for pedestrians (or tram) off of the existing roadway network.
Description: The current configuration of Sabino Canyon's roads and trails leaves visitors and the infrastructure vulnerable to flooding. In addition, the narrowness of the bridges limits concurrent passage of trams and pedestrians. This element would retain the existing narrow historic bridges for tram use while constructing a separate bridge at each stream crossing for pedestrians. Three new pedestrian bridges may be located in the following locations:

- Downstream of vented low water crossing 1;
- Downstream of crossing 3; and
- Upstream of crossing 4.

Costs: Costs are dependent on both the design and the span length. Span length also determines the number of columns and footings needed. However, a pedestrian bridge is lighter and requires a lower load bearing capacity than an equivalent span that would serve motorized traffic. Unit costs (per pedestrian bridge) can equal $750,000[147], but in the context of the Sabino Canyon road would probably be far less.

---

[147] See http://www.ci.mpls.mn.us/master-plans/above-falls/report/appendix_preliminary_cost_estimates.pdf

Safety: Risks of flood occurrences would be unchanged, but evacuation could be facilitated by the separate bridges which would also allow unimpeded access by first responder equipment. User conflicts between the tram and pedestrians would be resolved at the narrowest sections of the road on the bridges.

Cultural Landscape, Natural Environment, Historic Resources, Disruption: New bridges would introduce a new element to the cultural landscape. The effect on historic resources (e.g., the existing bridges) could be adverse because of adverse visual impact. Design of the new pedestrian bridge could help, however, to mitigate the visual impact – particularly on the approaches to the two bridges. Construction is likely to disturb the streambed edges. It is unlikely to degrade water quality because usage is limited to pedestrians only (i.e., no contaminant runoff). Disruption due to construction is likely to be moderate to high since the current road and bridges are needed for construction staging. Closures are likely during construction.

Technical Feasibility and Anticipated Response: There are no known technical difficulties. Public response is likely to be mixed, since this element radically changes the road prism and is likely to be seen by some as a major impairment to the cultural landscape.

Next Steps: Some visualization studies should be undertaken first along with a public process for review and input. More detailed cost estimates should be developed.

INF 08 – Eliminate planned overflow parking.
Description: An overflow parking lot would not be built.

Costs: This element would save the costs of planning, design and construction of the overflow parking facility, and an access pedestrian path back to the visitor center and staging area for the tram operation.

Safety: Reducing the impervious surface of the planned overflow lot would lower risk of flooding in general. However the increased congestion within the existing parking lot, and more access/egress from the existing lot to the street network, will increase the risk of vehicle-to-vehicle and vehicle-pedestrian collision. Evacuation risks would be unaffected by this action. User conflicts are limited to the existing parking lot, primarily the conflict between parking maneuvers and pedestrian movement.

Cultural Landscape, Natural Environment, Historic Resources, Disruption: Not building a new man-made structure would have a positive effect in general on the cultural landscape, natural environment, and historic resources. Some negative impacts related to increased air emissions and fuel consumption would result if this action leads to congestion and idling within the existing parking lot. Because construction is avoided, there would be no disruption to visitor activities or use of the current parking lot.

Technical Feasibility and Anticipated Response: There are no technical difficulties. Public response is apt to be negative since it reduces the amount and availability of parking. There could be a number of visitors during peak season that will be turned away due to a lack of available parking.

Next Steps: This is essentially a management decision, although it may be prudent to seek public input in a public outreach process.

Management Elements

MGMT 01 – Create and disseminate a disaster evacuation, rescue, and communication plan.
Description: Sabino Canyon and the surrounding Santa Catalina Mountains are susceptible to flash flooding, especially during the monsoon season (mid-June through September). The floods that occurred in 2006 demonstrated the susceptibility of transportation infrastructure to flooding and debris flows by destroying sections of road and bridge approaches. During flood events, the road and bridges are virtually impassable by pedestrian and vehicle traffic. A disaster plan created to facilitate evacuation, rescue, and sheltering of visitors would significantly improve safety in Sabino Canyon. The plan should include methods of detecting impending flood events and evacuation trails and aggregation points for sheltering-in-place. The plan should consider how to communicate to visitors regarding general and acute risks of flooding, what to do in case of flooding, and necessary considerations for evacuation, rescue, and sheltering-in-place.

Costs: A disaster evacuation, rescue, and communication plan can likely be in place within a 6-month to 1-year time period for $50,000 to $200,000, depending on the level of detail.

Safety: A disaster evacuation, rescue, and communication plan would assist visitors in evacuating or sheltering-in-place prior to a flash flood event. Such a plan would assist Forest Service personnel and state and county rescue workers in evacuating and retrieving visitors.

Cultural Landscape, Natural Environment, Historic Resources, Disruption: A disaster plan itself would have little consequence to the built environment, though physical improvements resulting from the plan such as signage, alert systems, and sheltering components may affect the natural view shed. Similarly, the plan itself would not impact the natural environment. Historic resources would not be affected by a disaster plan. By its nature, a disaster disrupts recreation in Sabino Canyon. The disaster plan would seek to minimize this disruption and facilitate evacuation, rescue, or sheltering in an orderly manner.

Technical Feasibility and Anticipated Response: A disaster evacuation, rescue, and communication plan is technically feasible, although feasibility of additional safety infrastructure would have to be considered by the planning process itself. Creation of an evacuation plan was favorably received by Forest Service staff and key Sabino Canyon stakeholders and can reasonably be expected to be of high importance to the general public. Its creation is necessary and should not be dependent on public enthusiasm.

Next Steps: A planning effort may naturally evolve from the "Monsoon Safety Awareness" campaign the Forest Service and members of the safety and rescue community have cultivated for the past two years.

Potential partner organizations[148] include:

---

[148] http://www.monsoonsafety.org/index.htm

- American Red Cross Southern Arizona Chapter;
- City of Tucson, Departments of Transportation and Stormwater Management;
- National Weather Service;
- Northwest Fire/Rescue District;
- Paluda Insurance Agency;
- Pima County Office of Emergency Management and Homeland Security;
- Pima County Health Department;
- Rural/Metro Fire Department;
- Southern Arizona Rescue Association;
- Tohono O'odham Nation;
- Tucson Electric Power;
- Tucson Fire Department; and
- Vaisala, Inc.

While that effort has focused on general flood safety, a disaster evacuation, rescue, and communication plan may be more specific to the geography, hydrology, and natural and built infrastructure in Sabino Canyon itself.

MGMT 02 – Develop aggregation points to shelter-in-place or facilitate evacuation for visitors within Sabino Canyon up to the end of Sabino Canyon Road.

Description: It is generally easier to rescue a concentrated group than dispersed individuals. To facilitate group rescues and evacuations, Sabino Canyon Recreation Area should have safe, signed areas where visitors can collect and wait out a flooding event together. These areas should be located to facilitate access by rescue crews, either by helicopter in the case of emergency, or by foot/vehicle after flooding has subsided. A covered facility should be considered and equipped with emergency supplies or emergency communications equipment. Challenges related to this element include how many supplies would be available and what visual impact would they have, and how would emergency supplies be protected against theft and vandalism.

Appropriate locations for aggregation points include: (1) Intersection of Telephone Line Trail and Bear Canyon Trail, (2) Opposite Rattlesnake Creek (on South Side), (3) Tram Stop 1 at Rattlesnake Creek, (4) Tram Stop 7, and (5) others identified by a disaster evacuation, rescue, and communication plan (see MGMT 01).

Costs: Costs would include those required for physical infrastructure and for communications efforts. Physical infrastructure includes basic signage ($18 each[149]) and improvements to areas to be designated aggregation points. Communications efforts include all efforts to inform visitors about the existence and function of the aggregation points. Exact requirements and costs would be identified during the creation of a disaster evacuation, rescue, and communication plan (see MGMT 01).

Safety: This element should improve visitor safety during flood events by providing and communicating safe locations for visitors to wait out storms and to provide specified locations to facilitate evacuation if needed.

---

[149] "Cost of Traffic Signs" Manual of Traffic Signs. http://www.trafficsign.us/signcost.html

Cultural Landscape, Natural Environment, Historic Resources, Disruption: There would be little impact to the cultural landscape, natural environment, or historic resources of this element if only signs are used to note the locations of the aggregation points. A compromise would need to be found between highly-visible signs and those that blend in with the natural landscape but may not be as visible to visitors. Allowing for helicopter landings would likely have some impact on the surrounding environment.

Technical Feasibility, Anticipated Response: A group shelter-in-place scheme would be technically feasible, and require little disruption to the canyon. Positive response to signed aggregation points is anticipated. Covered shelters and storage of emergency equipment may be seen as taking away from the natural environment and may be subject to vandalism. The Southern Arizona Rescue Association (SARA) may be willing to sponsor or monitor the materials stored at the shelter facilities.

Next Steps: The next steps include working with SARA to determine the most appropriate locations for aggregation points. It would make sense for this to be part of a larger safety/emergency plan for Sabino Canyon (see MGMT 01).

MGMT 03 – Develop flood detection and early warning system.

Description: Despite the existence of modern weather forecasting equipment in and above Sabino Canyon, there is no system to combine and interpret precipitation and stream flow readings, predict or detect potential flood events, and communicate flood conditions to canyon visitors. This element suggests improving the current data collection system, creating a detection/prediction system, and using a communication technique such as an air-raid siren to warn visitors of impending flash floods.

This element would provide additional data for early warning of potential flood events. The National Weather Service (NWS) and Pima County Regional Flood Control District monitor weather, precipitation and stream flow with gages in Pima and the surrounding counties using the NWS's Automated Local Evaluation in Real Time (ALERT) system. Four gauges provide precipitation data every 12 hours or at every millimeter of precipitation. They are located at: Sabino Creek @ Dam (2160), Sabino Creek 0.6 miles south of Marshall Gulch (2290), Mount Lemmon (1090), and White Tail (2150).

The U.S. Geological Survey collects stream-flow data at Sabino Canyon Dam. The gauge (09484000) provides real-time information about water discharge, gauge height, precipitation, and battery voltage. USFS can work with the NWS Tucson Weather Forecast Office, the Pima County Regional Flood Control District, and the USGS to add stream gauges and/or precipitation gauges within the canyon watershed in order to better model and monitor water flow. This data could be made available to USFS staff and integrated with development of a flood detection and early warning system.

Costs: Specific costs for research, design, and implementation of such a flood detection and warning system must be determined by weather prediction professionals. Air-raid sirens range roughly between $20,000-$80,000 per siren, with the total number of sirens depending on the range of the signal and the size of the park[150][151][152][153]. A stream flow gauge with cellular or radio communications device may cost between $5,000 and $7,000, while a precipitation gauge with cellular or radio communications device may cost between $3,500 and $5,000.[154]

Safety: Improved stream flow monitoring will not have a direct impact on preventing damage from flooding, but it will likely improve safety with respect to flooding by providing timely information so that visitors may evacuate or seek shelter prior to the arrival of the flood water. No user conflicts are expected from increasing water flow monitoring.

Cultural Landscape, Natural Environment, Historic Resources, Disruption: The cultural landscape will be negatively impacted by the addition of the monitoring devices. It is expected that most of the monitoring devices would be located toward the headwaters of the Creek, beyond the area that most visitors see. Some back-country visitors' wilderness experience will be impacted, and vandalism of the equipment may be of some concern. Furthermore, air-raid sirens may be placed at one or more visible locations within Sabino Canyon in order for warning alerts to effectively reach visitors. Visible placement may interrupt the continuity of the view shed of the natural environment. The signal of an air-raid siren may disturb wildlife in the canyon, although it is anticipated the siren would only be used on occasion under the direst flooding circumstances. The air-raid siren would have no impact on historical resources. Under normal circumstances, limited visitor disruption is expected. In extreme events the air-raid siren is actually intended to disrupt visitors in the canyon and provide a signal to evacuate or shelter-in-place.

Technical Feasibility and Anticipated Response: Implementing a flood detection and warning system is technically feasible but must be paired with proper evacuation and rescue planning, education of and communication with canyon visitors, and operations, management, and maintenance of the system (see MGMT 01 and MGMT 02). For example, prior to implementing flood detection and warning system, safety and evacuation officials must create a rescue and evacuation plan that specifies what actions visitors should take depending on their locations in the canyon. Officials need to communicate this plan and information about the flood warning system to visitors so that they know how to interpret the sirens. Officials must identify an organization to operate, manage, and maintain the system. Interest for a flood detection and early warning system was high both among Coronado National Forest Service staff and key stakeholders of Sabino Canyon and can reasonably be expected to be well received by the general public.

Next Steps: Next steps are to coordinate with NWS, Pima County Regional Flood Control District, and USGS to add additional sensors to the regional monitoring system and develop tools to provide immediate access to impending high water events to USFS Sabino Canyon staff. Such a system should be integrated with efforts to create a disaster evacuation, rescue, and communication plan (see MGMT 01 and MGMT 02).

---

[150] Ako, Diane. "State Civil Defense Warns of Lack of Disaster Warning Signs." *KHNL*. http://www.hawaiinews8.com/Global/story.asp?S=6338079
[151] *City Commission Agenda Memo: March 4, 2008.* Manhattan, KS http://www.ci.manhattan.ks.us/DocumentView.aspx?DID=4132
[152] Bernando, Rosemarie. "Officials roll out tsunami plans." *Honolulu Star Bulletin.* http://archives.starbulletin.com/2008/03/28/news/story03.html
[153] "Tornado Sirens" Town of Castle Rock, CO. http://www.crgov.com/Page.asp?NavID=1303
[154] Email communication with Eric Keith, Sales Manager, Vaisala Inc, "RE: waterflow and precipitation sensors", 9/21,2009.

MGMT 04 – Update and enforce time-separation strategies for different user types.

Description: This strategy would change the way that visitors have access to the facility. Currently, the tram runs between 9:00 am and 4:30 pm. Cyclists are prohibited from using Sabino Canyon between 9:00 am and 5:00 pm and are prohibited completely on Wednesdays and Saturdays. This element would investigate the current restrictions and update limitations on all visitors including pedestrians, bicyclists, tram riders, and hikers based on daily and weekly visitation patterns and tram ridership. This strategy is aimed at reducing visitor conflicts and providing explicit time for specific activities within the canyon. The Forest Service may seek to organize a meeting or series of meetings for different user groups to come together and talk about their concerns and desires for use of the canyon and then come to a mutually agreeable schedule for use.

Kennesaw Mountain National Battlefield Park has successfully developed time segregated use of the key mountain road. Private vehicles, which have access to Kennesaw Mountain Road on weekdays, are prohibited from driving there on weekends. A shuttle runs during key weekend hours when bicycles are also prohibited. Bicycles have use of the road on weekends before and after the shuttle hours and are permitted to mix with private vehicles on weekdays. Pedestrians are permitted to walk the road at all times, recognizing the other user groups will also be sharing the road.

Costs: This strategy would involve no capital cost. New signage may be needed to alert visitors to the new rules. Some operating costs and or volunteer time may be needed to enforce the time separation.

Safety: Conceptually, this strategy would improve user conflict safety issues since it would limit times when multiple user groups are in the canyon. It is possible that identifying a bicycle-only time would imply that cyclists were allowed to ride at higher speeds, creating more opportunities for bike-on-bike collisions and/or more serious single-rider accidents. In addition, if pedestrians do make their way into the canyon, they may be at higher risk than they currently are. Additional measures such as striping the road and posting use regulations may mitigate some of these safety concerns. This strategy will have no impact on the risk of flooding or flood evacuation safety.

Cultural Landscape, Natural Environment, Historic Resources, Disruption: This strategy will have minimal effects on cultural landscape, natural environment, or historic resources because little to no infrastructure changes would be required and no new visitor impacts to the environment would be expected. This element is designed to limit access to the canyon for some users during specific periods so that other users may obtain fuller use during those same periods.

Technical Feasibility and Anticipated Response: This strategy is technically feasible and relatively easy to implement. A potential challenge of enforcing a no-pedestrian period may arise as it would be a change to their normally free access to the canyon. A monitor at the head of the canyon could be used to prohibit many visitors on foot although those coming in from the back-country could be more difficult to manage. It is expected that prohibiting pedestrians from the canyon would be highly objectionable to the majority of visitors who currently walk there. When the Forest Service considered banning bicycle access in the early 1990s, there was an outcry in the bicycling community (which later negotiated the time separation of uses that is in effect today).

Similarly, allowing cyclists to back into the canyon during the period in which they are currently prohibited, may face opposition from pedestrians.

Limiting the hours of tram service would negatively impact visitors who would like to access the canyon using that mode, but would likely be positively received by pedestrians and other users who were given access to the canyon road during those time periods.

Next Steps: Next steps include monitoring the level of use of the canyon by the various user groups during different times of day. (i.e. comparing pedestrian visitation on days when no bikes are allowed compared to days when bikes are allowed during the same time period; tracking pedestrian use of the canyon the last half hour of bike access in the morning compared to the first bike free half hour (or vice versa in the afternoon)).

Hourly and daily tram ridership would also need to be tracked to determine if specific reductions in hours would allow the service to continue to be financially viable, while providing additional hours and/or seasons that were tram-free.

Explicitly monitoring arrival and ridership data would provide insight into whether having multiple user types in the canyon actually impacts whether pedestrians choose to use the canyon. It would also provide information to determine what changes in hours would have the least negative and/or potential greatest benefit to the various user groups.

The Forest Service would also need to talk with representatives of the various user groups to get input on the new times and obtain public acceptance of the plan.

MGMT 05 – Require the tram vehicles to conform to specified noise and air quality requirements.

Description: Common complaints of the tram are that it emits offensive exhaust and that it is noisy due to its engine noise and interpretation provided by the drivers. One way to limit noise in the canyon is to specify in the special use permit allowable exhaust and noise levels (see MGMT 06). By setting functional requirements rather than mandating specific technologies, the concessionaire may reduce emissions and noise levels using the most economic means at its disposal.

Costs: The cost to the Forest Service would be minimal, presuming that the concessionaire was responsible for having the testing done. Additional effort by the contracting staff would be required to update the contract if need be, and to actively monitor or review the test results. Repercussions for non-compliance would need to be identified and enforced with in order to enforce the requirements.

Safety: The major safety impact of this element would be improving air quality, particularly at the visitor center where tram vehicles can idle. Quieter vehicles could also benefit drivers who are constantly within earshot. The impact on user conflicts will be minimal. Unless silent electric vehicles are used for the transit service, it is likely that the vehicle will make adequate noise to alert pedestrians of its presence.

Cultural Landscape, Natural Environment, Historic Resources, Disruption: Reduced noise and air emissions will significantly improve visitors' experience of the cultural landscape and natural environment. The purpose of this element is to reduce the impact of the tram service on the environment and visitors.

Technical Feasibility and Anticipated Response: Air and noise tests are technically feasible. Since the concessionaire's current vehicles are not designed to drive on public roads, the tests would have to be done on-site. Visitors are likely to support such changes, while the concessionaire is likely to oppose such requirements. There is some concern that the current concessionaire would refuse to have such tests done, so enforcement and the consequences of failure to perform the tests or to meet the stated noise and air quality measures would be key.

Next Steps: USFS contracting staff needs to include air and noise testing requirements and processes for evaluation and consequences for non-attainment in the language of the next contract (see MGMT 06) and enforce the requirements.

MGMT 06 – Include/enforce shuttle service requirements in special-use permit.

Description: The special-use permit is a powerful tool the Forest Service can use to set and enforce a wide range of requirements with the tram concessionaire. The current special-use permit specifies hours of operation, allowable fees, safety requirements, and other operations and maintenance requirements. The terms of the special-use permit may be expanded to help the Forest Service achieve other goals related to the shuttle service. For example, one way to limit noise in the canyon is to specify in the special-use permit allowable exhaust and noise levels (see MGMT 05). By setting functional requirements rather than mandating specific technologies, the concessionaire may reduce emissions and noise levels using the most economic means at its disposal.

Another example addition to the special-use permit may be the requirement of the tram concessionaire to provide additional services, such as providing scheduled trips specifically for school groups. Details regarding cost recover for the concessionaire could also be specified in the agreement.

The key to using the special-use permit as a management tool is enforcing its conditions. The Forest Service must create a special-use permit which allows a concessionaire to make a reasonable profit while meeting operational and recreational goals.

Costs: Financial costs to the Forest Service include staff time required to write, review, and approve the special-use permit.

Safety: Although updating the special-use permit itself will have no affect on safety, it may be used as a tool to specify and enforce safety strategies such as space-time separation strategies (see MGMT 04) and health safety strategies such as lowering emissions (see MGMT 05).

Cultural Landscape, Natural Environment, Historic Resources, Disruption: Although updating and enforcing the special-use permit will have no affect on cultural landscape, natural environment, or historic resources, the permit strategies may improve these features (see MGMT 05). This would not limit visitor access to the canyon.

Technical Feasibility and Anticipated Response: Updating the special use permit is technically feasible, although care must be taken to make sure i) the new language is financially feasible for both the Forest Service and the tram concessionaire and ii) the new language is enforceable by the Forest Service.

Next Steps: Next steps include identifying priorities and requirements regarding the tram service and incorporating them into an RFP for the concession agreement. This will develop requirements that are reasonable and options that are available in the face of non-compliance. After choosing a concessionaire, the Forest Service must negotiate a special-use permit that enables it to meet its operational and recreational goals.

MGMT 07 – Transfer ownership of the tram vehicles to USFS and continue operation by a contractor.

Description: This element would have the USFS purchase either new vehicles, or the existing vehicles from the current shuttle operator. Operations and maintenance of the shuttle vehicles would be put out to bid. This option could be attractive because USFS would have more control of the type of vehicle used on the service (another option is to specify functional requirements of the tram in the special use permit, see MGMT 05 and MGMT 06). It would also increase the number of operators interested in running the service since they would not have to invest in specialty vehicles. Without a guaranteed long-term contract, many potential operators would be unwilling to invest in specialty vehicles that may be hard to re-use elsewhere if their contract is not renewed.

Altering the ownership/operating model may also reduce the cost of the service to visitors since the operator will not have to recoup the capital costs of the vehicles. The operator would only have to for operations and maintenance. It is recommended that maintenance records be requested to ensure that the vehicles are being adequately maintained.

Costs: The USFS could either buy new vehicles (see MOT 07, MOT 08, and MOT 09) or the existing vehicles. The existing vehicles are old beyond their expected service life (see MOT 07 and MOT 08), thus this is not a recommended solution.

Safety: This element would have little impact on the safety of visitors. It is possible that a newer vehicle would include more modern safety features.

Cultural Landscape, Natural Environment, Historic Resources, Disruption: This element would have the same impacts on the environment as any new vehicle might have, including potential sound mitigation and air quality improvements from the current vehicle. This element would not affect historic resources. This element would not cause user disruptions or limit visitor access to the canyon.

Technical Feasibility and Anticipated Response: New tram vehicles are available that meet the specifications required for Sabino Canyon Road. Funding may be available from the FTA Paul S. Sarbanes Transit in Parks Program (TRIP) which is a competitive application grant program to provide funding for capital expenditures associated with planning or operating alternative transportation services in Public Lands. Most visitors would not be aware of the contracting specifics of who owns/runs the shuttles as long as the service is satisfactory. It expected that visitors would appreciate a new vehicle. It is unknown as to the reaction of the current concessionaire, but as mentioned, the ownership of the vehicles by the USFS may make the concession more attractive to other potential operators.

Next Steps: Undertake additional research on the specific models of tram vehicles available that could operate on Sabino Canyon Road. It would be desirable to test the vehicle on the road to ensure that it could maneuver the narrow road, tight turns, and changes in elevation.

MGMT 08 – Provide the tram as a fare-free service for visitors.

Description: By providing fare-free transportation in Sabino Canyon to visitors, this element fundamentally alters the service concept of the tram from an interpretive tour to a point-to-point transportation service. The tram may be fare-free throughout the canyon, or it may be fare-free for only a portion (e.g., free between the parking lots and the visitor center but paid to enter the canyon).

It is expected that any fare-free service would increase the number of visitors using the shuttle. USFS has observed that the lower canyon does not hold as much visual and environmental interest as the upper canyon. A free shuttle would allow visitors to access the more "interesting" scenery in the upper canyon.

Costs: It is currently unknown how much the tram system costs to operate and maintain. These costs would have to be subsidized by public or private sources or by all visitors as an expanded amenity fee charged upon entrance to the recreation area. The fee charged to all visitors would be significantly lower than the fee currently charged on a ride-by-ride basis.

Safety: The safety of a free transit service is unclear because the demand for such a service would likely be significantly higher than the fee-based service offered currently. If demand for a free service can be met by the current number of vehicles and trip frequency, user conflicts may remain the same or even decrease as more pedestrians ride the tram to points inside the canyon. If demand for a free service exceeds the capacity of what is offered currently, additional tram vehicles may have to be added creating additional opportunities for conflicts with pedestrians or other trams.

Cultural Landscape, Natural Environment, Historic Resources, Disruption: Similar to the issue of safety, if the number of concurrent trips remains the same, the cultural landscape, natural environment, and historic resources will remain the same. If the number of concurrent vehicles increases, the cultural landscape could be degraded, the natural environment may be marginally affected by increased emissions and noise, and the historic resources would remain unchanged. This element would not limit visitor access to Sabino Canyon for any period of time.

Technical Feasibility and Anticipated Response: Implementing a free tram service would be technically feasible. It is likely that additional and/or replacement vehicles would need to be purchased. Anticipated response to such a service is mixed. During stakeholder meetings with USFS and stakeholder groups, three USFS members supported such a concept and one opposed it, while no stakeholders supported it and three opposed it.

Next Steps: Next steps include obtaining operations and maintenance costs from the current tram operator, obtaining more detailed feedback from stakeholders and visitors, and researching operating costs and management options to provide a free service.

MGMT 09 – Charge an expanded amenity recreation fee to pay for fare-free shuttle service.
Description: This element seeks to fundamentally alter the service concept of the tram from an interpretive tour to a point-to-point transportation service available to all visitors, similar to the concept described in MGMT 08. Under the authority of the Federal Lands Recreation Enhancement Act, the USFS currently charges a standard amenity recreation fee of $5 per car for a day pass, $10 per week and $20 for an annual pass. Ninety-five percent of this money is retained within the recreation area to pay for amenities, while 5 percent is provided to the regional unit of USFS. USFS is also authorized to charge an expanded amenity recreation fee for additional uses, including that of a transportation system. Thus, USFS could charge an additional fee to pay for the operations costs of a free tram system.

Currently, riders pay the tram concessionaire a fee of $8 for adults and $4 for children to ride the tram. The tram system operations and maintenance costs are not known. Free service is expected to increase users of the service. USFS has observed that the lower canyon does not hold as much visual and environmental interest as the upper canyon. A free shuttle would encourage visitors interested in a limited walk to access the more "interesting" scenery in the upper canyon. While it may seem that charging all visitors a higher fee would be unjust, the tram would be an amenity of Sabino Canyon Recreation Area similar to existing bathrooms and drinking fountains. While not all visitors use these facilities, they are available to all and seen as an enhancement to the visitor experience.

Costs: Since fees are already collected, it is not expected that charging an expanded amenity fee would cost USFS any additional overhead.

Safety: The effects this element would have on safety are unclear because the demand for a free shuttle would likely be significantly higher than the current tour-based service. If demand for a transportation service can be met by the current number of vehicles and trip frequency, user conflicts may remain the same or even decrease as more pedestrians ride the tram to points inside the canyon. If demand for a free service exceeds the current capacity, additional tram vehicles may have to be added.

Cultural Landscape, Natural Environment, Historic Resources, Disruption: Similar to the issue of safety, if the number of concurrent trips remains the same, the cultural landscape, natural environment, and historic resources will remain the same. If the number of concurrent vehicles increases, the cultural landscape could be degraded, the natural environment may be marginally affected by increased emissions and noise, and the historic resources would remain unchanged. This element would not limit visitor access to Sabino Canyon for any period of time.

Technical Feasibility and Anticipated Response: Implementing a transportation service funded by expanded amenity fees would be technically feasible. It is likely that additional and/or replacement vehicles would need to be purchased. Visitors who currently use the tram may see a decrease in the cost of their visit, while visitors who do not use the tram (now or in the future) may feel they are paying for someone else's benefit.

Next Steps: Next steps include obtaining operations and maintenance costs from the current tram operator and obtaining willingness-to-pay and demand information from stakeholders and visitors.

MGMT 10 – Institute a frequent rider pass.

Description: A common suggestion received by pedestrians and shuttle riders is that the shuttle could be a useful service for pedestrians to reach more remote areas of the canyon, but it is too expensive to be used on a regular basis as such. This element, similar to establishing a free shuttle service for all passengers (see MGMT 08), seeks to make the shuttle a viable mode of transportation rather than just an interpretation service.

Costs: Costs for instituting a frequent rider pass would be minimal and administrative in nature, although concessionaire revenue would be affected. Depending on the structure of the pass, revenues could either increase or decrease.

Safety: Instituting a frequent rider pass would have no effect on flood safety or evacuation capability, nor would it prevent potential user conflicts.

Cultural Landscape, Natural Environment, Historic Resources, Disruption: Instituting a frequent rider pass would not affect the cultural landscape, the natural environment, or historic resources. This element would not disrupt or limit access by canyon visitors in any way.

Technical Feasibility and Anticipated Response: Instituting a frequent rider pass is technically feasible. Public response is anticipated to be positive.

Next Steps: Next steps include conducting a market analysis for frequent rider service. In particular, the USFS and concessionaire need to understand rider demand, rider patterns, and a price-point (if one exists) that is affordable for frequent riders and generates acceptable revenue for the concessionaire.

MGMT 11 – Develop a parking reservation system.

Description: The existing main parking lot is too small to meet parking demand during peak hours on weekends during early spring particularly late March and April. This element seeks to establish a parking reservation system so that visitors may plan their trip in advance, based partially on when parking is expected to be available. Such a system would assume an average length of time cars remain parked in the parking lot and thus estimate the number of spots remaining at a given time. For example, people would sign up to arrive during a specific period of time. If the average car stays parked for two hours, the system could estimate how many spots would be available at any given time, and allow additional people to reserve parking spots for those times. The advantage of such a parking reservation system is that it would reduce situations in which the main parking lot is filled to capacity. The disadvantage of such a system is that it may deter visitors from coming. This element is similar to developing a reservation system for the tram (see MOT 06).

Costs: The cost of developing, maintaining, and administering a reservation system would vary based on the technology and complexity of such a system. The National Intelligent Transportation Systems (ITS) Architecture[155] documentation provides tools for estimating costs for various alternatives. The Internet has lowered the costs of developing and maintaining reservation systems.

Safety: A parking reservation system would not affect flood safety or evacuation within the canyon. It would not affect the potential for modal conflicts on Sabino Canyon Road.

Cultural Landscape, Natural Environment, Historic Resources, Disruption: Implementing a tram reservation system would not affect the cultural landscape, the natural environment, or the historic resources. Implementation of a parking reservation system may disrupt visitor access to the canyon, especially during the first few weeks as visitors become aware of the system and are educated.

Technical Feasibility and Anticipated Response: Instituting a parking reservation system is technically feasible, though it may be challenging to operate the lot close to, but not exceeding, full capacity during peak periods. Anticipated response for such a system is uncertain. Some people may value the ability to plan ahead, while others may be dismayed by elimination of spontaneity.

Next Steps: Next steps include further investigating visitor interest in a parking reservation system and understanding whether one would be useful with or without a new overflow parking lot. If such a system is deemed appropriate, the Forest Service would have to identify goals, requirements, and potential reservation system options, and rate those options according to requirements.

MGMT 12 – Charge entry fee for all users, per person.

Description: Current parking fees are based on vehicle entry, with the same fee paid for a motorcycle and a school bus. Currently fees are only charged to visitors parking at the Visitor Center. Visitors who walk, bike, or come by horseback are not currently charged for entry. A moderate per person fee would spread the cost to more users and may be able to raise more money. Conceptually such a change in fee structure would be done to support a free transportation service.

Costs: Expanding the current fee collection system would necessitate infrastructure improvements and additional staff time for collection and enforcement. Without a specific collection plan it is difficult to estimate these costs, although they would need to be sufficiently low to justify per-person fee collection.

Safety: There are no safety implications of changing the entry fee structure.

Cultural Landscape, Natural Environment, Historic Resources, Disruption: This element may impact the view shed if additional infrastructure such as booths and fences were used to facilitate fee collection and enforcement. Fences may impact the natural environment by segmenting animal habitats. Historic resources would likely remain unaffected. This element may disrupt visitor access to Sabino Canyon as visitors are educated and become acclimated to the new system.

---

[155] http://www.its.dot.gov/arch/index.htm

Technical Feasibility and Anticipated Response: It is feasible to collect a per-person fee for visitors entering via the main parking access areas when those lots are monitored. Collecting fees from all visitors is likely impossible. Each visitor could be required to carry a visitor "permit" with them at all times; this would require a significantly more time-intensive enforcement effort. 100% compliance is unlikely. Visitors who currently do not pay a fee are likely to be unhappy about the change in policy and will react negatively. Visitors who drive in alone may appreciate a reduced fee, while those who drive in as part of groups may begrudge the increase resulting from a per-person fee.

Next Steps: A study of the average number of visitors per vehicle and the amount of funding needed for the purpose for which the fee policy was being changed would need to be conducted in order to set the per person fee structure at an appropriate level. Additional effort would need to be spent exploring how to implement and enforce the policy fairly.

MGMT 13 – Maintain existing tram operation and service concept.

Description: This element seeks to 'do-nothing' with respect to the operation and service concepts of the tram. It would maintain the tram as a concessionaire-run service and maintain the current division of ownership and responsibility. It does not necessarily seek to maintain the existing concessionaire or tram vehicles and it allows for alterations in the level of service and fare structure if agreed to by the Forest Service.

Costs: Costs of this element are expected to remain the same as the existing system.

Safety: Flood safety and evacuation would be unaffected by this element. This element would not affect user conflicts within the canyon, though different concessionaires or vehicles operating under the existing operations and service concept may address user conflicts.

Cultural Landscape, Natural Environment, Historic Resources, Disruption: The cultural landscape, natural environment, and historic resources in the canyon would be unaffected. This element would not cause user disruption.

Technical Feasibility and Anticipated Response: This element is technically feasible. Response for this element was largely negative at a stakeholder meeting, likely in some part because people strongly associate the current concessionaire and vehicle fleet with the operations and service concept. Others may be opposed the current operating concept, perhaps because they desire significantly more or less service.

Next Steps: No additional steps are required for this element, although the Forest Service may wish to investigate the potential to engage other concessionaires or employ other vehicles under the existing concept of operations.

Motorized Elements

MOT 01 – Use trams for evacuation.

Description: During minor flood events, the trams are currently used to carry non-paying passengers back down across the flooded bridges. This element would continue that policy.

Costs: Using the trams for evacuation does not incur costs if the tram is on a regularly scheduled tour. It is unlikely the tram would be used on an ad-hoc basis specifically as an evacuation vehicle.

Safety: Using the trams for evacuation specifically increases the safety of visitors by facilitating their retreat from the canyon during mild flood events. It is important, however, to have defined protocols and to train tram drivers on what constitutes a "mild flood event", and when to proceed and when to not attempt a bridge crossing.

Cultural Landscape, Natural Environment, Historic Resources, Disruption: Using the trams for evacuation does not impact the cultural landscape, the natural environment, or the historic resources, nor does it disrupt the visitor experience.

Technical Feasibility and Anticipated Response: Using trams for evacuation is technically feasible with the current tram stock and sufficiently mild flood conditions. Anticipated response is expected to be positive.

Next Steps: The ability of a tram to navigate several inches of fast moving water should be a factor when considering new vehicles. This ability should also be considered if a holistic evacuation and rescue plan is developed.

MOT 02 – Remove the tram.

Description: There are two arguments for removing the tram altogether. First, the tram is considered an annoyance by some visitors. The fumes, engine noise, and noise from the driver interpretation negatively affect the visitor experience for those not riding the tram. The tram occupies much of the road, forcing pedestrians to either stop or walk single file so that the tram may pass. Similarly the trams forces pedestrians to wait while they cross the bridges. To avoid potential modal conflicts, cyclists are not allowed to ride during the day while the tram is operating. Second, the noise and exhaust may be detrimental to local flora and fauna, although damage to the environment has not yet been quantified.

Costs: Removing the tram would have no direct costs, though it could deter some visitors from coming to Sabino Canyon and thus reduce entrance fee revenue. Approximately 25-30% of visitors who arrive by private vehicle and pay the entrance fee ride the tram.

Safety: Removing the tram would reduce evacuation safety because the tram could no longer be used to carry people across flooded bridges during mild flood events.

Cultural Landscape, Natural Environment, Historic Resources, Disruption: Removal of the tram would affect the cultural landscape of Sabino Canyon in two distinct ways. For those who wish to return Sabino Canyon to a more natural state, the cleaner, quieter, less visited landscape would be an improvement. For those who rely on the tram for mobility and access, removal of the tram would mean an end to interaction with the canyon landscape and a thus an absolute barrier to any cultural landscape at all. Removal would improve the state of natural environment, though because effects of noise and pollution have not been quantified, it is unclear how much. Removal of the tram would have no impact on the Canyon's historic resources, but would reduce access to them. Removal of the tram would permanently disrupt access for visitors with mobility challenges, but it would end tram disruptions to walkers and bikers.

Technical Feasibility and Anticipated Response: Removing the tram is technically feasible. Response is anticipated to be sharply divided and contested.

Next Steps: A plan to remove the trams must include input from a wide variety of Sabino stakeholders and consider alternate means of providing access to individuals with mobility impairments.

MOT 03 – Develop aerial tram service.

Description: A significant challenge at Sabino Canyon is how to provide access to all visitors while minimizing conflicts among various modes. One potential method is to reduce the number of competing modes and volume of competing users from the roadway by creating an aerial tram or gondola system similar to those found at ski resorts or that operate at Sandia Peak in the Cibola National Forest near Albuquerque, New Mexico.[156] In addition to reducing conflicts on the road, an aerial tram service might be less impacted by landslides and flooding events since it has fewer ground connection points.

Figure 43 - Aerial tram at Sandia Peak, Cibola National Forest

Costs: A 2007[157] study of aerial trams estimated the costs at between $18 and $65 million per mile. An aerial tram built in 2008 at Jackson Hole Mountain Resort cost $13.5 million per mile.[158] Operations and normal and preventative maintenances costs may be expected to be around $250,000 a year[159]. While there is some reduced risk of damage due to landslides, aerial tram infrastructure may suffer from similar damage. Repairs to the aerial tram infrastructure would depend on the damage, but could be quite significant. In addition to the aerial infrastructure, the aerial tram would require a support road for construction and maintenance activities. Depending on the tram's alignment, the support road could either be the existing canyon road or a new special-purpose road.

Safety: The aerial tram would allow visitors to avoid mild flood events altogether. Similar to the existing shuttle system, the aerial tram would likely be halted during extreme flood events and may be at-risk to damage from flooding and debris flows itself. An aerial tram replacing the current tram vehicles would

---

[156] Picture taken by Brian Couch, Jr., http://www.flickr.com/photos/briancouchjr/2427322360/ , licensed under the Creative Commons.
[157] Reconnecting America. "Hercules Aerial Tram/Mobility Study and Report"
http://www.reconnectingamerica.org/public/display_asset/aerialtram
[158] Calculated from "Tram Specifics" Jackson Hole Tramformation. http://www.tram-formation.com//index.php?option=com_content&task=view&id=42&Itemid=63, "The New Jackson Hole Tram: Is It Worth It?" NJ.com. http://blog.nj.com/skiing/2008/12/the_new_jackson_hole_tram_is_i.html
[159] Lichtenstein, Grace. "Are Trams Going the Way of Wooden Skis?" The New York Times. http://travel.nytimes.com/2005/11/13/travel/13prac.html?_r=1&pagewanted=2

reduce the potential for user conflicts by removing motorized vehicles from the road. It also may attract pedestrians from the canyon road, thus reducing the number of concurrent users.

Cultural Landscape, Natural Environment, Historic Resources, Disruption: Installation of an aerial tram would significantly alter the canyon view shed. Furthermore, it would likely introduce additional noise that would be heard at all times along the aerial tram way rather than at specific times and points as is the situation with the current shuttle solution. Noise from the aerial tramway may affect the natural environment; however specific effects are unclear without further study. Introduction of an aerial tram would have no direct impact on historic resources. Construction of an aerial tram could be expected to disrupt all users for a period of 12-21 months.[160] Operation of an aerial tram could be expected to permanently disrupt the visitor experience due to alterations to the view shed and additional noise created by the tram's operations.

Technical Feasibility and Anticipated Response: A detailed feasibility analysis would have to be undertaken to determine technical feasibility. Even if an aerial tram may be built, the analysis should investigate the potential for damage due to flood events and debris flows. Response is anticipated to be largely negative, since the visual and aural intrusions would be more significant than the expected benefits.

Next Steps: An aerial tram should be part of a long-term, inclusive planning process taking into consideration the input of visitors and stakeholders. If the aerial tram option is feasible with respect to public opinion, a detailed technical feasibility analysis will be needed to study alignments, costs and benefits, funding, fee structures, and risks including the potential for natural and man-made disasters.

MOT 04 – Electric carts could be provided for mobility-impaired visitors by reservation.

Description: A compelling argument in favor of retaining the tram service is to continue providing mobility and access to individuals with mobility impairments. One way to advance discussions to remove the tram is to investigate alternatives that continue providing mobility to individuals with mobility impairments. A small fleet of electric carts reserved for these individuals is one such alternative. It is expected that an electric cart could make 2-3 round trips between charging. A staff member or volunteer would need to be made available to operate the cart for liability reasons.

Golf carts are used at Lake Mead National Recreation Area (NRA) as a means of transportation between employee housing, a trailer camp, the hotel and restaurant, and administrative buildings[161]. Golf carts are not used for recreation or interpretation at Lake Mead NRA and are limited to specific roads and paths.

---

[160] "Tram Specifics" Jackson Hole Tramformation. http://www.tram-formation.com//index.php?option=com_content&task=view&id=42&Itemid=63
[161] National Park Service (2008). Lake Mead National Recreation Area Golf Cart Access. Last accessed on 9/29/2009 from http://www.nps.gov/lame/planyourvisit/upload/Golf%20Cart_map%20series-2.pdf

Costs: Golf carts cost between $5,000-$7,000 each[162] to purchase and about $100[163][164] each to maintain each year. Facilities would need to be built to store, maintain and charge the vehicles. The cost for this will vary depending on the number of vehicles needed.

Safety: Introduction of electric carts in the canyon would not improve safety or flood evacuation in the canyon. In fact, cart drivers would have to agree not to drive their cart through any moving water as the car may not be heavy or have high enough clearance to avoid being swept by moving water. Introduction of electric carts could potentially increase the possibility of modal conflicts in the canyon. Whether conflicts are more or less likely than they are with the current tram system would depend on the number of concurrent carts, the driving rules, and enforcement of the driving rules. Since the carts are narrower than the tram, they would be better able to share the road with pedestrians. On the other hand, visitors are less likely to be familiar with either driving the vehicle or the roadway as compared to the current tram drivers.

Cultural Landscape, Natural Environment, Historic Resources, Disruption: Effects on the cultural landscape would depend largely on the number of electric carts concurrently used in the canyon. Electric carts are generally quiet and non-obtrusive, however too many carts could become chaotic and distracting from the natural environment. Providing electric carts to mobility impaired visitors would not affect the natural environment or historic resource. Electric carts would reduce the noise and air emissions in the canyon compared to the current tram vehicles. Introducing electric carts would create no disruption of access or use in Sabino Canyon.

Technical Feasibility and Anticipated Response: Introducing electric carts in Sabino Canyon is technically feasible, although specific carts would have to be researched carefully to ensure they I) have the range to make the return trip into the canyon and ii) have the power to ascend the hills in Sabino Canyon. Public response would depend on the number of carts concurrently used in the canyon, the driving rules, and enforcement of the driving rules. Limiting the speed of the carts to 15 mph would contribute to a safe and enjoyable environment.

Next Steps: Additional research should be done to identify carts that would work in Sabino Canyon. It is recommended that the Forest Service test the vehicle on-site. One or two vehicles could then be purchased and made available for visitors either on a first come basis or via a reservation system. As demand is better understood, additional carts could be purchased. It is believed that one or two vehicles could be stored and charged with Sabino Canyon's existing infrastructure. A storage facility would need to be constructed if the fleet grew larger.

---

[162] "Sample golf cart and utility vehicle prices from BuyerZone buyers" BuyerZone. http://www.buyerzone.com/industrial/golf_carts/prices-golf-carts.html
[163] (Estimates http://docs.google.com/gview?a=v&q=cache:MRWzXJ72Lx8J:www.nevadamo.org/archive_library/2005_Files/2005%2520bids/2004/030204_glfclub_golfcarts.pdf+yamaha+golf+car+maintenance+cost+annual&hl=en&gl=us
[164] "The DRIVE Compare" Yamaha Golf-Car Company. http://www.yamahagolfcar.com/vehicles/compare/9/1030/48/gas.aspx (Gas costs achieved using estimate for 1 gallon of gas per day of use (standard mpg is 20-28 mpg, equivalent to three round-trips on Upper Sabino Canyon Rd.) for 350 days a year at $2.50/gallon)

MOT 05 – Rent electric bicycles to assist people to get up canyon.

Description: A compelling argument in favor of retaining the tram service is to continue providing a speedy option to access the upper reaches of the canyon. One way to advance discussions to remove the tram is to investigate alternatives, such as renting electric bicycles. This element might be a good introduction of a bicycle concessionaire, similar to that described in element PBE 01 – Initiating bicycle guided tours. Such a service could be provided by a concessionaire. In order for such an option to be financially viable, bicycles must have access to the canyon at all times; if tram service is halted, this may be feasible. It's important to note that many persons with mobility impairments cannot use an electric bicycle, thus this is not a viable option for the mobility-impaired.

Costs: Electric bicycles cost about $1,200[165] each.

Safety: Electric bicycles would not facilitate evacuation from the canyon beyond what the tram currently provides, in fact, while the tram can drive over the bridges during small flood events, electric bicycles are much lighter and less stable and cannot. Electric bicycles would increase the potential for accidents with other users, even if the tram were eliminated.

Cultural Landscape, Natural Environment, Historic Resources, Disruption: Introduction of electric bicycles would change the cultural landscape of the canyon. While they would be quieter than the current tram, there would be many more bicycles than there are trams now, and the bicycles would degrade the pedestrian experience.

Electric bicycles would lessen emissions in the canyon but not otherwise impact the natural environment or historic resources. Because introduction of bicycles requires no fixed infrastructure, no significant closures or other disruptions are likely.

Technical Feasibility and Anticipated Response: Although acquiring electric bicycles is technically feasible, there are several additional challenges they would create. First, electric bicycles would not provide canyon access to visitors with mobility impairments. Secondly, it would require a change to the hours of allowed bicycle use, a move likely to be controversial.

Next Steps: Next steps would be to develop a request for proposals for interested concessionaires.

MOT 06 – Create an on-demand and/or reservation system for the mobility-impaired.

Description: This element involves maintaining a tram shuttle concept with either the current or new vehicles, but tailoring the service specifically for persons who are mobility-impaired, much like service vehicles found in airport terminals. The tram would be converted from a concessionaire-operated attraction to a Forest Service- or contractor-operated free amenity.

Reservations are a common way of allocating fixed resources on federal public lands. The National Recreation Reservation Service, accessible online at Recreation.gov, is a portal that allows users to reserve and pay for recreational vehicle (RV) sites, cabins and lookouts, tent sites, trailer sites, group sites, day use sites, horse sites, and boat sites. Reservations are also common for transportation services

---

[165] "E-Bikes" Tucson Electric Bikes. http://www.tucsonelectricbikes.com/store/categories/E%252dBikes/

provided on or near public lands. For example, (1) Denali National Park and Preserve allows individuals to make shuttle bus and interpretive tour bus reservations; (2) Private operators allow advanced reservations for mountain bike shuttles in Uinta-Wasatch-Cache National Forest; (3) Cumberland Island National Seashore has a reservation system for its ferry and island camping opportunities; and (4) The Appalachian Mountain Club operates shuttle service in White Mountain National Forest which requires advanced reservations. There is no known precedent of reservations for transportation systems specifically for individuals with mobility impairments.

Costs: Because the tram would no longer provide service to all individuals, service and associated operating costs could be significantly reduced. There would be no revenue from ticket sales, however, additional costs would be incurred to develop and operate a reservation system if this element is included.

Safety: Because fewer trams would be running, this element would slightly reduce evacuation capability during mild flood events. Reducing shuttle service would also decrease the potential for accidents and modal conflicts.

Cultural Landscape, Natural Environment, Historic Resources, Disruption: Providing tram service only to those who require it would improve the cultural landscape because fewer trams would be running and interfering with the natural surroundings. At the same time, limiting tram service would likely decrease the number of visitors to the canyon and decrease the distance many visitors travel up the canyon, thus reducing the diversity and quantity of environment experienced. Reducing tram service would reduce noise and emissions impacts on the natural environment, though technical analysis would have to identify quantitative impacts. Historic resources would not be affected. Because providing tram service only to persons with mobility impairments requires no fixed infrastructure, no significant closures or other disruptions at Sabino Canyon are likely.

Technical Feasibility and Anticipated Response: Providing tram service only to persons with mobility impairments is technically feasible, although the current operator has voiced concerns over this element's legality. Any reduction in tram service will be hailed by some and be criticized by others. Continuing to provide service to individuals with mobility-impairments will soften the criticisms.

Next Steps: To convert the tram concept into an amenity servicing persons with mobility impairments, the Forest Service should identify the volume of concurrent users who would require service by conducting survey of existing tram riders. USFS must also recognize that visitors will self-select on whether or not they require tram service due to "mobility impairment". This could end up approximating the current schedule of service currently provided.

MOT 07 – Replace with in-kind vehicle of same size/function.
Description: The current 48 and 60-person diesel and gasoline trams are roughly 30 years old and deemed by some visitors to be smelly, noisy, or unsafe. This element seeks to maintain the current tram concept but upgrade the trams with vehicles that are safer, quieter, and less polluting. There are options for replacement rolling stock, particularly electric, gasoline, diesel, or propane trams. Minimum requirements of the canyon road include minimum turning radius of 30 feet, maximum grade of 14%,

and maximum width of 8 feet and 6 inches. Several tram vehicles from vendors such as Trams International[166] and Maritime Applied Physics Corporation[167] meet these criteria, while more traditional bus vehicles are either too wide to cross the vented low-water crossings or too long to accommodate some of the hills and sags. The Forest Service should be able to find newer, safer, cleaner, and quieter replacement vehicles, though costs may be higher for state-of-the-art technology including power-trains driven by alternative fuel sources.

Costs: Trams vary widely in price based on age, fuel type, and physical dimensions and characteristics. Replacement trams of roughly the same size as those currently in service could be estimated to cost between $120,000[168] and $180,000[169], but actual pricing may vary by technology and vendor.

Safety: New trams of similar size and weight would not greatly alter the ability of the tram to assist with evacuation efforts during mild flood events. New trams would similarly not affect the potential for conflicts with other users in the canyon. New trams could address safety concerns of the current vehicles, namely that the current vehicles have no doors or sides to prevent riders from falling out.

Cultural Landscape, Natural Environment, Historic Resources, Disruption: New quieter, less polluting trams would improve the cultural landscape as well as the natural environment. They would likely have minimal affect on historic resources in the canyon.

Because providing new trams requires no fixed infrastructure, no significant closures or other disruptions at Sabino Canyon are likely.

Technical Feasibility and Anticipated Response: Assuming new trams having the proper dimensions and characteristics are available at reasonable cost, replacing the old trams should be technically feasible. New trams would address many visitor concerns, thus anticipated response is expected to be positive.

Next Steps: The next steps would be to identify necessary tram dimensions and characteristics required to operate in the canyon and then to research specific tram vehicles themselves. The Forest Service must also consider who will own the trams and how they will be paid for.

MOT 08 – Replace vehicles with larger or smaller vehicles but run at equivalent capacity.
Description: The current 48 and 60-person diesel and gasoline trams are roughly 30 years old and deemed by some visitors to be smelly, noisy, or unsafe. This element seeks to maintain the current tram concept but replace the trams with vehicles that are safer, quieter, and less polluting. This would better match rider demand with supply to avoid running large, noisy trams that are mostly empty or small trams at capacity.

Costs: Trams vary widely in price based on age, fuel type, and physical dimensions and characteristics. Estimates for replacement trams of different sizes than those currently in use are as follows: (1) 18-28

---

[166] http://www.tramfactory.com/
[167] http://www.mapcorp.com/
[168] "New Tram Set" TrolleyBrokers Online. http://www.trolleybrokers.com/vehicle_listing.php?type=Tram%20Set&condition=new
[169] "New Trailer" TrolleyBrokers Online. http://www.trolleybrokers.com/vehicle_listing.php?type=Trailer&condition=new

seat power cars: $70,000-$140,000 and (2) 24-36 seat trailers $40,000-$80,000.[170] The current tram operator has not provided daily statistics regarding ridership, thus no analysis has been done regarding optimal shuttle sizes. A thorough study would have to identify the specific dimensions and characteristics required by the trams at Sabino. Larger sized trams may require modifications to lifts and bays within a maintenance facility.

Safety: There are trade-offs associated with larger/smaller vehicles in relation to flood safety. Larger vehicles would run less frequently and therefore have fewer opportunities to help people. Larger vehicles would also be heavier and have greater efficacy navigating overflowing bridges. Smaller vehicles would likely run more frequently and therefore have more opportunities to help people, although they are lighter and may be less able to navigate flowing water. Similarly, larger vehicles that run fewer times may lessen the potential for user conflicts and accidents, while smaller vehicles may run more frequently and have greater potential for user conflicts.

Cultural Landscape, Natural Environment, Historic Resources, Disruption: Similarly, to safety, larger vehicles that run fewer times may increase quality of the cultural landscape, while smaller vehicles that run more frequently may decrease quality of the cultural landscape. Because replacing the current trams requires no fixed infrastructure, no significant closures or other disruptions at Sabino Canyon are likely.

*Technical Feasibility and Anticipated Response: R*eplacing the trams is technically feasible, but requires detailed data regarding daily trip patterns throughout the year so that it may consider an optimally-sized tram fleet. Anticipated response is expected to be positive to new trams, as long as they are safer, quieter, and less polluting.

Next Steps: The Forest Service must obtain from the tram operator the daily rider patterns and consider these in concert with other tram requirements including maximum width, weight, and other vehicle characteristics. The Forest Service must also consider who will own the trams and how they will be paid for.

MOT 09 – Replace trams with an enclosed vehicle design.

Description: In addition to safety and emissions complaints addressed by other elements this element specifically addresses noise created by the driver interpretation. Furthermore it adds the possibility of climate controlled tours of the canyon. Many National Forests and National Parks including Inyo National Forest, White River National Forest, and Bryce Canyon National Park utilize enclosed bus vehicles for transportation, although there is no precedent for using enclosed tram vehicles for interpretation.

Costs: No enclosed tram designs that meet the required road characteristics (see MOT 07) are known to exist at this time. Several companies including Arboc Mobility, StarTrans, Champion Bus, Inc., and Eldorado National manufacture enclosed cutaway vehicles. While these vehicles are enclosed and meet

---

[170] "RE: Inquiry on Tramp Costs" Email, Leah Munoz, Specialty Vehicles. 9/12/09.

the width requirements of the road, it is unclear whether they have an appropriate turning radius. In addition, they only seat 7 to 30 passengers, fewer than the existing trams.

Safety: Enclosed trams would not significantly alter either evacuation capabilities or the potential for accidents or user conflicts.

Cultural Landscape, Natural Environment, Historic Resources, Disruption: The cultural landscape would be improved for pedestrians in Sabino Canyon because they would not be subject to the noise from interpretation. The cultural landscape for riders would be diminished because their views would be obscured and limited by glass and they would not be able to breathe the air or feel the heat. The natural environment may suffer minimally more as an enclosed vehicle running air conditioning will likely be less fuel efficient than an open vehicle with no air conditioning. Operation of enclosed vehicles would have no significant impact on historic resources. Introducing enclosed trams requires no new fixed infrastructure, no significant closures or other disruptions.

Technical Feasibility and Anticipated Response: If these trams exist, introducing them to Sabino Canyon is technically feasible. Anticipated response by riders is expected to be negative, while response by non-riders may be indifferent to positive.

Next Steps: Next steps are to research dimensions, availability, and costs of enclosed tram vehicles. The Forest Service must also consider who will own and pay for the trams.

MOT 10 – Upgrade interpretation method/technology.

Description: This element addresses the noise created by the current interpretation public-address system on the trams. Specifically, this element seeks to upgrade the technology so that riders may still receive interpretation but non-riders will not be affected by noise. One potential system is one that allows users to plug headphones directly into the tram.

Self-guided tour options, such as those found at Alcatraz Island, part of Golden Gate National Recreation Area, are audio tours provided by headphones connected to personal audio devices. These systems are also popular at museums around the world. Newer systems, such as that found at Vicksburg National Military Park, utilize hand-held units triggered by GPS points throughout the park to provide an interactive experience. Grand Canyon National Park has a system that allows visitors to listen to park rangers give 2 minute audio tours at various points of interest on the South Rim[171].

Costs: A headphone-based interpretation system may be expected to cost about $250 per set[172].

Safety: Upgrading the interpretation technology is not expected to impact flood safety or user conflicts.

Cultural Landscape, Natural Environment, Historic Resources, Disruption: The quieter cultural landscape will be improved for non-riders, while riders will likely be unaffected.

---

[171] National Park Service (2009). Grand Canyon National Park – Interpretive Ranger Programs (U.S. National Park Service). Last accessed on October 5, 2009 from http://www.nps.gov/grca/planyourvisit/ranger-program.htm.
[172] "Tour-Guide Systems" Full Compass. http://www.fullcompass.com/category/Tour-Guide-Systems.html

The natural environment will benefit from less man-made noise and historic resources will remain unaffected. Because no fixed infrastructure is required by this element, no significant closures or disruptions to visitors are expected.

Technical Feasibility and Anticipated Response: Upgrading the interpretation technology is technically feasible. Anticipated response is expected to be positive.

Next Steps: Next steps are to research specific interpretation systems, either as part of replacement trams or as a separate add-on that could perhaps be used on the current trams as well as future vehicles.

MOT 11 – Add passenger safety equipment.

Description: This element seeks to address the safety issues of the current trams, namely that there are no doors or sides to the tram seats to prevent passengers from falling out. This is intended to be a short-term solution until the tram vehicles are replaced or discontinued.

Costs: Any safety features added to the current trams will likely be a custom solution, it is impossible to estimate a cost without further study.

Safety: Adding passenger safety equipment will improve tram passenger safety but not affect flood evacuation capabilities or conflicts with non-riders.

Cultural Landscape, Natural Environment, Historic Resources, Disruption: Adding passenger safety equipment will not affect cultural landscape, the natural environment, or historic resources, nor will it impose closures or other disturbances within the recreation area.

Technical Feasibility and Anticipated Response: Adding safety features to the current trams is probably feasible, although because it would be customized to the current trams, specific feasibility and cost will not be known without further study. Visitor response is anticipated to be indifferent.

Next Steps: The tram operator should be engaged to analyze potential safety improvements to the current vehicles which safely prevent riders from falling out or otherwise injuring themselves.

MOT 12 – Limit hours/days/seasons of tram.

Description: While some elements suggest maintaining the current tram concept, which runs year-round, and others suggest eliminating the tram altogether, this element seeks a balance between the two by reducing tram service by hours, days, or even seasons. This concept creates more times when non-riders do not have to compete for the road with the tram. Possible reductions include one or two hours a day, one or two days a week (similar to the current restraints on cyclists), a couple days a month, or even entire seasons out of the year (perhaps the summer when it the climate is hottest and visitation is lowest). This concept addresses time-separation strategies of different user groups (see MGMT 04). The special use permit could be used to change the service requirements to limit service to more constrained hours and seasons (see MGMT 06).

Costs: While this option would not incur additional costs for the Forest Service, it would reduce revenue for the tram operator. Aside from general estimates[173][174], the Volpe team has been unable to determine the costs associated with the current service being provided in Sabino Canyon. It is impossible to model cost impacts without more cost and hourly and daily ridership information from the tram operator.

Safety: Reducing the number of tram trips through the Canyon could reduce the number of conflicts between user groups. The tram service currently will provide transportation for visitors with medical emergencies or those that are stuck due to rising stream flow who haven't paid for the service. The reduction in frequency of service may increase the need for Forest Service staff to assist visitors stranded along the road in Sabino Canyon. These visitors are currently picked up by the tram. The number of people requiring this assistance is reported to be low.

Cultural Landscape, Natural Environment, Historic Resources, Disruption: Reducing tram service hours would improve the cultural landscape for non-riders and marginally improve the natural environment due to less emissions and noise. Historic resources would not be affected and closures or other disruptions in the canyon would not occur.

Technical Feasibility and Anticipated Response: Reducing operating hours of the tram is technically feasible, although this element and its financial implications on the operator's business must be taken into consideration. The service provider must be able to support the service from income from the service. It is expected that reductions in the current level of service would not be supported by the service provider. If the service provider refuses the changes requested by the Forest Service, it is possible that tram service within the Canyon could end. Any reduction in tram hours must be supplemented with clear and consistent communication via all information distribution channels. Response from non-riders is expected to be positive. Anticipated response from previous riders, expecting the service to run as it has in the past, will be negative.

Next Steps: To pursue this element the Forest Service should continue to engage stakeholders to determine their wishes and engage the tram operator to understand what is financially feasible. Ideally, the Forest Service would analyze current ridership patterns and operations costs to determine time periods that would be economically viable to reduce service. Service changes would likely not be possible until the current special use permit is renegotiated.

MOT 13 – Limit tram route to lower canyon only.

Description: This element recognizes that the physical infrastructure in the canyon is subject to the destructive forces of nature and that continued rebuilding of this infrastructure may not be financially feasible. Limiting the tram to the lower canyon, perhaps below Stop 4, signifies a 'retreat' of motorized vehicles from the canyon and represents a compromise between those who want to return Sabino Canyon to nature and those who want to continue providing motorized access.

---

[173] School bus drivers in Tucson on average earn $11/hour (May 2008 Bureau of Labor Statistics for Tucson, AZ).

[174] Tucson's Transit Service, Sun Tran, had an average total cost of $78 per hour in 2007. It is expected that this would be on the high end of costs for transportation operations in Sabino Canyon. $40 per hour might be the lower range of the cost spectrum. A service provider in PA charges $330/day.

Costs: Limiting the tram to below Stop 4 would have no cost to the Forest Service, although it could reduce the costs and revenues of the tram operator because fewer trams would operate concurrently and because the tram would likely have to lower its ticket price

Safety: Limiting the tram to below Stop 4 would generally keep riders closer to the visitor center and thus ease evacuation. Also, although the tram would not make scheduled runs beyond Stop 4, it may be possible to conduct special evacuation runs all the way to Stop 9 if necessary. Limiting the tram to below Stop 4 would significantly reduce potential for conflicts with non riders, especially above Stop 8 where the road narrows significantly. Below Stop 4, potential for user conflicts would likely remain the same.

Cultural Landscape, Natural Environment, Historic Resources, Disruption: Limiting the tram to below Stop 4 would significantly improve the cultural landscape for non-riders above Stop 4 and leave the cultural landscape below Stop 4 unchanged. This element would improve the natural environment above Stop 4 as well due to reduced emissions and noise. It would not affect historic resources in Sabino Canyon, nor would it create any closures or significant disturbances that would detract from the visitor experience.

Technical Feasibility and Anticipated Response: Limiting the tram to below Stop 4 is technically feasible. Anticipated response of riders would be negative while for non-riders it would be positive. Negative responses would best be mitigated by advertising this service change as a compromise between all users and the natural environment.

Next Steps: To pursue this element the Forest Service would need to engage the tram operator regarding how service changes would impact its business and whether this is an economically viable option. Service changes would likely not be possible until the current special use permit is renegotiated.

MOT 14 – Connect new parking lot to visitor center via tram.

Description: The visitor center is the information hub of Sabino Canyon. It is at the visitor center that visitors obtain safety information, learn about the natural environment and canyon ecosystems, and have access to food, water, and shelter. It is important that all visitors have easy access to the visitor center, especially during their first visit to Sabino Canyon. The proposed new overflow parking lot is located roughly ¾ miles from the visitor center in the direction opposite from the canyon. To walk to the visitor center and back would entail a 1.5 mile walk without even entering the canyon, and many visitors would be unlikely to make this trip because it is too far and would take too long.

As a result, the Forest Service would consider initiating tram service between the proposed new overflow parking lot and the visitor center. There are several options for this:

i) Build a new road and tram turn-around connecting the main canyon road to the new overflow parking lot. The tram would stop by the parking lot on the way to the visitor center and/or the canyon.

ii) Build a new walking path from the new overflow parking lot to the main canyon road. The tram would pick up passengers from this point and takes them to the visitor center and/or the canyon.

iii) Build an access road between the new overflow parking lot and the main parking lot (see AM 01) and run a free tram service to and from the visitor center.

Costs: Each of the three options would entail different costs.

i) To build a new road to 1/5 miles to the main canyon road is expected to cost $500,000. A roundabout (turnaround for the tram) could be expected to cost roughly $150,000. This option would likely require the tram to offer free trips from the proposed new overflow parking lot to the visitor center as the operator currently has no way to collect ticket fees on the tram itself. Conversely the tram could be offered as a free service (see MGMT 08) or paid for with expanded amenity fees (see MGMT 09) .

ii) To build a new walking path 1/5 miles to the main canyon is expected to cost $40,000. This option would likely require the tram to offer free trips from the new overflow parking lot to the visitor center as the operator currently has no way to collect ticket fees on the tram itself. Conversely the tram could be offered as a free service (see MGMT 08) or paid for with expanded amenity fees (see MGMT 09).

iii) To build a ¾ mile access road between the new overflow parking lot and the main parking lot is expected to cost roughly $2.5 million per mile, or $1.9 million (see AM 01). The new shuttle would be expected to be free (see MGMT 08) or paid for with expanded amenity fees (see MGMT 09) and the existing shuttle service concept could remain unchanged.

Safety: Initiating shuttle service between the proposed new overflow parking lot and the visitor center is not expected to significantly alter flood or evacuation safety. For options (i) and (ii), if the quantity of tram service remains the same, risk of accidents resulting from user conflicts is expected to stay the same. For option (iii), an additional tram driving on the same access roads with cars could create additional conflicts between cars, trams, and pedestrians.

Cultural Landscape, Natural Environment, Historic Resources, Disruption: Options (i) and (iii) will have the largest impact on cultural landscape and natural environment because they involve construction of additional roads, though the access road for option (iii) is not located near existing visitor areas and will have significantly less impact on the cultural landscape than option (i). Option (ii) involves building an additional walking path which will have minimal impact on the cultural landscape as well. Each of the three alternatives will marginally degrade the natural desert environment by increasing impervious surface area and segmenting natural habitats. Construction of each of the three alternatives will moderately disrupt users with noise and visual impacts but will not limit user access to the canyon.

Technical Feasibility and Anticipated Response: Each of the three options is technically feasible. Establishing tram service between the proposed new overflow parking lot and the visitor center is expected to receive positive feedback from those who park in the overflow lot, particularly at busy, peak-hour times. Feedback from repeat, non-tram-rider users of the canyon is likely to be less positive due to more intense tram activity.

Next Steps: Next steps include continuing outreach with visitors to identify a preferred option and conducting financial and logistical analysis of the tram service to test viability of each of the options outlined above. Service changes would likely not be possible until the current special use permit is renegotiated.

MOT 15 – Replace Sabino Canyon shuttle with more developed shuttle service in Bear Canyon.
Description: To reduce modal conflicts and to improve the cultural landscape of Sabino Canyon, this element discontinues shuttle service on Sabino Canyon Road and provides improved tram service in Bear Canyon. Interpretation, which is not provided on the current tram service in Bear Canyon, could be instated along this route.

Costs: This element would not incur additional costs but would decrease demand and revenue for the shuttle concessionaire. The Bear Canyon shuttle route is shorter and less popular, and the concessionaire currently charges less money for that route than for the Sabino Canyon route.

Safety: This element would remove the tram as a potential evacuation vehicle in Sabino Canyon (see MOT 01). It would also decrease the potential for modal conflicts in Sabino Canyon and increase the potential for modal conflicts in Bear Canyon. The result would be a net benefit to safety as there is far more pedestrian activity in Sabino Canyon.

Cultural Landscape, Natural Environment, Historic Resources, Disruption: Removing the tram would eliminate odorous emissions and mechanical and interpretive noise and thus improve the cultural landscape in Sabino Canyon. The cultural landscape in Bear Canyon may be enhanced with the addition of interpretation on the tram. The natural environment in Sabino and Bear Canyons may marginally improve and be degraded, respectively. Removing the tram from Sabino Canyon would not affect historic resources, nor would it disrupt users or prevent user access to the canyon.

Technical Feasibility and Anticipated Response: Removing tram service in Sabino Canyon and improving service in Bear Canyon is technically feasible, although it may not be financially feasible under the current concessionaire agreement. Anticipated response is likely to be mixed. Bicyclists and pedestrians will likely respond positively, while those who depend on the tram to reach the depths of Sabino Canyon may respond negatively.

Next Steps: Next steps are to consider a concessionaire arrangement that would make a Bear Canyon-only shuttle system financially viable. Service changes would likely not be possible until the current special use permit is renegotiated.

MOT 16 – Develop separate shuttle options and/or routes within CNF (to Mt. Lemmon and/or additional parking areas).
Description: This element seeks to develop a separate shuttle service from Sabino Canyon to other points within the Santa Catalina Mountains including Mt. Lemmon via the Catalina Highway or the Control Road, or activity areas along Redington Road. This would provide additional opportunities in the Santa Catalina Mountains and other districts of the Coronado National Forest and allow people to reach skiing, hiking and camping destinations without the use of their cars.

Costs: The costs of initiating, operating, and maintaining additional service outside Sabino Canyon could be determined only after determining the vehicle type, route, and operating characteristics (such as frequency and time). Capital costs would include the purchase costs of vehicles as well as the costs of storage facilities. Operations costs would primarily consist of drivers' wages and fuel.

Safety: The greatest impact of developing additional tram services would be to reduce the number of vehicles on the roadway network and particularly reduce the number of travelers unfamiliar with the road from driving them.

Cultural Landscape, Natural Environment, Historic Resources, Disruption: Instituting shuttle service elsewhere in Coronado National Forests would likely have little effect on the cultural landscape, natural environment, or historic resources if the shuttle route were confined to existing roads. Occasional transit vehicles would add little additional traffic to the roads and may replace trips that would have otherwise been made by private vehicle. An in depth analysis of this element would have to be conducted to more accurately estimate costs and benefits. This element would not disrupt users, prompt closures, or prevent general access to Sabino Canyon. A location with adequate parking would need to be found for people to leave their private vehicles while using the shuttle.

Technical Feasibility and Anticipated Response: This element is technically feasible, although financial feasibility would have to be determined. Demand for a shuttle service to other destinations within Coronado National Forest may not justify the capital or operating costs required

Next Steps: Next steps include conducting a demand analysis for other destinations within Coronado National Forest and conducting a transit study to determine details including destinations, vehicle types, routes, and schedules. Funding sources would have to be identified.

School Elements

SCH 01 – Provide free tram shuttle to transport student groups within the canyon.

Description: Currently kindergarten and elementary school students arrive at Sabino Canyon in caravans of private automobiles or on school buses. They are taken to the locations of the field trips (Cactus Picnic Area for kindergarteners and Sabino Dam for elementary school children) in those same vehicles. The presence of private automobiles in the canyon creates potential hazards. The drivers are not familiar with the narrow and rolling roadway and may not be looking out for pedestrians or know what to do when they meet an oncoming vehicle. The presence of these automobiles also degrades the cultural environment for pedestrians, and creates situations in which drivers may become lost or break the rules of the road. This element recommends ending the practice of allowing private cars and school buses into the recreation area (beyond the parking lot), and instead provides free rides to the field trip sites on the concessionaire's trams, removing safety issues and lessening the financial burden on already-cash-strapped schools.

Costs: Providing tram rides to school children would require additional drivers and fuel beyond those necessary for concessionaire to provide normally scheduled service during field trip times. For example, a kindergarten field trip may consist of as many as 60 children and 15 parents and teachers. The current tram vehicles only have capacity for 60 individuals, thus two tram vehicles would have to be used in order to transport all the children to the Cactus Picnic Area and back in a timely manner. Days of kindergarten trips, Tuesdays and Thursdays, are also the days of elementary school trips which have roughly the same number of children, parents and teachers. Thus on a given Tuesday or Thursday, as many as four concurrent trams would be needed to transport the children. Additional costs borne by the shuttle concessionaire would have to be addressed in the special use permit and ultimately subsidized by the recreation area and its partners.

An additional 'cost' is the transfer time between vehicles. It may take as many as 15 minutes to move the children from buses or cars into the trams, and another 5 minutes to get them off the trams. Increase in transfer time may reduce the amount of educational time spent at Sabino Canyon or increase the real cost of bus transportation to and from the schools (currently $150/hour per bus).

Safety: While providing free tram rides to school children would not affect flood safety or evacuation within Sabino Canyon, it would lessen the chance for accidents between parent-drivers and pedestrians on the canyon road.

Cultural Landscape, Natural Environment, Historic Resources, Disruption: Whether this element would improve or detract from the cultural landscape is a matter of debate. Clearly some patrons consider the trams a detractor from the cultural landscape, while others would consider a group of personal automobiles a detractor. Which transportation option is more desirable is a matter of opinion that needs to be considered. Transportation options that use fewer vehicles, such as trams or buses, are more fuel efficient than multiple automobiles, and will produce fewer emissions to disturb the natural environment. Instituting a tram service for school children would not affect historic resources, nor would it create user disruptions or closures within the canyon.

Technical Feasibility and Anticipated Response: This solution is technically feasible but is challenged by logistical and financial constraints described in the 'Costs' section of this element. The response by the public at large is expected to focus on the impact of additional trams traffic on pedestrians along the canyon roads. Two additional components that would make this element more feasible would be to limit the group size so that the entire group could fit on a single tram and alternating the days of the kindergarten and elementary school program. These changes would minimize the impact on the tram service provider.

Next Steps schools: Conduct additional outreach with pedestrians to determine their preferences, work with the SCVN to develop better understanding time constraints (particularly related to transfer times) for field trips, and discuss with partners including the tram operator, how to structure compensation for use school group use of the tram.

SCH 02 – Relocate educational facilities or build trails so that students can walk from the parking lot.

Description: To eliminate the need for private automobiles, school buses, or use of the tram within the recreation area, the location of field trips could be moved closer to the visitor center or new overflow parking lot. For example, a ¼ mile path may be built for the kindergarten students connecting the overflow parking lot to the Cactus Picnic Area (see AM 11), or the elementary school field trip site may be moved from Sabino Dam to an area within reasonable walking distance of the visitor center.

Costs: The cost would depend on the amount of infrastructure built. A ¼ mile path from the new overflow parking lot to the Cactus Picnic Area could be expected to cost $200,000 per mile, or $50,000[175]. Any new field trip location would require additional infrastructure such as toilet facilities and shade.

Safety: Built improvements or relocation of field trip locations would have no effect on flood safety or evacuation. They may reduce potential for user conflicts, particularly those between motorized vehicles and pedestrians on the canyon road. This element does increase risk of exposure to students. Parents, teachers, and field trip staff would need to be instructed to always carry plenty of water and first aid equipment for students.

Cultural Landscape, Natural Environment, Historic Resources, Disruption: This will improve the cultural landscape and natural environment by removing field trip vehicles from Sabino Canyon. It will have little impact on historic resources and may cause minor short-term noise disruptions if additional facilities (such as a pedestrian pathway) are built.

Technical Feasibility and Anticipated Response: SCVN has made a compelling argument for why they need access to the creek for their education program. Walking students to sites may be difficult due to the already constrained time necessary to cover the educational program. Mobility-challenged children and adults will still require accommodation with vehicular access.

Next Steps: To pursue this element, the Forest Service will need to work with schools and SCVN to identify potential trail improvements or new field trip sites that may allow students to walk. Response is expected to be positive.

SCH 03 – Purchase vehicle specifically for student group travel.

Description: A vehicle (or vehicles) would be purchased specifically for student group travel. New vehicles would not be subject to the same dimension and operating requirements as the tram. They could be wider and longer because they would not have to cross the bridges or make the tight turns that are further up the canyon road. New vehicles could be operated and maintained by the current concessionaire, SCVN, or another partner. New vehicles could also be used to pick students up from the schools and take them directly to the educational site within the recreation area. If this option is explored, the vehicles and the drivers will need to meet very specific criteria defined by State of Arizona.[176]

Costs: A new field trip vehicle could be expected to cost between $100,000 and $300,000, depending on the particular vehicle.

---

[175] *Trail and Path Planning: A Guide for Municipalities,* County of Chester, Pennsylvania (http://dsf.chesco.org/planning/lib/planning/trailguide/trailguideappc.pdf), using the average of a $106,700 estimate for a 10-ft wide non-motorized asphalt surface in Iowa and a $300,000 estimate for a 12-ft wide multi-purpose asphalt trail in Asheville, NC
[176] Arizona Department of Administration (2008). Minimum Standards for School Buses and School Bus Drivers. Accessed on September 17, 2009 from http://studenttransportation.azdps.gov/documents/2008MinStandards_007.pdf.

Safety: Providing tram rides to school children would not affect flood safety or evacuation within Sabino Canyon. It would lessen the chance for accidents between parent-drivers and pedestrians on the canyon road (see SCH 01).

Cultural Landscape, Natural Environment, Historic Resources, Disruption: Some patrons consider the trams a detractor from the cultural landscape, while others consider automobiles a detractor. Which transportation option is more desirable is a matter of opinion. Fewer vehicles, such as trams or buses, that are also more fuel efficient than automobiles, and would produce fewer emissions to disturb the natural environment. Introducing a vehicle(s) dedicated to student travel would not affect historic resources, nor would it create major user disruptions or closures within the canyon.

Technical Feasibility and Anticipated Response: Purchasing a vehicle (or vehicles) specifically to transport students from the main entrance of Sabino Canyon Recreation Area to field trip sites is technically feasible, though it may depend on available funding sources. Operations and maintenance would also need to be funded. Anticipated response by the public at large is expected to be positive, although additional vehicles on the canyon roads may affect pedestrians along the canyon roads.

Next Steps: Define what service is to be provided (solely within the canyon or to and from schools as well), identify potential funding sources, identify an operator and maintenance partner, and identify a proper vehicle.

Appendix E. Elements not represented in the transportation alternatives

A number of transportation elements in the filtered list were not incorporated into the transportation alternatives presented in this document. These elements may have either overlapped in concept with other elements in an alternative or not fit with the specific focus chosen for each of the alternatives. Many of these elements have merit, however, and may be incorporated into future discussions regarding the alternatives and the transportation systems connecting to and within Sabino Canyon.

Table C1 - Elements not represented in the transportation alternatives

Element ID	Element Description
AM 02	Institute 24-hour access control.
AM 03	Develop south-side access-egress from lot to avoid conflicts with school.
AM 04	Install a traffic signal at the recreation area entrance.
AM 06	Stripe and widen shoulders of roads to improve bicycle access.
AM 09	Improve Bear Canyon access point.
AM 10	Dedicated right-turn lane into Sabino Canyon parking lot.
AM 12	Install a southbound right-turn lane from Sabino Canyon Road to Skyline.
BPE 05	Develop equestrian tours.
BPE 06	Create additional or improve infrastructure for equestrian users.
MGMT 07	Transfer ownership of the tram vehicles to USFS and continue operation by a contractor.
MGMT 12	Charge entry fee for all users, per person.
MOT 03	Develop aerial tram service.
MOT 08	Replace vehicles with larger or smaller vehicles but run at equivalent capacity.
MOT 09	Replace trams with an enclosed vehicle design.
MOT 16	Develop separate shuttle options and/or routes within CNF (to Mt. Lemmon and/or additional parking areas).
SCH 02	Relocate educational facilities or build trails so that students can walk from the parking lot.